Corpus Studies in Contrastive Linguistics

Benjamins Current Topics

Special issues of established journals tend to circulate within the orbit of the subscribers of those journals. For the Benjamins Current Topics series a number of special issues of various journals have been selected containing salient topics of research with the aim of finding new audiences for topically interesting material, bringing such material to a wider readership in book format.

For an overview of all books published in this series, please see
http://benjamins.com/catalog/bct

Volume 43

Corpus Studies in Contrastive Linguistics
Edited by Stefania Marzo, Kris Heylen and Gert De Sutter

These materials were previously published in *International Journal of Corpus Linguistics 15:2 (2010)*.

Corpus Studies in Contrastive Linguistics

Edited by

Stefania Marzo
Kris Heylen
KU Leuven

Gert De Sutter
University College Ghent/Ghent University

John Benjamins Publishing Company

Amsterdam / Philadelphia

TM The paper used in this publication meets the minimum requirements of the American National Standard for Information Sciences – Permanence of Paper for Printed Library Materials, ANSI z39.48-1984.

Library of Congress Cataloging-in-Publication Data

Corpus studies in contrastive linguistics / edited by Stefania Marzo, Kris Heylen, Gert De Sutter.
     p. cm. (Benjamins Current Topics, ISSN 1874-0081 ; v. 43)
Includes bibliographical references and index.
   1. Contrastive linguistics. 2. Corpora (Linguistics) I. Marzo, Stefania. II. Heylen, Kris.
     III. Sutter, Gert De.
P143.C67   2012
410--dc23   2012013943
ISBN 978 90 272 0262 8 (Hb ; alk. paper)
ISBN 978 90 272 7377 2 (Eb)

John Benjamins Publishing Co. · P.O. Box 36224 · 1020 ME Amsterdam · The Netherlands
John Benjamins North America · P.O. Box 27519 · Philadelphia PA 19118-0519 · USA

Table of contents

Developments in Corpus-based Contrastive Linguistics

Stefania Marzo, Kris Heylen and Gert De Sutter
KU Leuven / KU Leuven / University College Ghent/Ghent University

Since the early 1990's Contrastive linguistics has undergone a clear revival and expansion. One of the major reasons for this is the access to multilingual corpora and the improvement of quantitative methodologies for empirical research (Salkie 1999, Johansson 2007, Gómez-González et al. 2008). The past decade has seen a plethora of studies falling under the rubric of what may be referred to as *corpus-based contrastive studies*, serving both theoretical and applied goals (among others Laviosa 2002, Granger et al. 2003, Granger & Petch-Tyson 2003, Butler et al. 2005, Johansson 2007, Gomez-Gonzalez et al. 2008, Xiao 2010).

These valuable volumes all testify to the interesting methodological and theoretical challenges this growing research field offers. The present volume brings together several articles that aim to have a closer look at these challenges. The viewpoint they offer grows out of the numerous insights provided by these previous studies.

The contributions all share the same descriptive and theoretical goal of providing more insight into differences and similarities between languages, and hence more insight in language and language variation in general. They cover a range of different linguistic domains (syntax, modality and discourse) and pursue different types of research questions (grammaticalization, pragmatic function, stylistic function, typological profile) and accordingly use different types of corpora (contemporary and historical texts, written and spoken discourse, different text types, such as academic discourse and political discourse). In total, five different languages are represented (English, French, Dutch, Spanish and Lithuanian) and, probably not surprisingly, English is used as language of comparison in each contribution. Before giving an overview of the individual contributions, we will dwell on a series of general issues raised in this compilation.

First, this volume substantiates the necessity of a fully-fledged corpus-driven approach in Contrastive Linguistics and its indispensable interaction with theoretical findings. The field of contrastive linguistics has already witnessed a clear shift from –what in Corpus Linguistics is called (Tummers et al. 2005) —

corpus-illustrated work, using hand-picked corpus examples, to *corpus-based* analyses, characterised by a systematic analysis of corpus instances and empirical verification of theoretically grounded hypotheses (e.g. De Sutter et al. 2012, Neumann 2012). The six papers all attempt to contribute to the establishment of a thorough corpus-based approach to contrastive studies and thus to enhance the testability, authenticity and empirical adequacy in this field. A firm empirical grounding in linguistics, however, does not stand in contrast with a solid theoretical hypothesis. On the contrary, the papers show that it is necessary to set up falsifiable hypotheses about the cross-linguistic differences under investigation and to translate them into research questions so that they become apt to empirical investigation.

Second, the papers showcase a relatively recent shift in the field of corpus-based contrastive studies, where more attention is paid to semantic and pragmatic phenomena (Aijmer 2009). Contrary to primarily form-based approaches, the study of semantic and pragmatic issues present a series of methodological challenges, since the latter have appeared to be more difficult to combine with a thorough corpus linguistic research (Adolphs 2008). This is due to the more complex nature of corpus retrieval and linguistic analysis of semantic and pragmatic phenomena, as these are typically not traceable on a formal level, but have to be identified and categorized on the basis of very subtle interpretation of the data. The case-studies in this issue show that a combination of qualitative and quantitative approaches is needed for an accurate verification of the hypotheses. The future challenge for corpus-based analyses is undoubtedly the development of this multi-methodological approach which is objective and verifiable.

Finally, the contributions also reflect the ongoing discussion on the usefulness of different types of multilingual data in contrastive studies (Mauranen 1999, McEnery & Xiao 2007, Hasselgård forthcoming). Previous research has already shown that translation corpora can be a valuable tool for linguistic description (James 1980, Johansson & Hofland 1994) and for pragmatic markers in general (Aijmer et al. 2006, Lauwers, Vanderbauwhede & Verleyen 2010) . However, recently, several experts have insisted on the importance of combining translation corpora with larger comparable corpora (Johansson 2007), as it is repeatedly shown that language use in translated texts differs systematically from original texts in that same language (Laviosa 2002).

The papers in this issue all witness a growing awareness in choosing the appropriate corpora in order to verify their hypotheses. Some authors effectively combine comparable and parallel corpora (Usoniene & Šoliene, Williams), others work exclusively with comparable corpora (Defrancq & De Sutter, Fetzer & Johansson, Kanté, Noël & Colleman).

The contributions

In the first paper, **Dirk Noël and Timothy Colleman** report on a diachronic investigation of two morphosyntactic configurations which a few centuries ago were used both in English and Dutch but which have almost completely disappeared in the latter language, the so-called "raising-to-object" (or "Accusativus Cum Infinitivo" — ACI) and the "raising-to-subject" constructions (or "Nominativus Cum Infinitivo" — NCI). In particular, the authors question the common assumption in Anglophone and Dutch linguistics, that the NCI pattern is a merely passive counterpart of the ACI construction.

Two empirical methods are used. After an analysis of the frequencies of *believe*-type raising-to-object and raising-to-subject constructions in two comparable diachronic corpora, a 'distinctive collexeme analysis' is performed. The latter looks for differences in collocational preferences and relates them to differences in constructional semantics. The combination of the frequency analysis with the distinctive collexeme analysis allows the authors to test and confirm the following hypotheses: First, that both in English and Dutch, the NCI construction has a clear symbolic value which differs from the passive and hence that it cannot be reduced to a mere combination of an ACI pattern and the general passive form. The second confirmed hypothesis states that, especially for English, the NCI pattern has always been more than a mere passive.

Bart Defrancq and Gert De Sutter focus on the use of so-called contingency hedges in English, French and Dutch, i.e. linguistic items that speakers use in order to temper viewpoints expressed in previous discourse (either their own viewpoint or others' viewpoints). From an onomasiological point of view, the authors observe that both in English and French there is only one linguistic item at speakers' disposal, viz. *depend* and *dépendre* respectively. In Dutch, however, three alternatives can be used to realise this same function: *afhangen, te zien zijn* and *liggen*. This observation leads the authors to formulate two research questions: (i) are the contingency hedges used differently in the three languages and (ii) which parameters govern the onomasiological variation in Dutch? Building on three comparable corpora of Dutch, French and English, the authors argue that in all three languages the contingency hedges are semantically related to a conditional or causal meaning, as they signal that viewpoints expressed or asked for in the preceding discourse depend on other information. From a syntactic point of view, they observe that the contingency hedges in English, French and Dutch have undergone a process of decategorialisation, as the syntactic environment in which they appear is fixed to a large extent (in terms of verb morphology, type of subject, argument realisation). Nevertheless, some of the Dutch contingency hedges can still be used in a more flexible manner. Finally, it is shown that the choice between the available Dutch alternatives mainly depends on the exact function of the contingency hedges and the region where it is uttered; the communicative situation in which it is used plays only a marginal role.

Ian A. Willams investigates the stylistic properties of medical research articles in English and Spanish. More specifically, the study compares how authors in the two languages use the stylistic device of first person self references ("I" and "we") in the method section to support rhetorical moves. A quantitative analysis of two comparable English and Spanish corpora shows that in both languages, just under half of the articles use first person self references. However, within these articles, the device is used significantly more in Spanish than in English. A qualitative analysis using collocation and colligation information shows that the function of first person self references in Spanish and English is quite different. Whereas in Spanish the first person is used across the whole methods section with an intersubjective function to establish a rapport between author and reader, English self references have a much more specific use in justifying an author's personal choice to deviate from standard procedure in setting up or analysing an experiment. Williams' analysis of Spanish translations of English articles shows that translations tend to follow the English rather than the native Spanish use of first person self references and thus that translated language can deviate from original language.

Like Defrancq and De Sutter, **Anita Fetzer and Marjut Johansson** study a clause construction that functions as a discourse marker. In two comparable corpora of English and French political debates on television, they analyse the hedging function of parenthetical clauses introduced by a first person cognitive verb (*believe/think* and *croire/penser*). The quantitative data shows that such constructions are more common in English than French political discourse. A further qualitative analysis shows that parentheticals introduced by *believe* and *croire* have a boosting function that emphasises the conviction of the speaker. *Think* and *penser* can have both a boosting and attenuating function. In the latter case the parenthetical has an intersubjective function that indicates to the hearer that a proposition is open for negotiation.

An analysis of the connectives that link the parentheticals to the previous discourse shows an interesting difference between English and French. English politicians seem to prefer a more confrontational style using negative and contrastive connectives to mark their disagreement with their opponents in the debate. French politicians on the other hand have a higher use of causative connectives that seems to put the consistency of their argumentation in focus.

Issa Kanté presents a French — English contrastive study on the lexico-semantic relation between noun complement *that*-clauses and modality. This paper deals with the complex verification of a series of hypotheses on the role of modality. In the first part, the author puts forward a series of pragmatic and semantic arguments with the intention of showing the relation between the modality of the head noun and the use of *that*-clauses. In the second part, this hypothesis is tested in a quantitative analysis of two monolingual corpora. In particular, the author analyses the mood alternation in clauses introduced by nouns belonging to three modality groups, viz. epistemic nouns (e.g. *certainty, certitude*), alethic nouns (e.g. *likelihood, vraisemblance*) and deontic nouns (e.g. *constraint, contrainte*). These analyses show that the use of the indicative or the subjunctive in *that* complement clauses is clearly correlated to the modality type of the head of the subordinate clause. Further, it is shown that this correlation is cross-linguistically different. Whereas both in English and in French the epistemic nouns generally select the indicative, with regard to the alethic and deontic nouns, the mood selection differs. In French both classes favour the subjunctive, whereas in English the former chooses the indicative while the latter selects the subjunctive.

Aurelia Usoniene and Audrone Šoliene address a central issue in functional typology with their study on modality in English and Lithuanian. Using both parallel and comparable corpora, they analyse the verbal and adverbal strategies in English and Lithuanian for expressing epistemic possibility. They show that both languages dispose of roughly the same repertoire for encoding epistemic modality, but that the distribution over the specific devices is quite different: Whereas English prefers modal auxiliaries, Lithuanian uses relatively more modal adverbs. Qualitative analysis shows that this can be traced to the strong grammaticalisation of English modal auxiliaries, which is lacking in Lithuanian. Interestingly, the analysis of translational correspondences shows a substantial amount of zero correspondences in both directions. Apparently, the need for expressing an epistemic stance in specific propositions diverges considerably between the two languages and is argued to be indicative of a difference in the conceptualization of epistemic modality in English and Lithuanian.

Acknowledgments

In editing the present volume we were supported by a group of reviewers: we thank Karin Aijmer, Chris Butler, Bert Cappelle, Bart Defrancq, Liesbeth Degand, Hilde Hasselgård, and Johan van der Auwera, for their insightful comments and advice. We are also grateful to the authors for their contributions and efficient collaboration. Most of the papers were originally presented at The 5th International Contrastive Linguistics Conference (ICLC-5) held in Leuven in 2008. We would like to thank the organisers of ICLC-5 for having contributed to the realization of this publication project.

References

Adolphs, S. 2008. *Corpus and Context. Investigating Pragmatic Functions in Spoken Discourse.* Amsterdam/Philadelphia: John Benjamins.

Ajmer, K., Foolen, A.P., Simon-Vandenbergen, A.-M., Fischer, K. 2006. "Pragmatic markers in translation: A methodological proposal". In K. Fischer (Ed.), *Approaches to Discourse Particles.* Amsterdam: Elsevier, 101–114.

Aijmer, K. (Ed.) 2009. *Contrastive Pragmatics.* Special issue of *Languages in Contrast*, 9 (1). (also published as a volume in Benjamins Current Topics, 2011)

Butler, Ch., Gómez-González, M.L. A. & Doval Suárez, S. M. 2005. *The Dynamics of Language Use: Functional and Contrastive Perspectives.* Amsterdam/Philadelphia: John Benjamins

De Sutter, G., Delaere, I. & Plevoets, K. (2012). "Lexical lectometry in corpus-based translation studies. Combining profile-based correspondence analysis and logistic regression modeling". In M. Oakes & J. Meng (Eds.), *Quantitative Methods in Corpus-based Translation Studies. A practical guide to descriptive translation research.* Amsterdam: Benjamins, 325–345.

Gómez-González, M. L. A., Mackenzie, J. L. & González Álvarez, E. M. (Eds.) 2008. *Current Trends in Contrastive Linguistics: Functional and Cognitive Perspectives.* Amsterdam/Philadelphia: John Benjamins.

Granger, S., Lerot, J. & Petch-Tyson, S. 2003. *Corpus-based Approaches to Contrastive Linguistics and Translation Studies.* Amsterdam: Rodopi.

Granger, S. & Petch-Tyson, S. (Eds.) 2003. *Extending the Scope of Corpus-based Research: New Applications, New Challenges.* Amsterdam: Rodopi.

Hasselgård, H. forthcoming. "Forthcoming: Parallel corpora and contrastive studies". To appear in R. Xiao (ed.) *Corpus-Based Contrastive and Translation Studies: Recent Developments.* Amsterdam: John Benjamins.

James, C. 1980. *Contrastive Analysis.* London: Longman.

Johansson, S. 2007. *Seeing Through Multilingual Corpora: On the Use of Corpora in Contrastive Studies.* Amsterdam/Philadelphia: John Benjamins.

Johansson, S. & Hofland, K. 1994. "Towards an English-Norwegian parallel corpus". In U. Fries, G. Tottie & P. Schneider (Eds.), *Creating and Using English Language Corpora.* Amsterdam: Rodopi, 25–37.

Laviosa, S. 2002. *Corpus-based Translation Studies: Theory, Findings, Applications.* Amsterdam: Rodopi.

Mauranen, A. 1999. "Will 'translationese' ruin a contrastive study?". *Languages in Contrast.* 2 (2), 161–185.

McEnery, A. M. & Xiao, R. Z. 2007. "Parallel and comparable corpora: What are they up to?" In: G. M. Anderman, M. Rogers (Eds.): Incorporating Corpora: Translation and the Linguist. Translating Europe. Clevedon: Multilingual Matters.

Neumann, S. 2012. *Contrastive Register Variation. A quantitative approach to the comparison of English and German.* Berlin: De Gruyter.

Salkie, R. 1999. "How can linguists profit from parallel corpora?". Paper given at the *Symposium on Parallel Corpora, University of Uppsala, 22–23 April 1999.*

Tummers, J., Heylen, K. & Geeraerts, D. 2005. "Usage-based approaches in Cognitive Linguistics: A technical state of the art". *Corpus Linguistics and Linguistic Theory* 1 (2), 225–261.

Xiao, R. (Ed.) 2010. *Using Corpora in Contrastive and Translation Studies.* Newcastle: Cambridge Scholars Publishing.

Believe-type raising-to-object and raising-to-subject verbs in English and Dutch

A contrastive investigation in diachronic construction grammar*

Dirk Noël and Timothy Colleman
The University of Hong Kong / Ghent University

The so-called 'raising-to-subject' pattern that verbs of the type *believe* can occur in is usually treated as the passive alternative for the so-called 'raising-to-object' pattern. In addition to broadening the empirical basis for the opposite claim that the English and Dutch raising-to-subject (or 'nominative and infinitive') patterns have a special functionality which is different from that of the passive construction, this paper specifically examines the stronger proposition that this has always been the case. It empirically investigates whether this proposition holds equally well for English and Dutch through a comparison of the frequencies of *believe*-type raising-to-object and raising-to-subject patterns in two diachronic corpora. The methodology makes use of Distinctive Collexeme Analysis.

1. Introduction

This paper reports on a contrastive, diachronic, constructionist investigation of two morphosyntactic configurations that a few centuries ago were shared by the grammars of English and Dutch but which only remained productive in the first of these two languages. The first is a pattern that consists of an active perception, cognition or utterance verb (which Givón 1990 has grouped as 'P-C-U verbs') complemented by a *to*-infinitive that has its own explicit subject, as illustrated by the bits in italics in (1) and (2). Both in Chomskyan and post-Chomskyan linguistics this pattern is usually referred to as 'raising to object', also outside formalist paradigms (see, e.g., Givón 1993). An older, non-transformational, term for it is 'accusative and infinitive' (or 'ACI', short for 'accusativus cum infinitivo'). We have used this term in previous work (Noël 2003, 2008; Noël & Colleman 2009a) and will continue to do so here for reasons that will become clear below, having to do with the origin of the pattern.[1]

(1) The former Lord Chancellor, Lord Hailsham, said he *believed the scientific community to be* a responsible one. (BNC A96 259)

(2) Elk *meent zijn uil* een valk *te zijn.* (Dutch proverb)
     "Everyone considers his owl to be a falcon."

The second pattern consists of a passive P-C-U verb complemented by a *to/te*-infinitive, as in (3) and (4), and is often referred to as 'raising to subject'. The alternative term is 'nominative and infinitive' (or 'NCI', short for 'nominativus cum infinitivo').

(3) BOMB DISPOSAL specialists were yesterday called out to beaches on the south-west coast of Scotland after *Second World War phosphorus canisters believed to be* from an undersea dump were washed ashore. (BNC K5D 9706)

(4) *De boten worden geacht* over een dag of vier Kaap Hoorn *te ronden.* (ConDiv *De Telegraaf* NIE_S2)
     "The boats are predicted to round Cape Horn in about four days."

The functionality of the ACI has received a considerable amount of attention in the linguistics of English, where it is usually contrasted with that of a matrix + *that*-clause construction, both in a synchronic (see Noël 1997, 2003; and the references there) and a diachronic perspective (see Fischer 1989, 1992; Los 2005; and the references there). Especially in historical English linguistics, the terms 'accusative and infinitive' and 'ACI' are not unusual. 'Nominative and infinitive' and 'NCI', on the other hand, are not commonly used in Anglophone linguistics, since the NCI pattern is usually perceived as merely the passive counterpart of the ACI and consequently is not given independent attention. Largely the same is true of Dutch linguistics, where the ACI has mainly been treated in historical accounts (e.g. Overdiep 1935, Duinhoven 1991, Fischer 1994), Zajicek (1970) being the only dedicated study of the ACI in Present-day Dutch. We have proposed in Noël (2008) and Noël & Colleman (2009a), however, that both in English and in Dutch NCI patterns usually have a symbolic value which is quite different from that of the passive and that therefore the NCI cannot in most cases be reduced to a combination of an ACI construction and the general passive construction. In construction grammar terms, the NCI is not merely the passive version of the ACI, but qualifies as a construction — or rather, a cluster of constructions — in its own right. We have also argued, specifically about the English NCI, that it has *always* been more than a mere passive, i.e. that the English NCI pattern was not first a passive before certain specific NCI constructions developed, particularly what we have called the 'evidential NCI construction' (Noël 2008).

Our objective in the present paper is to strengthen the empirical basis for both of these claims, and to establish whether the second one applies to Dutch as well, through a comparison of English and Dutch historical frequency data on the ACI and the NCI. We will start the paper with a summary presentation of the semantic potential of the English and Dutch NCI and of the evidence adduced so far in support of the claim that at least one specific NCI construction, the evidential NCI, has always been there in English (Section 2). We will then formulate and motivate the research questions addressed in the present paper (Section 3) and describe in detail where we went looking for answers and how we went about it (Section 4), followed by a presentation and discussion of our findings (Section 5).

2. Background

2.1 The plain passive NCI and three NCI constructions

In English, both the ACI and the NCI patterns are productive morphosyntactic configurations that allow a great variety of P-C-U verbs. However, not only is the variety greater in the case of the NCI, the NCI is also generally more frequent than the ACI. In the 100-million-word British National Corpus (BNC), the overall ratio is almost three to one, but for some representatives of the P-C-U class figures are much more dramatic, to the point that some verbs do not display the active pattern at all (e.g. *say, rumour, repute*; see Noël 2001 for details). This is the observation that led us to suspect that the NCI is not just a passive, because passives are not normally more frequent than actives (see, e.g., Biber et al. 1999). We have proposed in Noël (2008) that most NCI patterns have at least three uses and that a distinction should be made between a plain passive NCI (as in (5)), an evidential NCI (6) and a descriptive NCI (7). Only the first of these constitutes a mere combination of an ACI construction and the general passive construction. The other two are constructions in their own right, with specific semantic properties. The discussion of the examples will help to make clear this distinction.

(5) In this book authorities *are said to be* limited also by the kinds of reasons on which they may or may not rely in making decisions and issuing directives, and by the kind of reasons their decisions can pre-empt. (BNC ANH 148)

(6) AMERICAN ring doughnuts from The Delicious Donut Co are made from a flour which *is said to give* them a light, fluffy, and non-greasy consistency. (BNC A0C 1141)

(7)   A market can *be said to be* a place where buyers and sellers meet to make an exchange of goods (or services). (BNC K8W 508)

We call the NCI in (5) a "plain passive" (even though no active "equivalent", i.e. an ACI, with *say* is possible in Present-day English) because the meaning of the matrix verb (*said*) is very much part of the propositional meaning of the sentence, which refers to a spatiotemporally locatable utterance act: a statement made "in this book". In this example the meaning of *are said to* is very much "on-stage" (cf. Langacker 1987): if you remove it, the sentence becomes nonsensical, or at the very least conveys an altogether different meaning (*?In this book authorities are limited also by...*). The NCI is used here for the same information packaging reasons that motivate the use of the passive generally (compare: *The authors of this book say that authorities...*). In (6) and (7), on the other hand, the meaning of the *be said to* pattern is "qualificational" (cf. Aijmer 1972: 39; Nuyts 2001: 113). These sentences do not report on a specific utterance act. The meaning of *be said to* is "off-stage" here and you can safely remove the pattern, so that *said* can be argued to no longer be a matrix verb, but to be part of an auxiliary-like construction that modifies the meaning of the infinitive. Examples (6) and (7) have in common that the NCI is not used for information structural reasons (since it can be left out: *...a flour which gives them..., A market is a place...*), but they differ in that they illustrate two different form-meaning pairings.[2] In (6) the modifying construction has an evidential function, i.e. its writer uses the pattern to indicate that s/he has a *source* for the information s/he is conveying, so that s/he is not the (sole) judge of the factuality of the statement that American ring doughnuts are light, fluffy, and non-greasy (see Noël 2008 for further elaboration). In (7) the modifying construction connects a description with a descriptum (see Goossens 1991).

Other frequent instantiations of the "evidential NCI construction" in Present-day English are *be alleged to, be assumed to, be believed to, be claimed to, be considered to, be deemed to, be estimated to, be expected to, be felt to, be found to, be held to, be known to, be reported to, be seen to, be shown to, be supposed to, be taken to, be thought to* and *be understood to* (Noël 2008). Whether these can all realize the "descriptive NCI construction" as well remains to be seen. Two of these patterns can carry the additional meaning illustrated in (8) and (9), however.

(8)   Pupils *are expected to use* their Maths to solve problems. (BNC K9X 434)

(9)   You *were supposed to do* six and you only did four! (BNC KST 788)

In these examples *be expected to* and *be supposed to* instantiate a "deontic NCI construction".[3] The following examples illustrate that the same patterns can also be the realization of a plain passive (10)–(11) and the evidential NCI construction (12)–(13), and they can serve as further illustrations of the distinction between these two NCI uses. Note that in (12)–(13), *be expected to* and *be supposed to* have the same, somewhat paradoxical, function as *be said to* in (6): the writer has a source, which diminishes his/her responsibility for the information conveyed and at the same time adds to its reliability.

(10) Standards for exposure to benzene *are expected* by the UK government *to be set* in 1993: a level of 3 ppb is under consideration, although according to the World Health Organization there is "no known safe threshold dose". (BNC JC3 608)

(11) The mechanism *supposed* by Miller (1948) *to underlie* acquired equivalence is that introduced by Hull (1939) with his notion of secondary generalization. (BNC APH 1337)

(12) The Japanese economy *is expected to grow* by only 3.8% during fiscal 1991 compared with this year's 5.2%. (BNC ABD 953)

(13) Napoleon *is supposed to have* said "An army marches on its stomach." (BNC A77 422)

In Dutch the ACI and NCI are much less "part of the grammar" than in English. To illustrate the ACI construction in Present-day Dutch we resorted to presenting an archaism in the introduction, example (2), obviously a relic from a time when the pattern was more common in Dutch than it is now, because modern examples of the pattern are very hard to come by. In historical accounts the ACI is said to have had two usage peaks (see, e.g., Duinhoven 1991). It occurred more than sporadically at the start of the Middle Dutch period (generally taken to span the time from 1200 to 1500), but rapidly grew out of fashion again during that period. Later it enjoyed a brief moment of popularity in the early stages of Modern Dutch (late 16th and 17th century), mainly in the formal writings of authors who had had a classical training (van Leuvensteijn 1997). Subsequently it disappeared from the language, barring a few relics (c.f. Duinhoven 1991; Fischer 1994). Zajicek (1970:203) claims that the ACI still occurs with a limited set of P-C-U verbs in very formal administrative and didactic texts, but Duinhoven (1991:425) questions the grammaticality of most of the examples he offers, though he recognizes that the ACI is not altogether impossible in relative clauses. The Dutch NCI, on the other hand, has survived better than the ACI, but it is a far less prolific pattern there than in Present-day English. Corpus research of our own revealed that the only patterns that still occur today with any frequency are *geacht worden te* ("be considered/supposed to"), *verondersteld worden te* ("be supposed to") and, to a lesser extent, *verwacht worden te* ("be expected to"). While the 20 most frequent NCI patterns in Present-day English occur with a frequency of 340.47 tokens per million words in the entire BNC, and with a frequency of 433.45 and 710.53 tokens per million words respectively in a newspaper and a natural sciences sub-corpus of it, these three Dutch patterns together only occur with a frequency of 4.4 tokens per million words in a fragment of about 12.5 million words of the newspaper component of the Dutch ConDiv corpus (Noël & Colleman 2009a).

Like the English NCI, the Dutch NCI is not simply a passive, however, if at all. Most often it instantiates a deontic NCI construction as in (14), less often an evidential NCI construction as in (15) and occasionally also a descriptive NCI construction as in (16). We have exemplified them here for *geacht worden te* (for examples of the other patterns, see Noël & Colleman 2009a).

(14) Chefs van afdelingen *worden geacht* excessief of nutteloos surfen *te voorkomen*. (ConDiv NRC_NIEUWS07)
"Heads of departments are supposed to prevent excessive and useless surfing."

(15) Ze werden populair bij atleten en wielrenners omdat meer rode bloedlichaampjes *worden geacht* een "zuurstofvoorsprong" *te geven*. (ConDiv NRC_VARIA01)
"They [EPO hormones] became popular with athletes and cyclists because more red blood cells are thought to give an 'oxygen advantage.'"

(16) Kan de rechterlijke macht, nu in ons constitutioneel staatsbestel alle machten van de natie uitgaan, *geacht worden* de natie *te vertegenwoordigen*? (ConDiv DS961216)
"Since in our constitutional system all powers are vested in the nation, can the judicial power be supposed to represent the nation?"

Zooming in on the evidential NCI construction, we will now summarize our evidence so far for the claim that the arrival of this construction in English (and Dutch) cannot be separated in time from the NCI's introduction into these languages as a morphosyntactic possibility.

2.2 A concise and selective history of the evidential NCI

Though there is no complete consensus on the origin of the ACI and the NCI in the two languages considered here, the two late-20th-century authorities on these structures in English historical linguistics, Warner (1982) and Fischer (1989, 1992, 1994), agree that these patterns are calques from Latin which became thoroughly entrenched in the grammar of English in the 15th century. In Dutch historical linguistics the debate on whether they are native or of Latin origin seems not to have been settled yet (for a summary and references, see Noël & Colleman 2009a: 166) but there is agreement at least that when these patterns acquired a certain popularity in Early Modern Dutch (between 1500 and 1650) this was due to the influence of Latin. With regard to the NCI this raises the question of whether what was copied was simply a passive of the ACI — which went on to develop a number of "qualificational" functions through grammaticalization processes internal to English and Dutch — or whether there already was an evidential NCI in Latin. Comments in text-analytical work on the use of *dicitur* ("be said") and *creditur* ("be thought/believed/supposed") by Roman authors seem to suggest that the latter was the case (Noël 2008: 323–324).[4] One cannot therefore avoid the conclusion that, if the NCI was a borrowing from Latin, so must have been the evidential NCI construction. In other words, it is unlikely that the English and Dutch evidential NCI are the result of a grammaticalization of the passive NCI owing to the routinization resulting from frequent use that is typical of central cases of grammaticalization. The fact that many early examples of the NCI in English are clearly of an evidential nature supports this (Noël 2008: 324–325). It is a claim for which further support is needed, however, and it especially needs to be confirmed for Dutch.

3.   Problem: Have the English and Dutch NCI always been more than passives?

The research reported on in the present paper was designed to provide a type of evidence for the past constructional status of the NCI in both English and Dutch which does not rely on the analyst's interpretation of individual examples but which provides claims about this with a more objective, empirical basis. If the evidential NCI was borrowed from Latin — and hence was there from the start of the introduction of the NCI pattern in English/Dutch — and if the presence of this construction helps to explain the higher frequency of the NCI pattern relative to the ACI in Present-day English and Dutch, one might expect that the NCI has always been more frequent than the ACI in these languages. Research on the occurrence of these patterns in Middle English does not support this expectation (Warner 1982, Fischer 1992), nor does research on Middle Dutch, Fischer (1994: 111) reporting having found "no examples" of the NCI in the Middle Dutch sources she consulted.[5] However, while there is no relevant research on Early Modern English, Fischer (1994: 113) did find a "large number" of NCIs in a corpus of 17th-century Dutch she put together. The difference between these two observations on Dutch could be highly significant, also for English, because the influence of Latin on Dutch as well as English of course came in two completely different waves. There first was the influence of biblical and ecclesiastical Latin during the Middle Ages and later the influence of classical texts during the Renaissance. One could speculate that there was less need for an evidential construction in the religious texts that were influential for Middle English and Middle Dutch than in the scholarly texts that were important during the 17th century. Therefore, starting where earlier research suggests it might be meaningful to do so, we will trace back the history of the English and Dutch ACI and NCI to the 17th century, asking whether the NCI has consistently been more frequent than the ACI from then till now in both languages. If this turns out to be the case, one may assume the NCI to have had a different symbolic value from the passive from the moment the frequency of this morphosyntactic pattern was boosted under the influence of classical texts.

Next, inspired by the work by Gries & Stefanowitsch (Stefanowitsch & Gries 2003; Gries & Stefanowitsch 2004), we will try to find supplementary evidence for the special symbolic value of the NCI by asking whether the ACI and NCI have consistently displayed a different preference for certain verbs in the two languages. If indeed Latin *dicitur* and *creditur* served as a model for the evidential NCI, one might expect for instance that English verbs like *say* and *believe* and Dutch verbs like *zeggen* and *geloven*, and/or semantically closely related verbs, will have consistently preferred the NCI over the ACI. In more general terms, if from the moment the ACI and NCI patterns were introduced in English and Dutch the NCI had a number of specific semantic properties not shared by the active construction, most notably the evidential function, this should be evident from the kinds of verbs frequently attested in both patterns.

4. Methodology

The decision to start this contrastive diachronic investigation in the 17th century was also partly determined by the availability of two comparable corpora that were large enough to produce reliable frequency data on the phenomenon under investigation. The first one is the Corpus of Late Modern English Texts (CLMET) compiled at the University of Leuven by Hendrik De Smet, with texts drawn from the *Project Gutenberg* and the *Oxford Text Archive*. At the time the CLMET was downloaded for use in the present research (i.e. in the spring of 2006), it spanned a period from 1640 to 1920, divided into four sub-periods of 70 years each, ranging from 1.9 to 6.1 million words of running text (for an account of the principles behind the compilation of the corpus, see De Smet 2005). The comparable Dutch corpus is one that was compiled along the same principles as the CLMET for the purpose of the study reported on in Noël & Colleman (2009a). It consists of extracts from texts available online from the *Digitale Bibliotheek voor de Nederlandse Letteren* and the *Project Gutenberg* and spans the same period as the CLMET, the size of the four 70-year subcorpora ranging from 1.2 to 3.5 million words of running text.

English NCI patterns were identified in the CLMET by looking for past participle forms of P-C-U verbs immediately followed by *to*. The ACI patterns were identified by searching for any form of P-C-U verbs separated from *to* by 0 to 6 words. The verbs searched for constitute the union of three collections of verbs: (a) the verbs that were investigated in Noël (2001), i.e. the ones referred to there as "the sixty-odd *believe*-type verbs that Postal (1974: 297–317) lists in his chapter on 'The scope of raising in clause domains'", (b) the verbs that were included in Noël (2008) and Noël & Colleman (2009a), i.e. the ones that were identified as NCI verbs in the BNC by manually sifting the results of a query for any form of the verb *be*, followed by "any word", followed by the infinitival particle *to*, and (c) the verbs that were identified in the CLMET as NCI verbs by manually sifting the results of a query for any form of the verb *be*, followed by "any word", followed by *to be*. This produced a list of 138 English verbs, 74 of which turned out to occur at least once as an ACI and/or an NCI verb in the CLMET (i.e. the ones included in Table 1 below).

The Dutch ACI and NCI patterns were identified in the Dutch corpus by looking for any form of P-C-U verbs separated from *te* by 0 to 10 intervening words (the larger span as compared to the English queries being motivated by the relatively more free word order in Dutch). The verbs searched for were those that have either been said in the literature to still occur occasionally in ACI and/or NCI patterns today (Duinhoven 1991, Zajicek 1970, Noël & Colleman 2009a) or to have occurred in these patterns during the 17th century (Overdiep 1935, Duinhoven 1991, Fischer 1994). These selection criteria resulted in a list of 62 Dutch verbs, 42 of which were attested at least once in ACI and/or NCI patterns in the diachronic corpus (i.e. the ones listed in Table 2 below).

For each language, the absolute frequencies of the patterns subsequently formed the input of four separate *distinctive collexeme analyses*, i.e. one for each of the sub-corpora. For a full explanation and justification of this methodology we would like to refer to Gries & Stefanowitsch (2004), but very briefly what a distinctive collexeme analysis does is test the degree of association between two or more "competing" constructions C_1, C_2, etc. and the various lexemes occurring in a particular slot of these constructions, on the basis of the co-occurrence frequencies of lexeme x and C_1, x and C_2, etc. and the overall frequencies of C_1, C_2, etc. in the corpus (or the sub-corpus in our case). A lexeme is revealed by this test to be significantly attracted to one of the constructions under investigation if its observed frequency in that construction significantly exceeds the frequency expected on the basis of the overall distributions. If this procedure is repeated for all lexemes occurring in the investigated slot of either of the constructions in the corpus, the outcome is a list of so-called *distinctive collexemes* for each of the examined constructions, i.e. the lexemes which significantly prefer that construction over the other construction(s) (in this case, the verbs with a significantly above-average preference for the ACI over the NCI or vice versa). The analyses were carried out using version 3 of Stefan Gries' R-script for collostructional analysis (Gries 2004).

5. Results and discussion

5.1 General comments

The results of the frequency counts in each of the four parts of the two corpora are provided in Table 1 and Table 2, respectively. To allow comparison, the bottom row in both tables presents the totals as frequencies per million words.

Table 1. Observed frequency of the ACI and the NCI in the four CLMET sub-corpora

PCU verb	Period I: 1640–1710 (1,978,050 wds)		Period II: 1710–1780 (3,036,325 wds)		Period III: 1780–1850 (5,777,348 wds)		Period IV: 1850–1920 (6,103,660 wds)	
	ACI	NCI	ACI	NCI	ACI	NCI	ACI	NCI
admit	2	0	6	2	22	14	8	16
affirm	7	1	8	1	8	3	7	0
allege	1	0	0	1	2	3	0	7
announce	0	0	0	0	1	2	1	5
apprehend	4	0	6	1	1	1	0	0
approve	0	0	1	3	0	0	0	0
ascertain	0	0	0	0	5	2	2	2
assert	2	0	11	1	5	5	3	1
assume	0	0	0	0	1	3	18	11
avow	0	0	0	1	2	1	0	0
believe	36	2	47	6	161	24	142	31
calculate	0	0	1	1	1	0	2	7
certify	0	0	0	0	0	0	0	1
claim	1	0	0	0	0	1	1	4
compute	1	3	2	2	0	2	0	0
conceive	24	8	16	6	57	9	19	6
conclude	17	1	12	2	15	0	2	0
confess	20	2	4	7	6	1	2	0
conjecture	0	0	1	0	3	1	2	1
consider	5	1	6	3	40	9	29	21
declare	16	4	11	2	29	10	19	14
decree	0	0	0	0	0	1	0	0
deem	1	0	0	0	9	5	2	1

Table 1. *(continued)*

PCU verb	Period I: 1640–1710 (1,978,050 wds)		Period II: 1710–1780 (3,036,325 wds)		Period III: 1780–1850 (5,777,348 wds)		Period IV: 1850–1920 (6,103,660 wds)	
	ACI	NCI	ACI	NCI	ACI	NCI	ACI	NCI
demonstrate	1	2	0	0	1	3	1	4
deny	17	0	7	5	1	0	2	0
describe	2	0	1	0	6	5	2	0
detect	0	0	0	1	0	0	0	0
determine	0	0	1	2	2	0	0	0
discern	1	2	0	0	1	0	1	0
discover	3	2	20	6	17	5	12	6
establish	0	0	1	0	0	0	0	0
esteem	4	1	5	2	2	0	1	0
estimate	0	0	1	0	1	0	0	2
expect	10	2	24	20	99	118	208	139
experience	0	0	4	5	0	0	0	0
fancy	2	0	6	0	5	0	8	1
feel	1	1	4	0	40	6	69	9
find	108	19	132	76	52	137	37	92
grant	7	5	2	0	3	0	2	0
guarantee	0	0	0	0	0	1	0	1
guess	2	1	3	0	9	0	6	0
hold	9	1	8	5	25	15	31	38
imagine	23	5	23	13	39	2	33	5
judge	19	9	28	2	8	4	10	3
know	63	37	73	48	169	128	118	103
note	0	7	0	0	1	1	1	1
notice	0	0	0	0	0	0	2	1
observe	24	27	23	12	9	13	5	8
perceive	17	5	15	0	18	6	5	4
presume	5	14	0	2	3	6	2	3
presuppose	0	0	0	0	0	0	1	0
pretend	10	10	1	2	4	7	1	0
proclaim	2	1	0	0	3	0	1	0
profess	6	0	1	0	5	0	1	0
pronounce	0	1	8	3	29	9	15	5
propound	0	2	0	0	0	0	0	0
prove	17	6	16	6	34	22	21	15

Table 1. *(continued)*

PCU verb	Period I: 1640–1710 (1,978,050 wds)		Period II: 1710–1780 (3,036,325 wds)		Period III: 1780–1850 (5,777,348 wds)		Period IV: 1850–1920 (6,103,660 wds)	
	ACI	NCI	ACI	NCI	ACI	NCI	ACI	NCI
reckon	0	1	3	4	1	1	0	2
recognise	0	0	3	0	3	1	2	0
report	2	5	0	17	2	12	2	19
repute	0	3	0	1	0	3	0	6
reveal	0	0	0	1	0	0	1	0
rumour	0	1	0	0	0	0	0	2
say	4	157	0	243	0	318	0	196
see	12	17	10	14	3	31	19	45
show	7	3	13	0	13	7	36	18
state	1	0	1	2	11	14	5	6
suppose	33	70	120	224	137	218	101	196
surmise	0	0	0	0	1	0	0	0
suspect	4	5	16	3	16	1	9	1
take	58	15	76	3	26	2	33	15
think	31	56	11	46	16	43	18	36
understand	5	27	5	17	12	25	21	16
TOTAL (absolute)	664	551	809	839	1,216	1,271	1,108	1,132
(normalized per million words)	*335.7*	*278.62*	*266.44*	*276.38*	*210.49*	*220*	*181.51*	*185.43*

Table 2. Observed frequency of the ACI and the NCI in the four sub-corpora of a diachronic corpus of Dutch literary texts

PCU verb	Period I: 1640–1710 (1,188,932 wds)		Period II: 1710–1780 (2,471,692 wds)		Period III: 1780–1850 (2,625,226 wds)		Period IV: 1850–1920 (3,518,374 wds)	
	ACI	NCI	ACI	NCI	ACI	NCI	ACI	NCI
bedenken "think of"	0	1	0	0	0	0	0	0
begrijpen "understand"	0	0	9	1	0	0	0	0
bekennen "confess"	0	0	2	0	1	0	0	0
beschouwen "consider"	0	0	0	0	0	1	0	1
betonen "show, prove"	0	0	0	1	0	0	0	0

Table 2. *(continued)*

PCU verb	Period I: 1640–1710 (1,188,932 wds)		Period II: 1710–1780 (2,471,692 wds)		Period III: 1780–1850 (2,625,226 wds)		Period IV: 1850–1920 (3,518,374 wds)	
	ACI	NCI	ACI	NCI	ACI	NCI	ACI	NCI
betuigen "express"	0	0	1	0	0	0	0	0
bevinden "find"	16	0	15	4	2	6	0	2
beweren "state, claim"	1	0	4	0	0	0	1	0
bewijzen "prove"	0	1	4	0	2	1	0	0
considereren "consider"	0	3	0	0	0	0	0	0
denken "think"	4	0	12	0	2	0	1	0
erkennen "recognize"	1	0	3	0	1	1	0	0
geloven "believe"	5	0	15	0	2	0	1	0
gevoelen "feel"	1	0	0	0	0	0	0	0
hopen "hope"	5	0	2	0	0	0	0	0
houden "hold, consider"	1	0	1	1	1	3	0	1
kennen "know"	1	0	2	0	0	0	0	0
menen "be of the opinion"	5	0	15	0	4	0	5	0
merken "perceive"	3	0	0	0	0	0	0	0
noemen "call"	0	0	2	0	0	0	0	0
ondervinden "experience"	0	0	3	0	0	0	0	0
ontkennen "deny"	0	0	1	0	0	0	0	0
oordelen "judge"	32	1	33	5	8	1	0	0
rekenen "estimate"	0	0	3	5	4	6	0	1
schatten "estimate"	0	1	0	0	0	0	0	0
schrijven "write"	1	0	0	0	0	0	0	0
stellen "state"	1	0	1	0	1	0	0	0
sustineren "assume"	0	0	1	0	0	1	0	0
verhalen "tell"	1	0	0	0	0	0	0	0
verklaren "declare"	0	0	4	0	5	3	0	0
vermoeden "suppose"	0	0	1	0	1	0	1	0
vernemen "be told"	1	0	0	0	0	0	0	0
(ver)onderstellen "suppose"	0	1	8	9	2	1	3	5
vinden "find"	4	0	2	1	2	1	0	0
voorgeven "profess"	0	0	1	2	1	0	0	0

Table 2. *(continued)*

PCU verb	Period I: 1640–1710 (1,188,932 wds)		Period II: 1710–1780 (2,471,692 wds)		Period III: 1780–1850 (2,625,226 wds)		Period IV: 1850–1920 (3,518,374 wds)	
	ACI	NCI	ACI	NCI	ACI	NCI	ACI	NCI
voorstellen "present, imagine"	0	0	1	1	0	0	0	0
voorwenden "pretend"	0	0	0	2	0	0	0	0
verstaan "understand"	0	1	0	0	0	0	0	0
wanen "presume"	2	0	5	0	1	0	0	0
weten "know"	5	0	5	0	0	1	0	0
zeggen "say"	20	2	14	20	6	12	2	9
TOTAL (absolute)	120	11	172	53	53	43	18	28
(normalized per million words)	*100.93*	*9.25*	*69.59*	*21.44*	*20.19*	*16.38*	*5.12*	*7.96*

A brief glance at these normalized total frequencies suffices to show that both the ACI and the NCI consistently occurred far more frequently in English than in Dutch. Even at their respective frequency peaks — 100.93 ACI instances per million words in the first period and 21.44 NCI instances per million words in the second period — the Dutch frequencies are nowhere near the English ones, which range between 181.51 (Period IV) and 335.7 (Period I) per million words for the ACI and between 185.43 (Period IV) and 278.62 (Period I) for the NCI. In the last period, the Dutch frequencies have dropped to 5.12 instances per million words for the ACI and 7.96 for the NCI. Moreover, the majority of these instances is made up of just four verbs, viz. *achten* "consider", *menen* "be of the opinion", *veronderstellen* "suppose" and *zeggen* "say", corroborating earlier observations that the ACI and NCI are infrequent and lexically restricted patterns in the later stages of Modern Dutch (Fischer 1994, Noël & Colleman 2009a). In English, by contrast, both patterns are very much part of the grammar throughout the investigated period and many individual verbs attain respectable ACI and/or NCI frequencies, allowing for statistical comparison. In the next two subsections, we will first zoom in on these English data and then compare the observed trends to the situation in Dutch, to the extent that the data enable us to do so.

5.2 English

A comparison of the normalized frequencies in the bottom row of Table 1 reveals that the overall higher frequency of the English NCI relative to the ACI only came about in the 18th century.[6] Counter to the expectations formulated in Section 3, the ACI was more frequent than the NCI in the 17th century. However, unlike in Dutch (see below), the NCI was already well established at the start of the investigated time span, the proportion of ACI to NCI instances in the first period (1640–1710) being about six to five. In addition, if we start comparing the frequencies of the NCI and ACI patterning of individual verbs, we notice that there are a number of verbs that already preferred the NCI over the ACI in the 17th century. This is confirmed by the results of the distinctive collexeme tests for each of the four sub-corpora, summarized in Table 3. This table lists the distinctive ACI and NCI collexemes in each period, in order of diminishing "collostructional strength" (i.e. degree of association).[7] For instance, in the first period, *find* is the verb with the strongest preference for the ACI over the NCI, and *say* displays the strongest preference for the NCI over the ACI.

Table 3. Significant distinctive collexemes of the English ACI and NCI in the four CLMET sub-corpora, in order of diminishing collostructional strength

Period I (1640–1710)		Period II (1710–1780)		Period III (1780–1850)		Period IV (1850–1920)	
ACI	NCI	ACI	NCI	ACI	NCI	ACI	NCI
believe	suppose	believe	suppose	conceive	find	feel	suppose
take	under-	judge	think	imagine	see	imagine	pose
deny	stand	find	report	feel	sup-	expect	find
confess	think	perceive	under-	take	pose	take	report
conclude	note	show	stand	consider	think	conceive	see
imagine	presume	suspect		conclude	report	affirm	allege
conceive		assert		suspect	under-	show	think
declare		discover		pronounce	stand	suspect	repute
hold		conclude		declare		guess	
perceive		know		guess		fancy	
profess		declare		know		pro-	
expect		fancy		discover		nounce	
prove		affirm		perceive		judge	
know		conceive		acknowl-		know	
		prove		edge			
		observe		fancy			
				profess			
				prove			

Table 3 shows that six verbs display a statistically significant above-average preference for the NCI in the 17th century, viz. *say, suppose, understand, think, note* and *presume*. Three of these continue to display a significant preference for the NCI in subsequent centuries, viz. *say, suppose* and *think*, while one of them, *presume*, continues to be more frequent as an NCI verb but not in a statistically significant way. Other verbs that consistently prefer the NCI over the ACI but not in a statistically significant above-average way in all four sub-corpora are *see*, *report* and *repute*. Conversely, there are also verbs that display a consistent preference for the ACI, viz. *affirm, assert, conclude, consider, declare, deny, discover, fancy, guess, imagine, judge, perceive, profess, prove* and *show*, and four verbs do so statistically significantly in all four periods, viz. *believe, take, conceive* and *know*. For several of the other verbs just mentioned the ACI preference is statistically significant in three of the four periods; instances include *conclude, declare, perceive* and *prove*, all of which display a significantly above average preference for the ACI in the first three sub-periods (and a non-significant ACI preference in Period IV). The results therefore clearly point toward the existence of two subclasses of P-C-U verbs, distinguished by their constructional preferences, "ACI verbs" and "NCI verbs".[8] Moreover, such a distinction was already present at the start of the time span covered in this investigation. There is only one verb that changes sides, as it were, in a statistically significant way, viz. *find*, which demonstrates a significant above-average preference for the ACI in the first two time periods, but then a significant above-average preference for the NCI in the last two periods.

We think all of this is congruent with the hypothesis that the special symbolic value of the NCI is not a recent development and that, moreover, the history of the English evidential NCI goes back further than the 18th century. Though the NCI only overtook the ACI in frequency during that century, this does not mean that the NCI only developed its special functionality around then. It is merely the confirmation of a stylistic change that has been independently established to have taken its course during the 18th century and as a result of which a construction we would argue was already available increased in usefulness. Adamson (1998:662), for instance, has written that

> During the eighteenth century, an objectivising, generalising style had become the goal in most forms of public discourse, prompting writers to look for ways of eliminating, minimising or conventionalising the use of subjective features. In scientific writing, for instance, the impulse towards objective description led to the gradual emergence of the passive, which linguistically emancipates an experiment from its author's personal experience (by converting, for instance, "I saw the liquid boil" to "the liquid was seen to boil").

In our analysis the example of the "passive" given here is an evidential NCI.

The claim that the evidential NCI was already around before then is supported by the semantic nature of the verbs that already displayed a significant preference for the NCI in the 17th century. It cannot be a coincidence that most of these verbs are semantically closely related to either of the two Latin verbs *dicere* ("say") or *credere* ("believe, think"), which led to the Latin evidential constructions *dicitur* and *creditur. Be said to* is obviously equivalent to the former and *be thought/supposed/presumed to* are all equivalent to the latter. In other words, the semantics of these NCI verbs is compatible with the hypothesis that the evidential NCI is a calque from Latin.

The fact that there is a sizeable group of verbs that has consistently preferred the ACI above the NCI and a group that has consistently preferred the NCI above the ACI can be taken to confirm that the two patterns have always had a different symbolic value (at least for the period covered by the CLMET). It is not easy to detect what the members of each group have in common that distinguishes them from the other group, but one could argue that most of the verbs that consistently prefer the ACI over the NCI have a more specific meaning than the average NCI verb. *Affirm, assert, declare, deny* and *profess*, for instance, cannot be characterized as "basic linguistic action verbs" (Verschueren 1985), unlike *say*, the most typical NCI verb. Likewise *conceive, conclude, consider, fancy, guess, imagine, judge* and *take* are less basic cognition verbs than *think* and *suppose*. The same cannot be said of the typical ACI verbs *believe* and *know*, but they perhaps differ from the typical NCI verbs *think* and *suppose* in strength or commitment. *Believe* can be a near synonym of *think*, but it can also have the stronger meaning glossed by Dixon (2005: 140) as "think of something as true (when in fact it may not be, but the Cogitator will not accept that it may not be)". Similarly, *know* implies more commitment to the truth of a proposition than both *think* and *suppose*. One could hypothesize, therefore, that the specificity and/or the commitment entailed by the verbs typically occurring in the ACI pattern requires these verbs to have an expressed, topical "agent", which makes them less compatible with the NCI pattern, because this is usually agentless. It would also make these verbs less compatible with the typical "off-stage" meaning of the NCI.

If we compare the results of our distinctive collexeme analysis with Gries & Stefanowitsch' (2004) distinctive collexeme analysis for the active vs. the passive construction, displayed in Table 4, a few additional observations can be made with relation to the symbolic value of both patterns.

A first observation is that none of the verbs we considered are part of Gries and Stefanowitsch' list of the 20 most distinctive collexemes of the passive. Our verbs are all P-C-U verbs, but there are no P-C-U verbs among the verbs most typically associated with the passive. This alone might already be an indication that NCIs are not first and foremost passives. Gries & Stefanowitsch (2004: 110) conclude from their results that

> the distinctive-collocate collexeme analysis shows that passive voice is a construction in its own right with its own specific semantics. It encodes a situation where the referent of the passive-voice subject has come to be in some relatively stable end

Table 4. Collexemes distinguishing between active and passive (culled from Table 3 in Gries & Stefanowitsch 2004: 109)

active collexemes	passive collexemes
have	*base*
think	*concern*
get	*use*
say	*involve*
want	*publish*
do	*associate*
know	*bear*
see	*engage*
mean	*design*
like	*confine*
try	*entitle*
hope	*relate*
believe	*deposit*
remember	*compare*
feel	*derive*
suppose	*deal*
wish	*aim*
thank	*release*
enjoy	*attach*
ensure	*store*

state as a result of someone acting on it. The distinctive collexemes of the active-voice construction are either action verbs that do not lead to such end states, or they are states that are not brought about by someone acting on the entity in this state.

Utterance acts and acts of cognition and perception do not, of course, involve entities that are acted on, which predisposes P-C-U verbs to favouring the active voice. Yet still many of them have for a long time preferred the ostensibly "passive" NCI pattern over the active ACI.

A second and more crucial observation is that there are quite a few P-C-U verbs in the active column of Table 4 and four of them are verbs that consistently prefer the NCI above the ACI: *say, think, suppose* and *see*. This is an important fact: if these verbs both typically occur in the active voice construction *and* in the NCI pattern, the latter must be more than just a passive. Translated in constructionist terms, there exist NCI constructions that do not "inherit" the semantics of the passive construction (on "inheritance" in construction grammars, see Lakoff 1987: 508; Goldberg 1995: 73–74; Kay & Fillmore 1999: 7–8, 30–31).

A third and final observation is that two verbs that show an above-average preference for the active over the passive also display a consistent above-average preference for the ACI over the NCI, viz. *believe* and *know*. This would be consistent with a situation in a constructional network where the ACI is a daughter construction of the active construction. In other words, ACIs are actives, but NCIs are usually not passives, at least not semantically.

How to explain the fact that *find* changes from being a typical ACI verb to being a typical NCI verb? We would contend that this, too, can be related to the historical stylistic change affecting expository genres which we already referred to above. Additional support for it is supplied by Montgomery (1996), who has observed that 17th-century science writing offered "detailed descriptions of experiments, as a kind of 'historical' writing of what happened, told directly through the 'I' as a personal narrator of events, such that the reader would be brought as close to these events as possible" (Montgomery 1996: 93), whereas "[b]y the early 19th century, […], the actor-I had begun to disappear" (Montgomery 1996: 106). In an academic culture where the most reliable underpinning of information offered is observational or experimental evidence which is somehow "found", *find* is of course the quintessential evidential verb. It is consequently little surprising that it was first frequently used in the active voice and that it was subsequently recruited for use in the evidential NCI when changing evidentiality requirements boosted the frequency of this construction. The fact that *find* was first predominantly associated with the ACI and later with the NCI therefore substantiates the symbolic value of the latter.[9]

5.3 Contrasting English and Dutch

If we compare the normalized frequencies in the bottom row of Table 2 with the matching information in Table 1, we notice that the frequencies are not only consistently much lower in Dutch than in English, both for the ACI and the NCI, but the proportional relationship between the two patterns in the two languages is different as well. Whereas in English the NCI was only mildly less frequent than the ACI in the 17th century and then became the more frequent pattern, in Dutch the NCI started out being considerably less frequent than the ACI, remained much less frequent in the 18th century in spite of a rise in its frequency and a drop in the frequency of the ACI, and only in the second half of the 19th century became the more frequent pattern, though a very rare one compared to the English NCI. As was stated in Section 2.1 above, earlier research into the presence of both patterns in Present-day Dutch has shown that the ACI is (virtually) extinct and that only three verbs are attested in the NCI pattern with any frequency, viz. *achten* ("consider"), *veronderstellen* ("suppose") and *verwachten* ("expect") (Noël & Colleman 2009a). Overall, therefore, it seems clear that Dutch has moved from a situation where only the ACI was a true option, if not a very frequently taken one, to a situation where only the NCI is possible, though again not frequent (neither in type nor token frequency).

To corroborate this we computed a gamma coefficient of the relation between the numbers of observed ACI and NCI instances over time. This revealed that, in statistical terms, there is a significant linear increase in the proportion of the NCI in the combined total of ACI and NCI instances from the first period in our corpus to the last (effect of NCI versus ACI uses: $\gamma = 0.5970491$, ASE $= 0.05621057$).[10] In other words, in Dutch, the proportion of the NCI displays a significant linear increase as time goes by. There is no such trend in English: the figures in Table 1 do show a slight increase of the NCI proportion from Period I to Period II, but this is followed by a status quo. A conclusion can be that the Dutch NCI developed its special functionality later than the English one.[11]

As for the ACI and NCI frequencies of the individual verbs in the Dutch table, many of them are too low to allow meaningful comparison. It is technically possible to conduct collexeme analyses of these data, since the method of distinctive collexeme analysis can handle small frequencies, but, unsurprisingly, the results of these tests are far from spectacular. Only in Period II (i.e. the period with the largest absolute ACI and NCI frequencies) does the test reveal a number of statistically significant contrasts: *geloven* ("believe"), *denken* ("think") and *menen* ("be of the opinion") are significant ACI collexemes while *zeggen* ("say"), *(ver)onderstellen* ("suppose") and *rekenen* ("estimate") are significant NCI collexemes. Overall, however, and leaving aside statistical significance, the numbers that seem large enough to be indicative of constructional preferences suggest a preference for the ACI before the 19th century (i.e. in the first and second periods of the corpus), most notably in the cases of *achten* ("consider"), *bevinden* ("find"), *oordelen* ("judge"), *denken* ("think"), *geloven* ("believe") and *menen* ("be of the opinion"). At least two of these verbs seem later to have developed a preference for the NCI, viz. *achten* and *bevinden*, but the numbers are small and only NCI *achten* has survived to this day (Noël & Colleman 2009a). *Zeggen* ("say") preferred the ACI in the first period only and "already" developed a preference for the NCI in the 18th century, which is interesting in the light of a dedicated study of NCI *zeggen* in a large 19th-century Dutch corpus (Colleman & Noël 2009), which showed that *gezegd worden te* ("be said to") at one time used to be quite common as an evidential in formal varieties of written Dutch. Note, however, that the preference for NCI *zeggen* in Dutch is less marked and comes later than the preference for NCI *say* in English.

In sum, though we cannot underpin this claim with statistical evidence of the kind offered in the previous subsection, the fact that *achten, bevinden* and *zeggen* seem to have changed from preferring the ACI to favouring the NCI does constitute evidence that the Dutch NCI did not simply inherit the general semantic properties of the passive construction, unless one would wish to argue that the meaning of the passive has changed. The special functionality of the Dutch NCI surfaced later than that of the English NCI, however, and was never exploited to the same extent.

6. Conclusion

This paper has demonstrated differences between English and Dutch in the historical evolution of the entrenchment of their ACI and NCI patterns. Our main aim, however, was to test the hypothesis that the NCI has always had a symbolic value different from (or on top of) that of the passive construction. The empirical, non-interpretative evidence supplied here was inspired by and based in part on Gries & Stefanowitsch' (2004) distinctive collexeme analysis methodology. Distinctive collexeme analysis can provide evidence for the symbolic value of constructions through a measure of the degree of association between (alternating) constructions and the lexemes that fill them. We have shown that, in English, there is a subclass of P-C-U verbs which have for a long time (starting at least in the 17th century, possibly earlier) displayed a statistically significant above-average preference for the NCI. Several of these verbs display the same kind of preference for the active voice and this makes it very unlikely that the NCI, though "passive" in form, has a mainly "passive" symbolic value, or that this has ever been the case even. Our findings therefore corroborate the hypothesis that right from the start of the investigated period the English ACI and NCI were not just perspectival variants distinguished primarily by their active vs. passive information-structural properties, but had quite different symbolic values.

In Dutch, unlike in English, the NCI was decidedly less frequent than the ACI during the first half of the investigated time span and became the more frequent pattern only in the second half of the 19th century. Our data reveal a significant linear change in the preference of the examined verbs from the ACI in the 17th century to the NCI in the 20th century. The extent of the change is such that the ACI has all but disappeared from Dutch. The verbs that remain in the NCI today, *achten* ("consider"), *veronderstellen* ("suppose") and *verwachten* ("expect"), are all cognition verbs. Unless one can argue that the Dutch passive attracts an altogether different category of verbs than the English passive, the extremely close association between these three verbs and the NCI in Present-day Dutch, combined with the fact that one of them used to be closely associated with the ACI, is an indication that in Dutch, too, the NCI has a symbolic value different from the passive. However, the Dutch NCI seems to have developed this special functionality more recently than the English pattern.

Notes

* We are grateful for the comments of two anonymous referees and for the financial support of the University of Hong Kong Seed Funding Programme for Basic Research (contract no. 200611159021), the Research Fund of the University of Ghent (for the project "Meaning in between structure and the lexicon", contract no. GOA B/05971/01) and the Belgian Federal Science Policy Office (for the project "Grammaticalization and (Inter)Subjectification", contract no. IUAP P6/44). We also owe gratitude to Chan Tsz Ying and Fung So Hing for their help with sifting the data that went into Table 1.

1. The description and the examples of the ACI offered here should make clear that what we will be dealing with is the pattern which is sometimes called the "genuine", "learned" or "Latin-type" ACI (e.g. see Fischer 1989, 1992, 1994), i.e. the pattern containing what Postal (1974) termed 'B-element R-triggers' (verbs of the type of *believe* that "trigger Raising"). The term 'ACI' has also been used to refer to perception verbs and causative verbs (*make*, *let*) followed by "accusatives" and bare infinitives, and mandative verbs (e.g. *order*) followed by accusatives and *to*-infinitives, but these patterns do not constitute the object of investigation in this paper.

2. An anonymous referee has rightly pointed out that our paraphrase of (7) not only leaves out the NCI pattern but also the modal *can*, which might therefore be part of the descriptive NCI construction. However, we have noted in Noël & Colleman (2009a: 153) that modals (not necessarily *can*) are only an optional (though frequently occurring) part of this construction. An example without a modal cited there is:

   (i) When two grammatical items occur together in a specified syntagmatic relation, they
        are said to colligate and the combination is a colligation (as opposed to a collocation).
        (BNC H0Y 1159)

3. The reference to "additional" meanings should not be taken to mean that the deontic NCI construction has developed from another NCI construction, particularly the evidential one, though this has recently been suggested in the literature (for references and a paper-length discussion of this point, see Noël & van der Auwera 2009).

4. Moles (1991: 553), for instance, offers the following comment about the use of *dicitur* in the lines *risissi Cupido / dicitur atque unum surripuisse pedem* ("Cupid is said to have laughed and to have stealthily removed one foot") from Ovid's *Amores*: "'It is said', 'they say', 'there is a story' etc. are often used as 'distancing' formulae whereby the writer does not commit himself to the veracity of certain material, particularly when it is of a supernatural character". Space prevents a more elaborate discussion, but obviously, this shedding of responsibility for the truthfulness of a proposition through the invocation of an unspecified source is strikingly reminiscent of the effect of the NCI in some of the Present-day English and Dutch examples discussed above.

5. Fischer (1994) terms NCI patterns "second passives", following Warner (1982), who in turn borrowed the term from Lees (1960).

6. The general drop in the frequencies of the ACI and NCI is less relevant here and there is no space to discuss it. Suffice it to say regarding the frequency of the NCI that we have argued elsewhere that a comparison with its present-day frequency, established on the basis of the British National Corpus, suggests that the drop in its frequency in the genres that are well-represented in the CLMET (fiction and philosophy) must have been matched by a frequency rise in genres that are not represented there (journalism and science) (Noël 2008). We have no data on whether such genre distinctions are relevant to the ACI as well and on whether the frequency of the ACI continued to drop in the 20th century.

7. Only collexemes which are significant at the 95% level of statistical confidence ($p < 0.05$) are included in the table.

8. There are also a number of verbs which are not revealed by the tests to be significantly attracted to either the ACI or the NCI in any of the four investigated sub-corpora. Most of these are low-frequency verbs with too few attested ACI and NCI instances to allow for conclusions about their constructional behaviour (e.g. *avow, conjecture, surmise*). *Pretend* is the only verb with over 20 relevant instances which is attracted to neither of the two constructions in none of the four periods and which might hence be considered as truly "neutral" with regard to the ACI/NCI distinction (note, however, that the majority of relevant instances of *pretend* date from the first period, after which *both* its ACI and NCI uses seem to have dwindled).

9. For a paper-length elaboration of this point, see Noël & Colleman (2009b).

10. The gamma coefficient characterizes the strength of the association between two variables of which at least one is ordinal (in this case the period variable is inherently ordered, from Period I to Period IV). Values range from -1 (perfect negative linear association) to +1 (perfect positive linear association), with a value of zero indicating the absence of association. A .95 confidence interval (CI) is computed around the gamma coefficient as follows: CI = gamma +/- 1.96 * ASE (=Asymptotic Standard Error). For the association of NCI to ACI frequencies in Dutch, the gamma coefficient is 0.5970491 and the ASE is 0.05621057. This means that the .95 confidence interval is [0,486 ; 0,707]. Since this interval excludes the zero value, we can be 95% certain that there is a positive linear association: the number of NCI as opposed to ACI instances significantly increases from Period I to Period IV.

11. Our findings for Period I seem to be at odds with the claim in Fischer (1994: 113), namely that she observed a "large number" of NCIs in 17th-century Dutch. Since Fischer does not report exact ACI and NCI frequencies, it is impossible to compare her findings on this score with ours. However, her statement about the large number of NCIs in Renaissance Dutch must probably be seen in relation to the observed absence of such patterns in Middle Dutch, rather than as a claim about the synchronic relation between the ACI and the NCI in the 17th century.

References

Adamson, S. 1998. "Literary language". In S. Romaine (Ed.), *The Cambridge History of the English Language, IV, 1776–1997*. Cambridge: Cambridge University Press, 589–692.

Aijmer, K. 1972. *Some Aspects of Psychological Predicates in English*. Stockholm: Almqvist & Wiksell.

Biber, D., Johansson, S., Leech, G., Conrad, S. & Finnegan, E. 1999. *Longman Grammar of Spoken and Written English*. Harlow: Longman.

Colleman, T. & Noël, D. 2009. "*Gezegd worden* + *te*-infinitief: Een verouderde evidentiële constructie". [Dutch *gezegd worden* ("be said to") + *te*-infinitive: An archaic evidential construction.] *Tijdschrift voor Nederlandse Taal- en Letterkunde*, 125 (4), 385–403.

De Smet, H. 2005. "A corpus of Late Modern English texts". *ICAME Journal*, 29, 69–82.

Dixon, R. M. W. 2005. *A Semantic Approach to English Grammar*. Oxford: Oxford University Press.

Duinhoven, A. M. 1991. "Dat siet men wit ende reine wesen. A.c.i.-constructies in het Nederlands". *Nieuwe Taalgids*, 84 (5), 409–430.

Fischer, O. 1989. "The origin and spread of the accusative and infinitive construction in English". *Folia Linguistica Historica*, 8 (1–2), 143–217.

Fischer, O. 1992. "Syntactic change and borrowing: The case of the accusative and infinitive construction in English". In D. Stein & M. Gerritsen (Eds.), *Internal and External Factors in Syntactic Change*. Berlin: Mouton de Gruyter, 77–88.

Fischer, O. 1994. "The fortunes of the Latin-type accusative and infinitive construction in Dutch and English compared". In T. Swan, E. Mørck & O. Jansen Westvik (Eds.), *Language Change and Language Structure: Older Germanic Languages in a Comparative Perspective*. Berlin: Mouton de Gruyter, 91–133.

Givón, T. 1990. *Syntax: A Functional-typological Introduction*, Vol. 2. Amsterdam/Philadelphia: John Benjamins.

Givón, T. 1993. *English Grammar: A Function-based Introduction*, Vol. 2. Amsterdam/ Philadelpia: John Benjamins.

Goldberg, A. E. 1995. *Constructions: A Construction Grammar Approach to Argument Structure*. Chicago: The University of Chicago Press.

Goossens, L. 1991. "FG reflections on 'Tobacco is said to be harmful'". *Cahiers de l'Institut de Linguistique de Louvain*, 17 (1–3), 65–74.

Gries, S. Th. 2004. Coll.analysis 3, R-script for collostructional analysis. Available on demand from the author.

Gries, S. Th. & Stefanowitsch, A. 2004. "Extending collostructional analysis: A corpus-based perspective on alternations". *International Journal of Corpus Linguistics*, 9 (1), 97–129.

Kay, P. & Fillmore, C. J. 1999. "Grammatical constructions and linguistic generalizations: The *What's X doing Y?* construction". *Language*, 75 (1), 1–33.

Lakoff, G. 1987. *Women, Fire and Dangerous Things: What Categories Reveal about the Mind*. Chicago: The University of Chicago Press.

Langacker, R. W. 1987. *Foundations of Cognitive Grammar, Vol. 1: Theoretical Prerequisites*. Stanford: Stanford University Press.

Lees, R. B. 1960. *The Grammar of English Nominalizations*. Bloomington: Indiana University Press.

van Leuvensteijn, J. A. 1997. "Vroegnieuwnederlands (circa 1550–1650)". In M. C. van den Toorn, W. Pijnenburg, J. A. van Leuvensteijn & J. M. van der Horst (Eds.), *Geschiedenis van de Nederlandse Taal*. Amsterdam: Amsterdam University Press, 227–272.

Los, B. 2005. *The Rise of the To-Infinitive*. Oxford: Oxford University Press.

Moles, J. 1991. "The dramatic coherence of Ovid, *Amores* 1.1 and 1.2". *The Classical Quarterly*, 41 (2), 551–554.

Montgomery, S. L. 1996. *The Scientific Voice*. New York: The Guilford Press.

Noël, D. 1997. "The choice between infinitives and *that*-clauses after *believe*". *English Language and Linguistics*, 1 (2), 271–284.

Noël, D. 2001. "The passive matrices of English infinitival complement clauses. Evidentials on the road to auxiliarihood". *Studies in Language*, 25 (2), 255–296.

Noël, D. 2003. "Is there semantics in all syntax? The case of accusative and infinitive constructions vs. *that*-clauses". In G. Rohdenburg & B. Mondorf (Eds.), *Determinants of Grammatical Variation in English*. Berlin: Mouton de Gruyter, 347–377.

Noël, D. 2008. "The nominative and infinitive in Late Modern English: A diachronic constructionist approach". *Journal of English Linguistics*, 36 (4), 314–340.

Noël, D. & Colleman, T. 2009a. "The nominative and infinitive in English and Dutch: An exercise in contrastive diachronic construction grammar". *Languages in Contrast*, 9 (1), 144–181.

Noël, D. & Colleman, T. 2009b. "ACI and NCI *find* and the development of evidentiality in Modern English, with a note on Dutch *(be)vinden*". In S. Slembrouck, M. Taverniers & M. Van Herreweghe (Eds.), *From Will to Well: Studies in Linguistics Offered to Anne-Marie Simon-Vandenbergen*. Ghent: Academia Press, 337–346.

Noël, D. & van der Auwera, J. 2009. "Revisiting *be supposed to* from a diachronic constructionist perspective". *English Studies*, 90 (5), 599–623.

Nuyts, J. 2001. *Epistemic Modality, Language and Conceptualization: A Cognitive-pragmatic Perspective*. Amsterdam/Philadelphia: John Benjamins.

Overdiep, G. S. 1935. *Zeventiende-eeuwsche Syntaxis (Derde Stuk)*. Groningen/Batavia: Wolters.

Postal, P. M. 1974. *On Raising: One Rule of English Grammar and Its Theoretical Implications*. Cambridge, MA: MIT Press.

Stefanowitsch, A. & Gries, S. Th. 2003. "Collostructions: Investigating the interaction of words and constructions". *International Journal of Corpus Linguistics*, 8 (2), 209–243.

Verschueren, J. 1985. *What People Say They Do With Words: Prolegomena to an Empirical-Conceptual Approach to Linguistic Action*. Norwood, NJ: Ablex.

Warner, A. R. 1982. *Complementation in Middle English and the Methodology of Historical Syntax: A Study of the Wyclifite Sermons*. London: Croom Helm.

Zajicek, J. 1970. "Réflexions sur l'accusativus cum infinitivo". *Nieuwe Taalgids*, 63 (3), 198–208.

Contingency hedges in Dutch, French and English

A corpus-based contrastive analysis of the language-internal and -external properties of English *depend*, French *dépendre* and Dutch *afhangen, liggen* and *zien*

Bart Defrancq and Gert De Sutter
University College Ghent/Ghent University

This article reports on a detailed corpus-based and contrastive analysis of the syntactic, semantic and functional properties of English *depend*, French *dépendre* and Dutch *afhangen, liggen* and *zien* as markers of intersubjectivity. Based on three large-scale monolingual corpora of spoken English, French and Dutch, the results show that these intersubjectivity markers are semantically related to a conditional meaning of the verbs they are based on: viewpoints expressed or asked for in the preceding discourse are presented as valid only in particular circumstances. Furthermore, it is shown that the markers have undergone a process of decategorialisation, as they appear almost exclusively in third person present tense, and as the range of subjects that can be combined with these markers is more restricted than the non-intersubjective uses of these verbs. Finally, a detailed corpus analysis of the Dutch markers shows that their use is mainly determined by regional and functional parameters.

1. Introduction

Traditionally, contrastive linguistics is concerned with the description of formal correspondences and differences between languages against a semantic language-independent background often called 'tertium comparationis'. Several competing models exist to describe meaning language-independently, based on formal logic or deep structure (Krzeszowski 1990), semantic primes (Wierzbicka 1972), semantic maps (Anderson 1982), predicate types (Chesterman 1998), predicating fields (Weigand 1998), etc. In contrast with semantic information, pragmatic information appears to be considerably more difficult to model in a way that would be useful in contrastive studies. This is probably the reason why contrastive research into the mapping between form and pragmatic function is more often based on the use of parallel corpora than on carefully designed language-independent models of pragmatic function. The extensive contrastive research on discourse particles is a case in point in this respect (e.g. Aijmer 2002, Aijmer & Simon-Vandenbergen 2003, Simon-Vandenbergen & Aijmer 2003, Johansson 2007; for a recent exception, see Siepmann 2005).

The present paper aims to contribute to this kind of contrastive research of the syntax-pragmatics interface by focussing on a particular kind of hedges, called 'contingency hedges' in English, French and Dutch. More particularly, the formal, semantic and functional properties of English *depend*, French *dépendre* will be described and compared to their Dutch equivalents *afhangen* "to depend", *zien* "to see" and *liggen* "to lie".

The term 'contingency hedge' was first proposed by Moissinac & Bamberg (2004) in a study on discursive identity formation to describe the occurrence of *depend* in line 12:

(1)   – Group Discussion I/ 10-yr / Feb 2000 / 57:14–58:13
       Participants: M – Moderator; L – Lou, V – Vic; W – Wes, B – Ben

       01   M: ok guys what about you =
       02   L: = ° yeah yeah °
       03   M: is it important what girls look like↑
       04   B: uh-huh {nodding}
       05   V: mh-hmh
       06   M: yeah↑
       07   L: [{shakes head}]
       08   W: [ng-ngmh] [I dunno]
       09   M: [like what↑] like what
       10   B: <u>cute</u>
       11   M: cute
       12   W: <u>it depends</u>
       13   M: yeah↑ =
       14   V: =like Ben used to say he had a girlfriend but he never <u>did</u>
       15   B: YAH I DID
       16   V: which one↑ which one↑ {pointing at Ben}
       17   B: KAREN
       18   {Vic shakes his head 4 times while looking at Ben}

In their view, *it depends* is "a soft challenge to the status that [the hearer] has claimed and seemingly attained with the moderator" (Moissinac & Bamberg 2004: 12), i.e. the status of being a knowledgeable person in matters of female looks.

Taking stock of this example and its interpretation by Moissinac & Bamberg (2004), Defrancq & De Clerck (2009) define 'contingency hedges' as the use of particular linguistic items whose purpose is to mitigate viewpoints asserted or implicated in the preceding discourse by presenting them as dependent on parameters that were previously ignored. They studied approximately 900 examples of both *depend* and its French equivalent *dépendre* in spoken dialogues, and found that in both languages about half of these examples can be considered 'intersubjective', i.e. geared towards expressing stance in the interaction. A typical example of an intersubjective use is shown in (2), where *depend* allows the speaker to signal that a straightforward answer is not to be expected:

(2)   S1   Now it also goes on to say that's going to affect electricity prices which will rise, now how will that compensate with, with nuclear electricity?

       S2   Erm well *it depends* erm the, the economics of power production are extremely erm er complex and, and t to a certain extent arbitrary erm and erm I mean there, there are various ways that the government can actually get out of this fix because obviously it's caused a lot of concern to close the, the mines, and one is actually to, to subsidize the mines and put the price on to electricity bills er.

[BNC F8N 103, from Defrancq & De Clerck 2009]

Example (2) can be contrasted with (3), where *depend* is used non-intersubjectively, and expresses a social relationship between the individuals referred to by the subject and the prepositional phrase:

(3)   [...] and in the High Court case, we've just said, how can an employee be independent when *he depends* upon his employer for his future work.

[BNC JNP]

Defrancq & De Clerck (2009) also observe that the hedging achieved by means of *depend* and *dépendre* mostly aims at providing justification for behaviour that may be felt to be uncooperative (e.g. not answering a question), a breach of consensus (e.g. denial) or a retraction. By using a verb like *depend*, a speaker signals that answering a question may be difficult because of lacking information in the question or that the hearer's viewpoint (or even the speaker's own viewpoint) is true only in particular cases.

From a contrastive point of view, French and English do not appear to differ much as far as pragmatic functions are concerned and the verbs they recruit for these functions. However, French and English do differ with regard to the extent to which these verbs are affected by a process of decategorialisation (Hopper & Traugott 1993), i.e. the tendency of lexical items to lose the distinctive properties of the lexical category they belong to (Hopper & Traugott 1993). The precise effects of that process show significant divergence. More particularly, it has been shown that intersubjective uses of *depend* and *dépendre* have lost to a large extent the typical grammatical properties of their paradigm, i.e. mainly person, tense, aspect and modality markers and argument structure.

In this paper, we extend the research carried out by Defrancq & De Clerck (2009) by investigating the form and use of contingency hedges in Dutch and compare them with what is already known about contingency hedges in French and English. One important difference between Dutch on the one hand, and French and English on the other, is that the former possesses several verbs that can be used as contingency hedges. The verb *depend* in line 12 in (1), for instance, can be translated by Dutch *afhangen* "to hang", *liggen* "to lie" and *zien* "to see", as in the expressions *'t hangt ervan af*, *'t is te zien* and *'t ligt eraan*.

Two main questions emerge in this particular situation. First, from a contrastive linguistic point of view, how do the three Dutch alternatives relate to English *depend* and French *dépendre*? In other words, can Dutch *afhangen*, *zien* and *liggen* be used with the same functions as their English and French counterparts? Can the same process of decategorialisation be observed in the Dutch data and, if so, to what extent are the verbs already decategorialised? Second, from a monolingual point of view, how do Dutch *afhangen*, *zien* and *liggen* relate to each other? Is it a case of free variation or complementary distribution, and, if the latter applies, which parameters determine the variation?

Possible answers to the second question can be found in functional specialisation and regional or register divergence. As contingency hedging consists of several subtypes (e.g. hedging of answers to questions and hedging of assertions made by the hearer; cf. Section 5), it is reasonable to assume that some items specialise for some functions and others for other functions. The variation can also be considered from an extralinguistic, regional perspective. The Dutch language area consists of two large areas, viz. Flanders and the Netherlands, which are linguistically considerably different. Previous research has shown that both areas have to some extent unique lexical and constructional devices (e.g. Taeldeman 1993, Haeseryn 1996); in other cases, it has been found that the linguistic repertoire is used differently (e.g. Deygers & Van den Heede 2000, De Sutter et al. 2005, Grondelaers et al. 2008). Consequently, the relevant question here is whether language users in Flanders use these contingency hedges in a different way than language users in the Netherlands. Finally, since — as previous (sociolinguistic) research has convincingly shown — one of the main parameters that guide language users to choose between competing alternatives is the type of communicative situation (e.g. Finegan & Biber 1994, De Sutter et al. 2005), it is investigated to what extent the use of Dutch *afhangen*, *zien* and *liggen* depends on the register in which they are used.

This paper will deal with both above-mentioned questions. The first, contrastive question will be dealt with in Section 3 and 4. More particularly, these sections are concerned with the semantic and formal properties of the verbs under scrutiny. By doing so, we are able to shed light on the extent to which a decategorialisation process has taken place when these verbs are used as contingency hedges. The second, monolingual question will be answered in Section 5. There, it is investigated to what extent the choice for one of the three competing forms is determined by the type of intersubjective function that has to be realised, the region where it is realised and the type of communicative setting in which it is realised. Section 2 is devoted to a description of the corpora that are underlying the analyses in this paper. More particularly, three large-scale monolingual corpora of English, French and Dutch are used, i.e. the spoken part of the British National Corpus, the Valibel corpus and the Corpus of Spoken Dutch (CGN) respectively. Finally, the main conclusions will be presented in Section 6, which also discusses some perspectives for future research.

2. Data

The data for this study are extracted from the spoken part of the British National Corpus, the Valibel corpus of Belgian French and the Corpus Gesproken Nederlands (Corpus of Spoken Dutch; Oostdijk 2000). The English and French data are discussed in detail in Defrancq & De Clerck (2009). All selected corpora represent late-twentieth-century spoken English, (Belgian) French and Dutch. The Dutch and English corpora contain approximately 9 and 10 million words respectively, and they are distributed over different types of registers, such as classroom discussions, lectures, meetings and broadcasted commentaries. Moreover, the Dutch corpus is also stratified for national variety (Belgian Dutch vs. Netherlandic Dutch). The French corpus contains 3.5 million words and is restricted to only one type of spoken discourse, viz. interviews.

From the description above, it becomes clear that the French corpus is designed quite differently from the English and Dutch corpora. Consequently, when interpreting the results in the next sections, we will have to take into account these design differences. More particularly, the results for French will only be representative for Belgian French (regional limitation) in an interview setting (register limitation). In contrast, the results for English and Dutch represent various types of spoken registers in British English and Belgian and Netherlandic Dutch. Although one could argue that the results for French on the one hand and Dutch and English on the other are therefore not comparable, we still believe that the description of the inventory of semantic, formal and functional properties of French *dépendre* is generalizable to spoken French in general and to other types of registers, and hence can be compared to the English and Dutch inventories. Obviously, future research has to confirm this. In contrast, the frequency distributions of the semantic, formal and functional properties of the French, English and Dutch contingency hedges will have to be compared with more caution, as different registers and different regions affect the extent to which linguistic resources are used. We will return to this issue in the concluding section.

As the second part (Section 5) of this paper aims at revealing the influence of region and register on the choice between the Dutch competing contingency hedges, a full overview of the structure of the Dutch corpus, the Corpus of Spoken Dutch, is needed. Table 1 shows that the corpus is structured along a regional dimension (Netherlandic texts vs. Belgian Dutch texts) and a register dimension (14 different communicative settings). The table moreover shows that some of the register types in some of the regional varieties contain very few data, such as business negotiations in Belgian Dutch (n = 0) and sermons, lectures and speeches in Netherlandic Dutch (n = 5,565). We will take these proportional differences into account when interpreting the results in the next sections.

Table 1. Structure of the Corpus Gesproken Nederlands

		Regional dimension	
		Belgian Dutch	Netherlandic Dutch
	face-to-face conversations	878,383	1,747,789
	interviews with teachers	315,554	249,879
	telephone conversations	808,263	1,253,741
	business negotiations	0	136,461
	broadcasted interviews and discussions	250,708	539,561
Register dimension	political discussions, debates, meetings	138,819	221,509
	lessons	105,436	299,973
	broadcasted spontaneous commentaries	78,022	130,377
	broadcasted reportages, current affairs	95,206	90,866
	broadcasted news programme	82,855	285,298
	broadcasted commentaries	65,386	80,167
	sermons, lectures, speeches	12,510	5,565
	university lessons, lectures	79,067	61,834
	read aloud texts	351,419	551,624
		3,261,628	5,654,644

All instances of *depend, dépendre, afhangen, liggen* and *zien* were retrieved from the three corpora, provided they met the following selection criteria: (i) In the case of *depend, dépendre, afhangen, liggen*, all occurrences of the infinitive or any conjugated form in a non-analytic tense. This rules out prepositional forms such as *depending on* and adjectival forms such as *dépendant* ("dependent"). As these forms are hardly ever used as verb forms, their omission does not affect the statistics. (ii) In the case of *zien*, all occurrences of the infinitive, as this is the only way in which the verb can be used as a contingency hedge (in combination with a deontic use of *zijn* "be", see below). (iii) All occurrences should be connected in some way to causality. As will be explained in Section 3, the intersubjective uses of these verbs involve a particular kind of conditional relationship which in most cases is connected to a causal meaning of the verbs.

The total number of retrieved occurrences that complied with these selection criteria is 2,383: 918 occurrences for English, 897 for French and 568 for Dutch. Table 2 provides an overview of the frequency of these verbs used intersubjectively and non-intersubjectively. As some of the instances appeared to be unclassifiable, a third category 'indeterminate' is added to Table 2. This typically covers examples where the utterance preceding the use of one of the verbs has not been transcribed, is incomplete, overlaps with another utterance, etc.

Table 2. Frequency of the intersubjective and non-intersubjective use of the English, French and Dutch verb forms

		Intersubjective	Non-intersubjective	Indeterminate
English	*depend*	42.0% (386/918)	51.0% (468/918)	7.0% (64/918)
French	*dépendre*	53.8% (483/897)	44.3% (397/897)	1.9% (17/897)
Dutch	*afhangen*	53.1% (179/337)	38.6% (130/337)	8.3% (28/337)
	liggen	60.1% (110/183)	30.6% (56/183)	9.3% (17/183)
	zien	89.6% (43/48)	4.2% (2/48)	6.2% (3/48)

What these figures show is that English *depend* is used more often non-intersubjectively (51.0%) than intersubjectively (42.0%). Its French and Dutch counterparts, on the contrary, occur in more than half of the instances as intersubjectivity markers: Dutch *afhangen* is used in 53.1% of the cases as an intersubjectivity marker, followed by French *dépendre* (53.8%), Dutch *liggen* (60.1%) and Dutch *zien* (89.6%). Thus, the extent to which these verbs are used as contingency hedges varies considerably (all verb forms treated separately: $\chi^2 = 69.6$, df = 4, $p < .0001$; all Dutch verb forms grouped together: $\chi^2 = 43.5$, df = 2, $p < .0001$ — statistics without the indeterminate category).[1] In order to better grasp the differences in Table 2, we also performed a residual analysis. This enables us to answer the question which of the verb forms contributed most to the observed statistically significant differences. From this analysis it emerges that intersubjective *zien* is used more frequently than expected (residual: 3.9) and intersubjective *depend* less frequently than expected (residual: −3.2).

On the basis of the proportions in Table 2, Dutch *afhangen* appears to be a closer equivalent of French *dépendre* and English *depend* than both other Dutch verbs. Conversely, *liggen* and *zien* appear to have specialised within the field of causality, in the expression of intersubjective meaning. As Section 4 will show, this specialisation goes hand in hand with an increased frequency of formal features that are typical of a grammaticalisation process. Zooming in on the intersubjectivity markers in Dutch, it emerges from Table 2 that Dutch contingency hedges are most frequently expressed by *afhangen* (n = 179) and least frequently by *zien* (n = 43).

The statistical package R 2.7.0 (2008) was used for the statistical analyses presented below. It is important to note that the focus will be on the interpretation of the analyses, not on the technical details (cf. Agresti 1996). For all statistical tests performed in this study, significance cut-off level was set at .05: all p-values smaller than .05 indicate statistical significance, p-values larger than .05 indicate non-significance.

3. Semantic analysis of the contingency hedges

Depend and *dépendre* convey fairly similar meanings. In English the verb can be used, although it rarely is in Present-day English, in a concrete meaning referring to a particular position of an object, whereby one end of the object is higher up than the other one. This is illustrated by the following example, taken from the OED online:

(4) The branches of the damsons depended so low.

(JEFFERIES *Gt. Estate* 146, <u>1880</u>)

In French, the concrete meaning rather refers to the action of taking off an object from a hook, as illustrated by (5), taken from the *Grand Robert*:

(5) Dépendre un tableau.
     "Take off a painting."

In most cases, however, the English and French verbs are used to refer to several kinds of abstract relationships between individuals and concepts. Example (3) in Section 1 illustrates the use of *depend* to refer to a social relationship, whereas (6) and (7) are illustrations of conditional relationships between two entities:

(6)   Database technology *depends* on the development of an appropriate data model for structuring and manipulating the data.   [BNC CGA]

(7)   la désignation des futurs administrateurs de tous ces organes euh / *dépendra* de leur connaissance de l'anglais   [Valibel]
      "the appointment of the future Board members of all these bodies erm will depend on their knowledge of English"

The relationship of both (6) and (7) with the meaning conveyed in (4) and (5) is likely to be a metaphorical one, as described by Sweetser (1990), mapping a connection from the real world domain to the epistemic domain of causality.

As Defrancq & De Clerck (2009) show, the intersubjective uses of *depend* and *dépendre* are semantically related to the conditional meaning of examples such as (6): they signal that viewpoints expressed or asked for in the preceding discourse cannot be confirmed or provided without taking into account other bits of information. This again is an illustration of a metaphorical process described by Sweetser (1990), mapping a connection from the epistemic domain to the speech act domain.

In Dutch, the verbs that are used in contingency hedges are semantically very different. *Afhangen* is the prototypical equivalent of *dépendre* and *depend*; in its most concrete meaning it refers to the state of an object that is attached to another object by the upper side only and that is not supported by any other means, as in (8):

(8)   a dat komt door al die *afhangende* planten die hier uh allemaal voor je neus opeens…
      "oh, that is because of all these plants that are hanging down that erm all in front of you…"

As its French and English equivalents, *afhangen* can also refer to states and events that are causally connected to other states and events. In most cases, the causal connection is presented as potential, i.e. as a condition. In (9), for instance, the number of people must first be known before the subsidy can be calculated:

(9)   maar zou 't niet zo zijn dat de subsidies *afhangen* van 't aantal toeschouwers?
      "but wouldn't it be the case that subsidies depend on the number of people watching?"

Afhangen also refers to situations in which an individual cannot live a normal life without the support of another individual, as in (10):

(10)   dus dat zou goed zijn want daardoor zoudt hij kunnen blijven. en *hangt* ie
        niet meer *af* van die studiebeurs.
        "so that would be good, because then he would be able to stay and not
        depend any longer on a scholarship."

Finally, the intersubjective use is illustrated in (11), where S2 tells S1 that there is
no straightforward answer to the question if the nature of the dance is not taken
into account:

(11)   S1   dans maar ja dat moe* kan je moeilijk sport noemen hè?
        S2   *hangt* een beetje van *af* welke dans waarschijnlijk

             "dance but okay you real* you cannot really call that a sport, can you?
             depends a bit on what kind of dance probably"

Liggen is a multifunctional verb in Dutch. In its most concrete meaning it refers to
a particular position of an object. Much like English *lie*, which it is etymologically
related to, *liggen* is used to describe the position of an object that is situated on
another object and whose vertical extension in space is smaller than its horizontal
extension (Lemmens 2002). Example (12) illustrates this meaning:

(12)   als je begint met uh 't is er heel mild en 't is er altijd lekker weer en je kunt
        altijd aan 't strand *liggen* en in de winter kun je altijd schaatsen da 's lastig.
        "if you start saying erm the temperatures are very mild and it is always good
        weather and one can lie on the beach at all times and in winter one can skate
        that's a problem."

Liggen can also indicate a causal connection. Unlike *afhangen*, it mostly refers to
an actual cause, not to a potential one. In (13), for instance, the discontinuous *wh*-
item *waar-aan* ("to what") is in fact held responsible for the sneezing:

(13)   dus als er af en toe een nies tussendoor komt dan uh weet je waar 't aan *ligt*.
        "so if you hear me sneeze from time to time, you erm know how come."

The intersubjective uses of *liggen* are also related to the causal meaning of the verb.
Here again, the idea is that a viewpoint cannot be confirmed or provided without further information being available. In (14), for instance, S2 signals that S1's
previous assertion cannot be confirmed if no information is available about one's
preferences in matters of housing:

(14)   S1   nou 't is ook niet een streek waar je nou ja ik bedoel je zit hier overal
             nogal ver vandaan denk 'k.
        S2   ja *ligt* er*aan* wat je zoekt natuurlijk hè.

> "well it's not exactly an area where you well I mean it is a bit remote I think
> yeah depends what you're looking for, doesn't it."

The meaning extension from the content domain to the illocutionary domain is probably supported by the fact that, in a number of causal cases, *liggen* is used in an epistemic sense. In (15), the speaker signals that his/her view is strictly personal and may be due only to his/her own situation of not being a twelve- or fifteen-year-old:

(15) S1 zo wat jeugdliteratuur betreft heb je daar 't idee dat er op dit moment veel goeie dingen op de markt zijn die ook op school of op boekenlijsten zouden kunnen?

  S2 uhm. ik ik heb het idee maar *'t kan aan mij liggen* omdat ik misschien zelf geen twaalf- of vijftienjarige meer ben dat het uhm dat het zeer verbreedt.

> "as far as youth literature is concerned do you have the impression that nowadays there is a lot of good stuff available that could be put on reading lists in schools?
> erm my impression is but it could be me as I'm no longer a twelve- or fifteen-year-old that it's erm widening a lot."

Finally, *zien* is the prototypical equivalent of English *see*. It refers to a visual perception or cognition process, which probably underpins its use as a contingency hedge. To understand this, it is important to point out that in intersubjective uses, the verb is always in the infinitive and combined with an inflected form of *zijn* ("to be", underlined in the example), as in (16):

(16) S1 ja maar we kunnen dat niet gebruiken voor opname denk ik want dat gaat te veel lawaai zijn met de pan en …

  S2 xxx. ah ja ja. *'t is te zien* hoe dat jij kookt natuurlijk.

> "yeah but we can't use that for recording I think because there will be too much noise with that pan and…
> xxx oh yeah yeah it depends on how you cook of course."

Zijn is used as a modal or aspectual verb in cases like this, combining aspects of deontic modality and future tense, a combination which is quite common. Literally, in intersubjective cases, *zien* refers thus to an observation that still has to be made. In other words, the information that such an observation could provide is not available at the time of speech. The fact that the speaker presents it as relevant in the given context implies that it is in some way connected to the viewpoints expressed or implied in the preceding discourse.

4. Formal analysis of the contingency hedges

Traugott (1995) and a number of other scholars have pointed out that lexical items that are used with intersubjective functions are more prone to decategorialisation (as defined by Hopper & Traugott 1993, Heine 1993). This is a process whereby lexical items such as nouns and verbs lose the typical grammatical properties of their paradigm (Hopper & Traugott 1993: 106–107), i.e. mainly person, tense, aspect and modality markers, and argument structure. Typical examples are the English modal verbs and the Romance future tense that developed out of Latin *habere*. Defrancq & De Clerck (2009) have shown that person and tense markers of intersubjective *depend* and *dépendre* are affected, as well as their argument structure.

In both languages, 96% or more of the intersubjective cases appear in third person and present tense. As Table 3a shows, this proportion is much higher than in non-intersubjective cases (third person present tense vs. other verb forms: English: $\chi^2 = 128.9$, df = 1, $p < .0001$; French: $\chi^2 = 28.8$, df = 1, $p < .0001$). The size of those differences, quantified in terms of odds ratios, is 14.07 (C.I. = 8.19–24.19) for English and 15.47 (C.I. = 5.12–46.78) for French. This means that the choice for intersubjective *depend* and *dépendre* (vs. non-intersubjective *depend* and *dépendre*)

Table 3a. Morphological appearance of intersubjective and non-intersubjective *depend* and *dépendre*

English	Intersubj.	Non-IS	French	Intersubj.	Non-IS
depends	96.1% (370/385)	63.7% (298/468)	dépend	99.4% (480/483)	91.2% (362/397)
depend	0.3% (1/385)	5.7% (27/468)	dépendons	0% (0/483)	0.3% (1/397)
depending	0% (0/385)	1.3% (6/468)	dépendent	0% (0/483)	1.3% (5/397)
aux$_{mod}$ + depend	1.8% (7/385)	23.3% (109/468)	dépendre	0% (0/483)	2.8% (11/397)
has + depended	1.8% (7/385)	5.6% (26/468)	dépendra	0.2% (1/483)	1.3% (5/397)
had + depended	0% (0/385)	0.4% (2/468)	dépendrait	0% (0/483)	1.3% (5/397)
			dépendais	0% (0/483)	0.3% (1/397)
			dépendait	0.4% (2/483)	1.5% (6/397)
			dépendaient	0% (0/483)	0.3% (1/397)

is 14 times (English) and 15 times (French) more likely when the third person present tense of *depend* and *dépendre* is used.

In Dutch *afhangen*, *liggen* and *zien*, used as contingency hedges, all display the same feature (cf. Table 3b): nearly all occurrences of *liggen* are in 3rd person singular and present tense, as well as nearly all occurrences of the inflected verb form that combines with *zien*. In the case of *afhangen*, 3rd person singular and present tense account for 93.8% of the occurrences. Non-intersubjective uses *afhangen* and *liggen* clearly display a larger variety of tense markers than intersubjective uses. Only *afhangen* occurs with other person markers than 3rd person singular. In the case of *zien*, the number of non-intersubjective uses is insufficient to allow any comparison. The discrepancies for *afhangen* and *liggen* are statistically significant. Comparing third person present tense with the other verb forms yields the following significant results: *afhangen*: $\chi^2 = 21.3$, df = 1, $p < .0001$; *liggen*: $\chi^2 = 21.1$, df = 1, $p < .0001$. The size of the differences, quantified in terms of odds ratios, is 5.2

Table 3b. Morphological appearance of intersubjective and non-intersubjective *afhangen*, *liggen* and *zien*

Dutch	*afhangen*		*liggen*		*(te) zien (zijn)*	
	Intersubj.	Non-IS	Intersubj.	Non-IS	Intersubj.	Non-IS
3sg present	93.8% (168/179)	74.6% (97/130)	99.1% (109/110)	76.8% (43/56)	95.3% (41/43)	100.0% (2/2)
3sg past	0.6% (1/179)	7.7% (10/130)	0%	10.7% (6/56)	0%	0%
3sg future	5.0% (9/179)	9.2% (12/130)	0.9% (1/110)	1.8% (1/56)	0%	0%
3sg condit.	0.6% (1/179)	0.8% (1/130)	0%	7.1% (4/56)	0%	0%
3sg modal v.	0%	5.4% (7/130)	0%	3.6% (2/56)	0%	0%
3pl present	0%	1.5% (2/130)	0%	0%	0%	0%
3pl past	0%	0%	0%	0%	0%	0%
3pl future	0%	0%	0%	0%	0%	0%
3pl condit.	0%	0%	0%	0%	0%	0%
3pl modal v.	0%	0%	0%	0%	0%	0%
other	0%	0.8% (1/130)	0%	0%	0%	0%
indeterminate	0%	0%	0%	0%	4.7% (2/43)	0%

(C.I. = 2.54–10.62) for *afhangen* and 33 (C.I. = 5.88–184.59) for *liggen*. This means that the choice for intersubjective *afhangen* and *liggen* (vs. non-intersubjective *afhangen* and *liggen*) is 5.2 times (*afhangen*) and 33 times (*liggen*) more likely when the third person present tense is used.

A second indicator of decategorialisation is the type of subject that can be combined with the intersubjectively used verbs. As can be seen in Table 4a, the range of subjects both *depend* and *dépendre* combine with is extremely limited. In more than 70% of the English intersubjectivity cases, the subject is either *it* or a demonstrative pronoun. Most of the remaining cases (28%) even do without a subject altogether. In contrast, the non-intersubjective uses of these verbs combine with a larger variety of subjects. NPs, subordinate clauses (grouped under "other" in Table 4a) and quantifiers account for approximately 40% of the non-intersubjective instances. For the English data, this is statistically confirmed when contrasting the categories zero-subject, *it*-subject and *that*-subject on the one hand and the other subject types on the other hand: $\chi^2 = 172.2$, df = 1, $p < .0001$. The size of the odds ratio is 35.83 (C.I. = 17.0–75.57), signifying that the choice for intersubjective *depend* (vs. non-intersubjective *depend*) is almost 36 times more likely when the zero-subject, *it*-subject or *that*-subject is used. In French, demonstratives and the universal quantifier *tout* represent more than 99% of the observed subjects. As shown in Table 4a, non-intersubjective uses of the French verb are the only ones that can be combined with other types of subject. Once again, this

Table 4a. Subject realisations with intersubjective and non-intersubjective *depend* and *dépendre*

English	Intersubj.	Non-IS	French	Intersubj.	Non-IS
Ø	28.0% (108/386)	7.8% (36/468)	Ø	0.2% (1/483)	0% (0/397)
it (all)	66.6% (257/386)	46.8% (219/468)	*ça / cela*	86.7% (419/483)	81.4% (323/397)
that (all)	3.6% (14/386)	5.6% (26/468)			
(all / some of) this	0% (0/386)	1.1% (5/468)			
all	0.5% (2/386)	0.9% (4/468)	*tout*	13.1% (63/483)	9.3% (37/397)
a lot / much / great deal	0.5% (2/386)	4.5% (21/468)			
other	0.8% (3/386)	33.3% (156/468)	other	0% (0/483)	9.3% (37/397)

is statistically confirmed by contrasting *tout* and demonstratives on the one hand and the other subject types on the other: $\chi^2 = 41.6$, df = 1, $p < .0001$, odds ratio = 50 (C.I. = 9.63–254.79). In other words, the choice for intersubjective (vs. non-intersubjective) *dépendre* is 50 times more likely when the universal quantifier or a demonstrative is used.

In combination with the morphological appearance of the verb, the restriction on subjects clearly points to a process of chunking, whereby previously independent items are blended into a new 'chunk', which is retrieved from the memory as one single item (Haiman 1994).

In Dutch too, the range of subjects that can combine with contingency hedges is more limited: either *het*, its short form *'t* and demonstrative *dat* are used, totalling between 60.9% (*liggen*) and 97.6% (*zien*) of the intersubjective cases, or the contingency hedges are used without any subject at all (16.8%, 38.2%, 2.3% for *afhangen*, *liggen* and *zien* respectively). The range of subjects that can be combined with the non-intersubjective use of *afhangen* is larger: compare the quantifiers *alles* and *veel*, the NP and the embedded interrogative in Table 4b, where it can be seen that these are combined with non-intersubjective *afhangen*, but hardly with intersubjective *afhangen*. Beside these, the non-intersubjective cases also

Table 4b. Subject realisations with intersubjective and non-intersubjective *afhangen*, *liggen* and *zien*

| Dutch | *afhangen* | | *liggen* | | *(te) zien (zijn)* | |
	Intersubj.	Non-IS	Intersubj.	Non-IS	Intersubj.	Non-IS
Ø	16.8% (30/179)	7.7% (10/130)	38.2% (42/110)	10.7% (6/56)	2.3% (1/43)	0% (0/2)
't	26.3% (47/179)	21.5% (28/130)	27.3% (30/110)	44.6% (25/56)	76.7% (33/43)	100% (2/2)
het	6.1% (11/179)	16.2% (21/130)	2.7 % (3/110)	12.5% (7/56)	0% (0/43)	0% (0/2)
dat	49.7% (89/179)	32.3% (42/130)	30.9% (34/110)	28.6% (16/56)	20.9% (9/43)	0% (0/2)
veel	0.6% (1/179)	3.1% (4/130)	0% (0/110)	0% (0/56)	0% (0/43)	0% (0/2)
alles	0% (0/179)	2.3% (3/130)	0% (0/110)	0% (0/56)	0% (0/43)	0% (0/2)
NP	0% (0/179)	13.1% (17/130)	0% (0/110)	0% (0/56)	0% (0/43)	0% (0/2)
embedded interrogative	0.6% (1/179)	3.8% (5/130)	0.9% (1/110)	3.6% (2/56)	0% (0/43)	0% (0/2)

combine with the already mentioned *'t, het, dat,* and zero-subject (zero subject, *'t, het, dat* vs. the other subject types: $\chi^2 = 35.15$, df = 1, $p < .0001$; odds ratio = 25.41, C.I. = 6.83–94.54).

Non-intersubjective cases of *liggen* and *zien,* however, do not confirm the hypothesis of larger combinatorial possibilities (*liggen:* $\chi^2 = 0.36$, df = 1, $p > .05$; *zien:* too many empty cells to compute the chi-square statistic), as these are almost exclusively combined with the same types of subjects as the intersubjective cases (*het, 't,* demonstrative *dat* and no subject at all). One possible explanation for this, besides the insufficient data regarding non-intersubjective *zien,* is that the non-intersubjective uses of these verbs are also undergoing an independently motivated process of decategorialisation.

With respect to morphological variability and subject types, intersubjective *liggen* and *zien* appear to be more decategorialised than *afhangen. Afhangen* displays greater morphological variation (6.2% of forms other than 3rd person singular, compared to 0.9% and 0% in the cases of *liggen* and *zien* respectively). It combines with quantifier subjects and combines more than the other verbs with full forms of pronominal subjects (*het* and *dat: afhangen:* 55.8%; *liggen:* 33.6%; *zien:* 20.9%). *Liggen* and *zien* are therefore probably better analysed as parts of chunks, such as *dat ligt eraan* and *'t is te zien,* whose first morpheme can vary minimally or be absent. *Afhangen* is slightly less constrained than both its Dutch equivalents and its English and French counterparts; its morphology is slightly richer: 6.2% of forms other than 3rd person singular, compared to 3.9% and 0.6% in English and French respectively) and its subjects are more varied (four types total 98.8%, whereas in English three types total 98.2% and in French two types total 99.8% of the occurrences).

Decategorialisation also affects a verb's argument structure. In the cases investigated here, the argument structure consists of a subject, discussed earlier, and a prepositional phrase (*dépendre, depend, afhangen, liggen*) or a direct object (*zien*).[2] As shown in Defrancq & De Clerck (2009), the prepositional phrase is less frequent in intersubjective uses, which are prone to decategorialisation, than in non-intersubjective uses. The frequent absence of an argument may indeed be interpreted as a precursor to loss of argument structure. As Defrancq & De Clerck (2009) do not provide the actual data on the absence of the prepositional phrase, we cannot draw a comparison with English and French. The relevant Dutch data are presented in Table 5.

Only 70.2% of all intersubjective occurrences in the data set possess a prepositional or a noun phrase, compared to 89.4% of the occurrences that have been analysed as non-intersubjective. In all cases except *zien,* for which we have insufficient data, the frequency of cases where the argument has been omitted is considerably higher in intersubjective contexts (*afhangen:* $\chi^2 = 10.9$, df = 1, $p < .001$; *liggen:* $\chi^2 = 17.0$, df = 1, $p < .0001$ — statistics without the indeterminate category).

Table 5. PP / NP argument realisations with intersubjective and non-intersubjective *afhangen, liggen* and *zien*

Dutch	afhangen		liggen		(te) zien (zijn)	
	Intersubj.	Non-IS	Intersubj.	Non-IS	Intersubj.	Non-IS
No PP / NP	24.6%	9.2%	36.4%	5.4%	20.9%	50%
	(44/179)	(12/130)	(40/110)	(3/56)	(9/43)	(1/2)
PP/NP	74.9%	90.0%	60.9%	91.0%	74.4%	0%
	(134/179)	(117/130)	(67/110)	(51/56)	(32/43)	(0/2)
Indeterminate	0.5%	0.8%	2.7 %	3.6%	4.7%	50%
	(1/179)	(1/130)	(3/110)	(2/56)	(2/43)	(1/2)

Liggen clearly is more strongly affected than *afhangen* in this respect, as the proportion of argumentless cases increases from 5.4% in non-intersubjective contexts to 36.4% in intersubjective contexts, compared to an increase from 9.2% to 24.6% in the case of *afhangen*. This can also be observed in the odds ratios: the odds ratio for *afhangen* equals 3.2, the odds ratio for *liggen* equals 10.1, signifying that the choice for intersubjective *liggen* (vs. non-intersubjective *liggen*) is 10 times more likely when there is no PP, whereas the choice for intersubjective *afhangen* (vs. non-intersubjective *afhangen*) is "only" 3 times more likely when there is no PP. Omission of the noun phrase is less frequent in combination with *zien* than with the other verbs: only 20.9% of its occurrences do not possess an argument.

In French and English, decategorialisation also manifests itself through the absence of the preposition, which introduces the PP. As shown by Defrancq & De Clerck (2009), two cases have to be distinguished: omissions that are expected on the basis of local incompatibilities between prepositions belonging to the matrix and the embedded clause; unexpected omissions that are not motivated by local constraints. Example (17) is an illustration of an expected omission, where the presence of the preposition *on* belonging to the argument structure of *depend*, would not be tolerated:

(17)   "Depends from which standpoint you view it," Petrova replied.
　　　　　　　(BNC EDV666 in Defrancq & De Clerck 2009)

Example (18) is an example of an unexpected omission, where the preposition could have been present:

(18)   Erm I mean it depends what you're looking for I mean.
　　　　　　　(BNC FMD269 in Defrancq & De Clerck 2009)

As the preposition *on* is part and parcel of the verb's argument structure, unmotivated omissions as in (18) seem to suggest that the argument structure undergoes changes. Table 6 (based on Table 6 in Defrancq & De Clerck 2009) summarises the number of expected and unexpected omissions in intersubjective and non-intersubjective uses of *depend* and *dépendre*:

Table 6. Deletion of the preposition in the English and French data

	English *depend*		French *dépendre*	
	Intersubj.	Non-IS	Intersubj.	Non-IS
Expected omission	6.9% (21/306)	2.3% (10/440)	16.8% (53/316)	5.4% (17/312)
Unexpected omission	53.3% (163/306)	16.4% (72/440)	29.7% (94/316)	11.5% (36/312)
Preposition maintained	39.8% (122/306)	81.1% (357/440)	53.5% (169/316)	83.0% (259/312)

In English, more than 60% of the intersubjective occurrences where *depend* is followed by a noun phrase, a gerund or an embedded interrogative have no preposition. In an overwhelming majority of these cases there is no direct motivation for its omission. In French, omissions are less frequent than in English (46.5%) in intersubjective contexts and they are more frequently motivated. Nevertheless, in nearly one third of the occurrences there is no preposition where one would be expected. In both languages, unexpected omissions occur substantially more often in intersubjective cases than in non-intersubjective ones (*afhangen*: $\chi^2 = 108$, df = 2, $p < .0001$; *liggen*: $\chi^2 = 200$, df = 2, $p < .0001$).

In Dutch, on the other hand, the preposition seems to resist better than in French and English. Only five examples of *afhangen* and two of *liggen* have been found where an embedded interrogative is used without a preposition. There seems to be no specific relationship between omission of the preposition and intersubjectivity either, as the absence of the preposition affects both intersubjective (19)–(20) and other cases (21):

(19)   S1   rijdt de gij eventueel met den*d auto?
       S2   uh i*a dat dacht ik te doen. maar dat *hangt* een beetje *af* of Il nu den auto nodig heeft ja of nee.

       "would you be going by car?
       erm y* that's what I was planning to do. but depends a bit if Il needs the car or not."

(20)   uh … ja helemaal niet kom je d'r dat red je dus niet hè? 't *ligt* helemaal *wat* voor inkomen je hebt.
       "erm … yeah not at all do you manage so you don't manage, right? it all depends what kind of income you've got."

(21)   dus je stemt ook je hele leven lang op die partij. dat *hangt* niet *af* of jou
        inkomen toe of afneemt. snap je?
        "so one votes an entire life time for that party. it doesn't depend whether
        your income increases or decreases. you see?"

We can conclude that intersubjective uses *of depend, dépendre, afhangen, liggen*
and *zien* show clear signs of decategorialisation: they appear most typically in 3rd
person singular and present tense, their subjects belong to a small range of options
and they can be used without a subject, as well as without a prepositional phrase.
In English and French, decategorialisation is well advanced: in intersubjective
uses, *depend* and *dépendre* occur in fixed chunks, such as *it depends* and *ça depend*.
In Dutch *liggen* seems to be the most decategorialised verb and *afhangen* the least,
whereas *zien* occupies an intermediate position. *Liggen* is indeed always used in
the present tense, it appears more often than the other verbs without a subject and
without a prepositional phrase. *Zien* is morphologically strongly decategorialised,
but its argument structure is less affected than that of *liggen*. Finally, *afhangen* is
morphologically less decategorialised than the other verbs, as it is used in other
tenses than the present tense in the corpus.

5.   Onomasiological perspectives on contingency hedges in Dutch: Region, register, function

In this final section, the research focus shifts from a contrastive-linguistic analysis
to a monolingual, onomasiological analysis of the three Dutch verbs *afhangen*,
liggen and *zien*, which can all be used as contingency hedges. More particularly, the central question in this section is on what grounds language users in the
Dutch language area choose between these contingency hedges. Are the hedges
completely interchangeable, i.e. do they relate to each other as free variants, or do
language-internal or language-external parameters determine the variation (to a
certain extent)?

The effect of three well-known parameters on the choice between the Dutch
contingency hedges will be investigated, viz. the language-external parameters **region** and **register** and the language-internal parameter **function**. By investigating
the region and register parameter, we want to find out whether the choice between
the alternatives is determined by the region where they are used (Section 5.1) and
the communicative situation in which they are used (Section 5.2). The function
parameter must enable us to answer the question whether the competing hedges
have undergone a process of functional specialisation (Section 5.3).

5.1 Region

The effect of the regional background of language users is well-studied in Dutch (sociolinguistic) language studies. More particularly, it has been repeatedly shown that language use in the main national varieties of Dutch, viz. Belgian Dutch in Flanders and Netherlandic Dutch in the Netherlands, is considerably different, even to such an extent that Dutch can be considered a pluricentric language (Clyne 1992, Geeraerts 2004). Systematic differences between both regional varieties can be observed on the phonetic, morphological, lexical and syntactic level (e.g. Deygers & Van den Heede 2000; De Sutter et al. 2005; Grondelaers et al. 2001, 2008; Plevoets et al. 2008). Grondelaers et al. (2001), for instance, observe that the presence vs. absence of Dutch er "there" in Netherlandic Dutch and Belgian Dutch presentative constructions is explained by structurally and proportionally different statistical models. In other words, the er/ø alternation exists in both varieties, but language users of those varieties use it differently.

This and similar observations are traditionally traced back to a different standardisation process in Flanders and the Netherlands, which is, in turn, due to a number of historical and demographic developments that have occurred since the sixteenth and seventeenth century. While the standardisation process in the Netherlands started in the sixteenth century and progressed in the centuries to follow, standardisation in Flanders only started in the late nineteenth century, as a consequence of centuries of occupation by foreign nations (Spain and Austria) and the dominance of the French language (Geeraerts 2004). Even though recent lexical research has shown that both regional varieties have converged since the 1950's, systematic differences can still be observed when comparing the varieties of Dutch in Flanders and the Netherlands (cf. Geeraerts et al. 1999 for an overview).

Against this background, it is obviously relevant to investigate to what extent Netherlandic Dutch and Belgian Dutch use *afhangen*, *liggen* and *zien* differently. Table 7 shows the frequencies of the intersubjective uses of *afhangen*, *liggen* and *zien* in Netherlandic and Flemish data.

The table clearly shows that the regional parameter affects the choice of the intersubjective verbs significantly ($\chi^2 = 139$, df $= 2$, $p < .0001$): *afhangen* is found in both areas, but is substantially more frequent in Belgian Dutch (61.5%) than in

Table 7. Regional distribution of the Dutch contingency hedges

	afhangen	*liggen*	*(te) zien (zijn)*
Belgian Dutch	61.5%	4.5%	100%
	(110/179)	(5/110)	(43/43)
Netherlandic Dutch	38.5%	95.5%	0%
	(69/179)	(105/110)	(0/43)

Netherlandic Dutch (38.5%), especially considering the fact that the Netherlandic part of the corpus contains substantially more data than the Belgian part (3.2 million for Belgian Dutch and 5.6 million for Netherlandic Dutch, cf. Section 2; $\chi^2 = 46.7$, df= 1, $p < .0001$). The other verbs appear to be typical of one particular area: *liggen* is predominantly used in the Netherlands (95.5%; $\chi^2 = 89.1$, df= 1, $p < .0001$), where it is more frequent than *afhangen* ($\chi^2 = 7.04$, df= 1, $p < .001$) and is only marginal in Belgium (4.5%). *Zien*, on the other hand, is never used in the Netherlands as a contingency hedge. In Belgium, it is a regular alternative for *afhangen*, albeit one that is less frequently used than *afhangen* ($\chi^2 = 28.4$, df= 1, $p < .0001$). It is also interesting to note that language users in Belgium seem to use the contingency hedge more often: the total frequency of verbs involved in hedging is nearly the same in Belgium (n = 158) and in the Netherlands (n = 174), even though the corpus contains substantially more data from the latter area than from the former ($\chi^2 = 16.9$, df= 1, $p < .0001$).

5.2 Register

There is a massive amount of (sociolinguistic, variational) evidence showing that language users vary their language according to the communicative context (or 'register') in which they are involved (Finegan & Biber 1994, Biber 1995). Language users can shift the way they speak and write as a response to communicative-situational stimuli or in order to generate social meaning. A relevant question in this respect is to what extent the three Dutch contingency hedges are typical for different types of register.

As pointed out above, CGN distinguishes between 14 different registers (cf. Section 2). In order to avoid too many empty cells, we have grouped registers according to three dimensions: spontaneous vs. prepared speech, private vs. public speech and monologic vs. dialogic speech. Moreover, it proved necessary to exclude some data from the analysis, especially when their inclusion would have implied a multiplication of zero-frequencies. Belgian Dutch data regarding intersubjective *liggen* (n = 5) and Netherlandic data regarding intersubjective *zien* (n = 0) have been ignored for this reason (cf. Section 5.1). The following analyses have therefore been carried out on two verbs from each area: *afhangen* and *liggen* in the Netherlands and *afhangen* and *zien* in Belgium.

Table 8 presents the frequencies of the relevant verbs in spontaneous and prepared registers. Unsurprisingly, intersubjective uses appear to be on the whole more typical of spontaneous registers, as these are the registers where speakers react more often and more directly to each other's viewpoints. This difference between spontaneous and prepared registers is significant both in Netherlandic Dutch ($\chi^2 = 94.1$, df= 1, $p < .001$) and Belgian Dutch ($\chi^2 = 107.8$, df= 1, $p < .0001$).

Table 8. Register distribution of the Dutch contingency hedges: spontaneous vs. prepared speech

Belgian Dutch	*afhangen*	*(te) zien (zijn)*	Netherlandic Dutch	*afhangen*	*liggen*
Spontaneous speech	86.4%	97.7%		82.6%	94.3%
	(95/110)	(42/43)		(57/69)	(99/105)
Prepared speech	13.6%	2.3%		17.4%	5.7%
	(15/110)	(1/43)		(12/69)	(6/105)

Moreover, in spontaneous speech (vs. prepared speech) the frequency of the area-specific items *zien* and *liggen* is higher than *afhangen*: whereas *zien* and *liggen* are used in only 6.2% (1/16) and 33.3% (6/18) of the cases in prepared speech, their frequency increases in spontaneous speech to 30.7% (42/137) and 66.5% (99/156) respectively.[3] This difference between spontaneous and prepared registers in the choice between *afhangen* on the one hand and *liggen* and *zien* on the other hand is statistically significant in Netherlandic Dutch ($\chi^2 = 4.9$, df = 1, $p = 0.03$), and border significant in Belgian Dutch ($\chi^2 = 3.1$, df = 1, p-value = 0.07). In terms of odds ratios, the odds for *liggen* (vs. *afhangen*) increases 3.5 times in Netherlandic Dutch spontaneous speech vs. prepared speech (C.I. = 1.28–9.46).

Table 9 shows the frequencies of the three contingency hedges in private and public speech. It can be seen that private speech displays more intersubjective work than public speech, which is expected, as private speech is usually more interactive than public speech. This difference in the amount of intersubjective verbs between private and public speech is significant both in Netherlandic Dutch ($\chi^2 = 76$, df = 1, $p < .001$) and Belgian Dutch ($\chi^2 = 84.9$, df = 1, $p < .0001$). Additionally, the distinction between private and public speech also appears to determine the choice of contingency hedge in Netherlandic Dutch only, where it is highly significant ($\chi^2 = 17$, df = 1, $p < .0001$), and yields an odds ratio of 0.15 (C.I. = 0.06–0.37). Thus, the odds for *afhangen* (vs. *liggen*) decreases (1 / 0.15 =) 6.7 times in private speech compared to public speech. So, the most salient feature concerns the public registers, which show a significant increase of the use of *afhangen* in the Netherlands. In the Flemish data, the choice between *afhangen* and *zien* is not dependent on the distinction between private and public speech.

Table 9. Register distribution of the Dutch contingency hedges: private vs. public speech

Belgian Dutch	*afhangen*	*(te) zien (zijn)*	Netherlandic Dutch	*afhangen*	*liggen*
Private speech	86.4%	90.7%		68.1%	93.3%
	(95/110)	(39/43)		(47/69)	(98/105)
Public speech	13.6%	8.3%		31.9%	6.7%
	(15/110)	(4/43)		(22/69)	(7/105)

Table 10. Register distribution of the Dutch contingency hedges: dialogic vs. monologic speech

Belgian Dutch	*afhangen*	*(te) zien (zijn)*	Netherlandic Dutch	*afhangen*	*liggen*
Dialogic speech	92.7%	97.7%		97.1%	100%
	(102/110)	(42/43)		(67/69)	(105/105)
Monologic speech	7.3%	2.3%		2.9%	0%
	(8/110)	(1/43)		(2/69)	(0/105)

Table 10 gathers the frequencies of the three Dutch verbs in dialogic and monologic speech. As monologues leave little room for interaction, the frequencies of intersubjectively used verbs are very low in that category (Netherlandic Dutch: $\chi^2 = 164.1$, df $= 1$, $p < .001$; Belgian Dutch: $\chi^2 = 117.3$, df $= 1$, $p < .0001$). The examples that have been found typically illustrate hedging carried out by the speaker with regard to assertions s/he made previously (cf. Section 5.3). The difference between dialogic and monologic registers does not appear to determine the choice of verbs either in Belgian Dutch ($\chi^2 = 0.6$, df $= 1$, $p > .05$), or in Netherlandic Dutch ($\chi^2 = 1$, df $= 1$, $p > .05$).

On the whole, it has become clear that the contingency hedges appear much more frequently in spontaneous, private, dialogic speech, both in Netherlandic and Belgian Dutch. However, the three register dimensions we studied in this section appear to determine the choice of contingency hedges only in Netherlandic Dutch, in contrast to Belgian Dutch. More particularly, the general pattern that seems to emerge is that the area-specific item *liggen* is more typical of spontaneous and private registers. In Belgian Dutch, both *afhangen* and *zien* are not dependent on any type of register.

5.3 Function

The last parameter we investigate is intersubjective function. As pointed out above, the three verbs are all used as contingency hedges, but Defrancq & De Clerck (2009) distinguish several subtypes of uses. According to the kind of speech act that precedes it, they distinguish the following subtypes: hedging of answers to questions, hedging of answers to leading questions, hedging of assertions made by the hearer, and hedging of assertions made by the speaker him/herself. These subtypes can be exemplified by the following English examples respectively (quoted as 18–20 in Defrancq & De Clerck 2009):

(22) S1 What's the difference between a glide and a diphthong?
     S2 Er I not really sure it *depends* on what you mean in that particular
        context.   (BNC G4W)

(23)   S1   Well are we then not going to have another Co-Chair?
       S2   Well it *depends* how you want to deal with it   (BNC DCH 830)

(24)   S1   There was there was a case of one girl who back in nineteen sixty eight
            she killed two boys when she was eleven. And she got out after ten years.
            Whereas whereas if you did that to a grown up you'd probably be in
            there for about thirty years or something. If it was in America you'd be
            chaired.
       S2   It *depends* where you were not every State does.   (BNC KPA2942)

(25)   So I said well I said, I usually try to get here quarter past ten or soon after
       but it all *depends* on traffic because I live the other end of the town.

                                                                      (BNC KB0)

The subtypes differ slightly with regard to the inferences the speaker invites the
hearer to draw: in the case of answers to questions, the speaker seeks to compensate for behaviour that is potentially perceived as uncooperative, as s/he does not
answer the question directly. The inference the hearer is expected to draw is that
the speaker is cooperative, but that it is impossible to give a straightforward answer
by lack of information about crucial parameters. Claiming ignorance is a classical
strategy in justifying evasive answers (cf. Clayman 2001, Haddington 2005).

In the case of answers to leading questions and replies to assertions made by
the hearer, the main concern of the speaker is to avoid disagreement, as the expression of disagreement is a potential face-threatening act. By using *depend*, the
speaker avoids contradicting what the hearer has said or implied. S/he maintains
consensus on part of the meaning, but restricts the field of consensus by making it
contingent upon specific criteria. By suggesting that there are cases that do not fall
under the criteria, the speaker invites the hearer to infer that there is an alternative
viewpoint, which is not in contradiction with his/her own. This is a typical case of
the strategies discussed in Myers (1998): in case of direct disagreement between
participants, speakers tend to present the disagreement within a shared view, by
agreeing with one aspect of the view they oppose.

In the last case, the speaker seeks to maintain coherence with viewpoints s/he
expressed previously in the interaction, while retracting them partially. Retracting
often occurs after a first quick answer by the speaker, as in (26), where S2 retracts
an affirmative answer :

(26)   S1   What, can you die on half of one?
       S2   *Yeah. Depends* on what's in it.
       S1   Ooh Ecstasy the d
       S2   It depends what you're body's like, you can die of anything.
                                                                      (BNC KP63328)

In Dutch all three verbs can be used for all functions. Examples (27) to (30) illustrate the different pragmatic subtypes for *afhangen*:

(27) S1 en lukt dat een beetje? leren die mensen snel Nederlands of?
     S2 uhm *dat hangt* ook weer *af* van het land van herkomst.

   "and does it work? do these people learn Dutch quickly?
   erm again it also depends on the country they come from."

(28) S1 maar mensen die hier twee drie jaar wonen hun kinderen gaan
        ondertussen naar school hier die kun je toch niet buitengooien?
     S2 wel *dat hangt* er natuurlijk van *af*.

   "but you cannot just throw people out of the country who have been living
   here for two three years and have children attending school here, can you?
   well it depends of course"

(29) S1 da 's een beetje gek van dan nog koffiepauzes te voorzien.
     S2 ja ja ja ja ja.
     S1 of zelfs in de namiddag helemaal ook geen koffiepauze maar op 't einde
        een drink.
     S2 *dat hangt* ervan *af* hè. als ze mmm ... ja. dat hangt er een beetje van af
        hè hoe la hoe dat…

   "it's a bit weird to schedule a coffee break then
   yeah yeah yeah yeah yeah
   or no coffee break at all in the afternoon but a reception at the end.
   it depends you know. if they erm … yeah. it depends a bit you know
   how late…"

(30) hè soms is het dan natuurlijk ook wel een ontgoocheling. als je 't dan in de
     realiteit ziet. uh 't *hangt* ervan *af* of dat uh enfin hoe de schrijver…
     "you know from time to time it is of course disappointing. when you see the
     real thing. erm it depends if erm I mean how the writer…"

The crucial question to be answered in this subsection, is whether the availability of several verbs in Dutch leads to a situation where individual verbs privilege specific functions. Table 11 shows a functional breakdown of the frequencies of *afhangen*, *liggen* and *zien*. The figures show that the choice of verbs indeed depends on the type of function ($\chi^2 = 31.2$, df = 6, $p < .0001$): *afhangen* is predominantly used in contingency hedges of answers to questions and of assertions made by the speaker himself, *liggen* is mostly used to hedge assertions by the hearer and *zien* is specialised in the field of hedging the speaker's own assertions. When comparing the frequencies for each of the functions, it becomes clear that *afhangen* is

Table 11. Distribution of intersubjective functions over the Dutch contingency hedges

	afhangen	liggen	(te) zien (zijn)
Hedging of answers to questions	39.7% (71/179)	26.4% (29/110)	16.3% (7/43)
Hedging of answers to leading questions	4.5% (8/179)	2.7% (3/110)	2.3% (1/43)
Hedging of assertions by the hearer	16.2% (29/179)	40.0% (44/110)	20.9% (9/43)
Hedging of assertions by the speaker	39.6% (71/179)	30.9% (34/110)	60.5% (26/43)

most frequently chosen when a speaker wants to hedge an answer to a question (71 instances out of 107 instances of such hedges), an answer to a leading question (8/12) and one of his/her own assertions (71/131). *Liggen* is chosen more often when assertions made by the hearer need to be hedged (44/82). The most salient facts about functional specialisation are the high frequency of *zien* in the field of hedging of assertions made by the speaker, its low frequency in other areas and the relatively high frequency of *liggen* in the area of hedging the hearer's assertions.

These are interesting facts in three respects. First of all, as has been observed in Section 4, *liggen* and *zien* are more decategorialised than *afhangen*, which probably implies that they have a longer history as hedges. Their increased frequency in particular functions could therefore reveal a diachronic pattern: as hedging of assertions is relatively more often ensured by "older" hedges and hedging of answers to questions by a "newer" hedge, it seems reasonable to assume that hedging of answers is the first intersubjective function these lexical items are recruited for.

Secondly, if we take into account that *liggen* and *zien* are area-specific items, whereas *afhangen* is used in the entire Dutch-speaking area, it appears that the division of labour between the verbs is organised differently. In both areas, the verb that is "area-specific" seems to specialise for a particular function: in the Netherlands, *liggen* specialises in the hedging of assertions by the hearer, while Flemish *zien* specialises in the hedging of own assertions. In both areas, *afhangen* covers the field that is not covered by the other verb, levelling out the differences in terms of functions between the Netherlands and Flanders.

Finally, the differences in frequency could also point to social and cultural differences between the two Dutch-speaking areas. Considering that *zien* is overwhelmingly used in Belgian Dutch and *liggen* in Netherlandic Dutch (see Section 5.1), the figures seem to suggest that Belgian Dutch (Flemish) speakers use hedging more for what they themselves say, whereas Dutch speakers use it more to counter viewpoints expressed by other speakers. To test this hypothesis, which is in line with some hard-weathered stereotypes about the Dutch and the Flemish, we cross-classify the total frequencies of the Dutch verbs with region and function. These results are shown in Table 12:

Table 12. Distribution of the Dutch contingency hedges over region and function

	Belgian Dutch	Netherlandic Dutch
Hedging of answers to questions	31.6% (50/158)	32.8% (57/174)
Hedging of answers to leading questions	4.4% (7/158)	2.9% (5/174)
Hedging of assertions by the hearer	19.0% (30/158)	29.9% (52/174)
Hedging of assertions by the speaker	45.0% (71/158)	34.4% (60/174)

Even though differences can be observed, they are not statistically significant ($\chi^2 = 6.8$, df $= 3$, $p = 0.08$). This means that speakers in both areas resort to hedging in similar circumstances.

6. Conclusions

The analyses have revealed some interesting facts about French, English and Dutch verbs used as contingency hedges. First of all, Dutch offers more lexical items than French and English to express contingency hedging. In French and English, this type of hedging relies on only one verb: *dépendre* and *depend*, respectively. In Dutch, speakers use three verbs: *afhangen*, *liggen* and a modal form of *zien*. In most cases, the hedging function of the verb is connected to an existing conditional-causal meaning: viewpoints expressed or asked for in the preceding discourse are presented as valid only in particular circumstances. The semantic basis of the intersubjective use of *zien* is different: a future perception is said to be needed to check the validity of a viewpoint.

Second, all verbs show signs of decategorialisation, as expected when lexical items become used as markers of intersubjectivity. The extent to which verbs are affected varies. *Afhangen* is less affected than its French and English counterparts and also less affected than both other Dutch verbs. The most significant cross-linguistic difference with regard to decategorialisation is that the omission of the PP's preposition is much more frequent in French and English than in Dutch, where hardly any prepositions are omitted.

The choice of particular items mainly depends on regional and functional parameters. Only *afhangen* is regularly used in both the Netherlands and Flanders. Each of the remaining verbs is clearly specific for one of the areas: *liggen* in the Netherlands and *zien* in Flanders. Evidence has been found in support of the idea that the verbs under investigation have a different functional profile: *liggen* is used more often than expected to hedge assertions made by the hearer, while *zien* mainly appears in contexts where the speaker hedges his/her own assertions. The suggestion that hedging of hearer assertions is more typical of the Netherlands and hedging of speaker assertions more typical of Flanders could not be substantiated. On the other hand, the functional profiles suggest another hypothesis: as *liggen* and *zien* have probably been used for a longer period of time than *afhangen*, lexical items seem to be recruited first as hedges for answers. Hedging of (speaker or hearer) assertions seems to be acquired in a later stage. It would of course be interesting to check this idea on the basis of diachronic data.

Finally, register variation appears to be only partly explanatory for the use of particular items as contingency hedges. On the whole, the area-specific items *liggen* and *zien* are more typical of private and spontaneous speech than the area-neutral *afhangen*. However, only the Netherlandic Dutch showed statistically significant variation on this point.

Notes

1. It should, however, be noted that *liggen* is most often used as a verb denoting the position of an object and that *zien* is most often used as a perception verb. These meanings have not been taken into account in Table 2, as they are not connected with causality (see Section 2).

2. Prepositional phrases of these verbs can occur without a preposition. These cases will be discussed below.

3. Totals between brackets represent the total number of occurrences of both verbs in prepared speech. In Belgian Dutch, for instance, there are 16 occurrences of *afhangen* (15) and *zien* (1) in prepared speech.

References

Agresti, A. 1996. *An Introduction to Categorical Data Analysis*. New York: Wiley.
Aijmer, K. 2002. "What can translation corpora tell us about discourse particles?" *English Corpus Studies*, 9, 1–15.
Aijmer, K. & Simon-Vandenbergen, A. M. 2003. "The discourse particle *well* and its equivalents in Swedish and Dutch". *Linguistics*, 41 (6), 1123–1161.

Anderson, L. B. 1982. "The 'Perfect' as a universal and as a language-particular category". In J. Hopper (Ed.), *Tense-aspect: Between Semantics and Pragmatics*. Amsterdam/Philadelphia: John Benjamins, 227–264.

Biber, D. 1995. *Dimensions of Register Variation. A Cross-linguistic Comparison*. Cambridge: Cambridge University Press.

Chesterman, A. 1998. *Contrastive Functional Analysis*. Amsterdam/Philadelphia: John Benjamins.

Clayman, S. 2001. "Answers and evasions". *Language in Society*, 30 (3), 403–442.

Clyne, M. G. 1992. *Pluricentric Languages: Differing Norms in Different Nations*. Berlin: Mouton de Gruyter.

Deygers, K. & Van den Heede, V. 2000. "Belgisch-Nederlandse 'klassiekers' als variabelen voor lexicaal variatie-onderzoek: Een evaluatie". *Taal en Tongval*, 52 (2), 308–328.

Defrancq, B. & De Clerck, B. 2009. "Intersubjective positioning in French and English: A contrastive analysis of 'ça dépend' and 'it depends'". *Languages in Contrast*, 91 (1), 37–71.

De Sutter, G., Speelman, D. & Geeraerts, D. 2005. "Regionale en stilistische effecten op de woordvolgorde in werkwoordelijke eindgroepen". *Nederlandse taalkunde*, 10 (2), 97–128.

Finegan, E. & Biber D. 1994. "Register and social dialect variation: An integrated approach". In D. Biber & E. Finegan (Eds.), *Sociolinguistic Perspectives on Register*. New York/Oxford: Oxford University Press, 315–347.

Geeraerts, D. 2004. "Cultural models of linguistic standardization". In A. Soares da Silva, A. Torres & M. Gonçalves (Eds.), *Linguagem, Cultura e Cognição. Estudos de Linguística Cognitiva 1*. Coimbra: Almedina, 47–84.

Geeraerts, D., Grondelaers, S. & Speelman, D. 1999. *Convergentie en Divergentie in de Nederlandse Woordenschat. Een Onderzoek naar Kleding- en Voetbaltermen*. Amsterdam: Meertens Instituut.

Grondelaers, S., Speelman, D. & Carbonez, A. 2001: online. "Regionale variatie in de postverbale distributie van presentatief er". *Neerlandistiek.nl* 01.04. Available at: http://www.neerlandistiek.nl/01.04/ (accessed December 2009).

Grondelaers, S., Speelman, D. & Geeraerts, D. 2008. "National variation in the use of er 'there'. Regional and diachronic constraints on cognitive explanations". In G. Kristiansen & R. Dirven (Eds.), *Cognitive Sociolinguistics. Language Variation, Cultural Models, Social Systems*. Berlin/New York: Mouton de Gruyter, 153–203.

Haddington, P. 2005. "The linguistic NEG + POS pattern and two action combinations as resources for interviewee stance taking in news interviews". In L. Kuure, E. Kärkkäinen & M. Saarenkunnas (Eds.), *Kieli ja sosiaalinen toiminta — Language and Social Action. AFinLA Yearbook*. Publications de l'association finlandaise de linguistique appliquée 63, 85–107.

Haiman, J. 1994. "Ritualization and the development of language". In W. Pagliuca (Ed.), *Perspectives on Grammaticalization*. Amsterdam/Philadelphia: John Benjamins, 3–28.

Haeseryn, W. 1996. "Grammaticale verschillen tussen het Nederlands in België en het Nederlands in Nederland: Een poging tot inventarisatie". In R. Van Hout & J. Kruijsen (Eds.), *Taalvariaties. Toonzettingen en Modulaties op een Thema*. Dordrecht: Foris, 109–126.

Heine, B. 1993. *Auxiliaries: Cognitive Forces and Grammaticalization*. Oxford: Clarendon Press.

Hopper, P. & Traugott, E. 1993. *Grammaticalization*. Cambridge: Cambridge University Press.

Johansson, S. 2007. *Seeing through Multilingual Corpora: On the Use of Corpora in Contrastive Studies*. Amsterdam/Philadelphia: Benjamins.

Krzeszowski, T. P. 1990. *Contrasting Languages: The Scope of Contrastive Linguistics*. Berlin/New York: Mouton de Gruyter.

Lemmens, M. 2002. "The semantic network of Dutch posture verbs". In J. Newman (Ed.), *The Linguistics of Sitting, Standing and Lying*. Amsterdam/Philadelphia: Benjamins.

Moissinac, L. & Bamberg, M. 2004. "*It's weird, I was so mad*: Developing discursive identity defenses in conversational "small" stories of adolescent boys". Special Issue of *Texas Speech Communication Journal*. Also available at: http://www.clarku.edu/~mbamberg/Material_files/Discursive_Adolescent_Identities.doc (accessed December 2008).

Myers, G. 1998. "Displaying opinions: Topics and disagreement in focus groups". *Language in Society*, 27 (1), 85–111.

Oostdijk, N.H.J. 2000. "Het Corpus Gesproken Nederlands". *Nederlandse Taalkunde*, 5 (3), 280–284.

Plevoets, K., Speelman, D. & Geeraerts, D. 2008. "The distribution of T/V pronouns in Netherlandic and Belgian Dutch". In K. P. Schneider & A. Barron (Eds.), *Variational Pragmatics. A Focus on Regional Varieties in Pluricentric Languages*. Amsterdam/Philadelphia: John Benjamins, 181–209.

R Development Core Team 2008. *R: A language and environment for statistical computing*. Vienna: R Foundation for Statistical Computing. Available at: http://www.R-project.org (accessed January 2009).

Siepmann, D. 2005. *Discourse Markers across Languages*. Oxon: Routledge.

Simon-Vandenbergen, A.-M. & Aijmer, K. 2003. "The expectation marker *of course* in a cross-linguistic perspective". *Languages in Contrast*, 4 (1), 13–43.

Sweetser, E. 1990. *From Etymology to Pragmatics: Metaphorical and Cultural Aspects of Semantic Structure*. Cambridge: Cambridge University Press.

Taeldeman, J. 1993. "Welk Nederlands voor de Vlamingen?" In L. De Grauwe & J. de Vos (Eds.), *Van Sneeuwpoppen tot Tasmuurtje. Aspecten van de Nederlandse Taal- en Literatuurstudie*. Gent: Bond Gentse Germanisten, 9–28.

Traugott, E. C. 1995. "Subjectification in grammaticalisation". In D. Stein & S. Wright (Eds.), *Subjectivity and Subjectivisation*. Cambridge: Cambridge University Press, 31–54.

Weigand, E. 1998. "Contrastive Lexical Semantics". In E. Weigand (Ed.), *Contrastive Lexical Semantics*. Amsterdam/Philadelphia: John Benjamins.

Wierzbicka, A. 1972. *Semantic Primitives*. Frankfurt: Athenäum.

Cultural differences in academic discourse

Evidence from first-person verb use in the methods sections of medical research articles

Ian A. Williams
University of Cantabria

This corpus-based study examines first-person verbs in Methods sections in English and Spanish. Quantitative analysis was based on rhetorical Move categories and qualitative analysis on linguistic profiles (collocation, colligation, semantic preference and semantic prosody). Both the English and Spanish subcorpora had more texts without first-person verbs than with this verb form. However, in the texts with this feature, the frequency was significantly higher in Spanish and the distribution of the rhetorical Moves associated with the first-person forms was also significantly different. The qualitative analysis revealed that in the English texts, the first-person signals the reasoned choice of a non-standard procedure (32 tokens) compared to only seven standard procedures, whereas in the Spanish texts the distribution was even (25 and 26 tokens, respectively). The results support cross-cultural differences in discourse functions that have implications for both translation and academic writing in cross-cultural contexts.

1. Introduction

Recently, increasing attention has been paid to the use of first-person forms in academic discourse from different perspectives: cross-cultural (Vassileva 1998), cross-disciplinary (Kuo 1999; Hyland 2001; Harwood 2005a, 2005b), and intergeneric (Tang & John 1999, Hyland 2002). These studies have examined aspects such as singular versus plural forms, and inclusive versus exclusive meaning, and have established taxonomies and associated functions. However, little attention has been given to first-person use in the individual sections (Introduction, Methods, Results and Discussion) that make up the standard IMRAD format (Paton 1976: 1115; Swales 1990: 133) of the research article (RA) and there is a need for empirical contrastive data for specific language pairs that would serve to establish guidelines for decision-making in translation. In a previous study (Williams 2010), the combined use of discourse analysis (Move analysis) and linguistic profiling (collocation, colligation, semantic preferences and semantic prosody) revealed significant differences between English and Spanish in the discourse functions of first-person verbs in the Results section of biomedical RAs. In the texts published in English language journals, these verbs were mainly associated with the presentation of methodological choices that deviated from standard procedures or were ad hoc decisions taken after consideration of some of the results. In contrast, in the Spanish texts these forms were used predominantly in statements of results.

Within the IMRAD framework of biomedical RAs, the communicative function of the Methods section is to describe how the individuals or material under observation (patients, animals, tissue, etc.) are selected and to identify the methods, apparatus and statistical procedures in sufficient detail to allow the results to be reproduced. Swales (1990: 166–170), in his overview of the section in a number of disciplines, observes that the methods are "merely labeled rather than characterized", that the sections show little thematic continuity and lack the cohesive features of pronominal reference and lexical repetition. Readers must, therefore, draw heavily on their background knowledge and experience to establish the coherence of the texts, which "often read like checklists". Commenting on a sample text taken from the literature, Swales noted the "bald Past tense narrative" (1990: 120) and the impersonal style focussing on the method rather than on the protagonists: "There are no problems, no matters of discussion, no questions of choice [...], no evidence of failure, and no statements of rationale" (Swales 1990: 120).

However, Skelton (1994: 456), who examined the rhetorical structure of the Methods section in 50 RAs from the *British Journal of General Practice*, identified three fundamental rhetorical moves, "which were extremely likely to occur and maintained a strong order", and three optional moves, referred to as "tied" moves because they "could not exist on their own, invariably appearing with the principal move". The moves can be summarised as follows: (M1) characterisation of the study population, plus optional (M1a) assertion regarding the inclusiveness or homogeneity of the sample, and/or adjustments to and exclusions from the original population; (M2) description of procedures, plus (M2a) justification of a method; (M3) reference to statistical tests to be used, plus (M3a) justification of a statistical choice (for illustration see Table 1 and Section 2.2). The three optional moves, when present, are likely to include the subjective features absent from the text analysed by Swales. In the light of the differences found in the previous study (Williams 2010), it seemed likely that the presence of the researchers in the discourse of the Methods section would reflect differences in the ways authors handle the moves and reveal differences in discourse style relevant in cross-cultural situations. This study examines first-person use both quantitatively and qualitatively in the Methods section of a large bilingual corpus of biomedical RAs.

2.   Material and Methods

2.1   The corpus

The study was performed on a bilingual computerised corpus composed of 192 RAs (approximately 500,000 words) with the typical IMRAD format, and divided into three subcorpora: 64 English source language (SL) texts (157,650 words); their 64 Spanish target language (TL) texts (185,000 words); and a comparable subcorpus of 64 Spanish native language (NL) texts (140,250 words) (see Appendix). This study used only the Methods sections, comprising 41,850, 49,570 and 30,265 words, respectively. The corpus was compiled by randomly selecting 8 RAs for each of the eight English-language medical journals with Spanish editions. The corresponding SL texts were then located in the English-language journals, and finally the comparable NL subcorpus was created by similar random selection of articles from Spanish journals covering the same specialities as the SL and TL subcorpora, namely, general medicine (2 journals), cardiology, dermatology, gynaecology and obstetrics, ophthalmology, paediatrics, and surgery.

This design with both parallel and comparable components allows contrasts from different viewpoints: interlinguistic analysis confronts similar text types in two languages; intralinguistic analysis contrasts TL with NL texts; and comparison of SL and TL texts provides insights into actual translation practice.

2.2   Rhetorical categories in the Methods section

The three main moves and associated tied moves identified by Skelton (1994) are defined and illustrated from the English SL subcorpus in Table 1.[1]

2.3   Methods and Analyses

All first-person verbs in the Methods section were located with the concordancing program of *WordSmith Tools* (Scott 1998) and the sentences in which they appeared were classified according to Skelton's categories. Quantitative analyses compared the subcorpora for number of texts with and without first-person verbs and, when this feature was present, for frequency of occurrence and distribution in relation to the rhetorical moves illustrated above. In this last analysis, when two verbs occurred in the same category in a context, only one was counted in order to ensure independence of the data. Qualitative contextual analyses created linguistic profiles based on extended units of meaning (Sinclair 1991, Tognini-Bonelli 2001). These consist of collocation, colligation, semantic preference and semantic prosody, reflecting lexical, grammatical, semantic and discourse functional

Table 1. Move categories in the Methods section according to Skelton (1994)

Move	Descriptor	Example
M1	Characterisation of study population	1. *The study group comprised* 286 patients who underwent valve repair for mitral regurgitation over a 22-month interval [...]
M1a (tied)	Assertion regarding the inclusiveness or homo-geneity of the sample, and/or adjustments to and exclusions from the original population	2a. *All patients had moderately severe or severe (3+ to 4+) mitral regurgitation* on preoperative echocardiographic or cardiac catheterization study, or both. 2b. Patients who underwent mitral valve replacement as the primary procedure and those whose mitral valve was predominantly stenotic *were excluded from the study.*
M2	Description of procedures	3. After the capsule is clean of all cortical material, *a vitrectomy probe is inserted into the eye and an inferior peripheral iridectomy is performed.*
M2a (tied)	Justification of a method	4. The iridectomy is done at this time *because it is easier to perform while the silicone is still kept behind the posterior capsule.*
M3	Reference to statistical methods to be used	5. The risk to patients of a second brain tumour after commencement of radiotherapy was estimated *by the Kaplan-Meier survival method.*
M3a (tied)	Justification of a statistical choice	6. Patients were censored on reaching age 85 *since tumour incidence rates for the very elderly may be unreliable.*

patterning, respectively. The individual lexical verbs that collocate with the first-person were examined, and for colligation, which is the "interrelation of grammatical categories in the syntactical structure" (Firth 1968: 183), the tense of these verbs was studied together with associated features such as fronted adjuncts and subclauses. Semantic preference was considered as the general categories to which the verb collocates belong (procedural, perception, possessive, desiderative, etc.). For semantic prosody, which is, according to Sinclair (1996: 88), "the functional choice which links meaning to purpose", broad rhetorical functions (e.g. state a procedure, make a comment, refer to current text) were considered in order to establish the nuances associated with first-person use in English and Spanish.[2] These profiles were then used to establish strategic options for Spanish-English and English-Spanish translation for the different rhetorical categories. The results of the application of the strategies were tested with the same statistical methods as those used to compare the English SL and Spanish NL subcorpora, the data from which are taken as reference values (Williams 2006).

Categorical variables were assessed with the χ^2 test, with Yates' correction for 2×2 tables when indicated. First-person frequencies were analysed with a binomial distribution test. A p value ≤ 0.05 was considered significant.

3. Results

3.1 Quantitative analysis

The number of texts with and without first-person forms showed a similar distribution in the SL and NL subcorpora, with more texts without these forms than those containing this feature (Table 2). Overall, the SL texts included 58 and the NL texts 70 first-person verbs. When this difference was analysed by the binomial distribution test, assuming even distribution of the first-person verbs in the two subcorpora and taking into account their relative size (SL-to-NL ratio 58:42), it was found to be statistically significant ($p = 0.001$). In the English SL texts, a first-person form appeared every twelve sentences (35 tokens per 10,000 words), compared to once every seven sentences in the Spanish NL texts (59 per 10,000 words).

Table 2. Comparison of texts with and without first-person forms in the English SL and Spanish NL subcorpora

Subcorpus	Texts with no 1st Person	Texts with 1st Person	χ^2 Value	p Value
English SL subcorpus	42	22	0.034	0.854
Spanish NL subcorpus	40	24		

For the χ^2 analysis of first-person tokens according to rhetorical category (Table 3), the two statistical method categories (M3 and M3a) were combined because of the small numbers. The significant difference between the subcorpora is due mainly to the higher frequency of first-person verbs in the description of plain procedures (category M2) in the NL texts (29 vs. 11 tokens), and, to a lesser extent, to a higher frequency of the M2a category in the SL texts (26 vs. 18 tokens). The Spanish texts also had a higher proportion of plain statements of statistical methods (5 of 10) than did the English texts (one of five).

Table 3. Distribution of first-person forms according to rhetorical function in the English SL and Spanish NL subcorpora (figures in brackets are percentages)

Subcorpus	Move 1	Move 1a	Move 2	Move 2a	Move 3 + 3a	χ^2 Value	p Value
English SL subcorpus	8 (14)	6 (11)	11 (20)	26 (46)	5 (9)	10.251	0.036
Spanish NL subcorpus	9 (13)	4 (6)	29 (41)	18 (26)	10 (14)		

3.2 Qualitative analysis: Linguistic profiles

Table 4 shows the linguistic profile for first-person use in the English texts.[3]

Table 4. Linguistic profile of first-person use in the English SL texts

Collocation		Colligation		Semantic Preference		Semantic Prosody	
Verb		**Tense**		**Verb type**		**Functions and Features**	
use	10	Past	46	Procedural	33	To state a non-standard proce-	
estimate	3	Present	5	Speech Act	11	dure	32
exclude	3	Pres. perfect	2	Cognitive	6	– linked to rationale (22)	
ask	2			Desiderative	4	– based on choice (5)	
collect	2	**Syntax**				– involving novelty (4)	
compare	2	Fronted				– related to study design (6)	
find	2	adjunct	10				
include	2	Adverb				To present subjects/methods	13
invite	2	Subclause	15				
measure	2	– preceding (11)				To express standard methods	7
perform	2	– included in (4)					
						To make a comment	6

The most frequent lexical verb collocate was the procedural verb *use* (10 tokens), with *estimate* and *exclude* appearing three times, and another 8 verbs appearing twice. The outstanding associated grammatical feature was past tense (46 of 58 instances, 79%). Syntactically, there were fronted adjuncts in 10 contexts, but no preference for a specific type was apparent:

> (1)   *As a check for response bias at later stages of the study* **we also asked** whether subjects had ever suffered from pain in their shoulders, elbows, wrists, hips, or knees.

Of the 15 adverbial subclauses, 11 preceded the associated first-person main-clause verb and 4 subclauses contained the first-person form. The main associated clause types were purpose clauses (5 instances), all of which were pre-posed and non-finite, as in example (2), and general conditional clauses (5 cases) introduced by *if, where* or *when(ever)* as in (3).

> (2)   *To calculate the magnitude of visual field change* **we used** the main indexes MD and CLV.

> (3)   *Whenever specimens from both eyes were examined,* **we used** the means of the measurements obtained for our calculations.

The outstanding semantic preference was for a procedural verb (33 tokens, 57%). Other associated verb types were speech act verbs expressing either interaction between researchers and subjects under study, e.g. *ask, invite, instruct* (cf. example 1) or communication between authors and readers, e.g. *define, describe, publish, refer*, and *report*:

(4)   As shown in Color Fig 1, **we refer** to the outermost terminations of aqueous channels that abut the internal boundary of the JXT as cul-de-sacs.

The main related communicative function is to state a procedure. However, the contextual analysis allowed qualification of this function. These forms are used preferentially with non-standard procedures (32 contexts), the use of which may be justified by explicit presentation of rationale, as in example (5), or based on personal choice or decision, as in (6), or involving some kind of novel aspect of the study, as in (7), where the author is the first to investigate these "cul-de-sacs", and so has to demonstrate the validity of the chosen method.

(5)   However, when it was impossible to unravel sufficiently reliably the proportion of the various types of operations **we omitted** it from the review.

(6)   **We decided** to use a 90% threshold to define desaturation because pilot data had shown that episodic fills in SaO_2 to <80%, the definition chosen in our studies on infants, are so rare in children that **we would not have obtained** informative results if **we had used** the same definition in the present study.

(7)   To test whether the orientation of sections alters the cul-de-sac measurements, **we compared** numbers and lengths of cul-de-sacs in sections taken meridionally and along the long axis of the canal at 90° to the meridional plane in the same specimen (No. 0433).

It should be noted that these three examples all contain more than one significant feature. The verb *omit* in (5) expresses an implicit choice; the decision in (6) is based on the evidence of a pilot study and is justified in a hypothetical conditional clause; and in (7), in addition to the novel concept of "cul-de-sac", the author also expresses the rationale behind the comparison in the non-finite purpose clause, which makes the first-person syntactically appropriate. These examples, therefore, contain clusters of linguistic features that indicate to the reader that something significant is being pointed out. The rationale is usually expressed in the accom-panying subordinate clause, but occasionally is presented as a separate comment:

(8)   **We have aspirated** the nucleus with this cannula in eyes not filled with silicone oil (not included in this series) and **found** that this is always easily done in patients younger than 40 years.

One further possibility is that researchers provide details that pertain specifically to the design of the current study. Here the associated verb is more likely to be cognitive, such as *hypothesise, consider* or *estimate*, as in (9):

(9)   **We estimated** that a trial with 80% power and a two-sided level of significance of 0.05 would require 80 patients (40 per arm) to detect the following differences between the two groups in qualitative assessment of right-ventricular wall motion.

In contrast, there were only 7 contexts in which the procedure presented by the authors appeared to be a routine method or a standard technique.

(10)   **We also collected** data from a standard 12-lead electrocardiogram (ECG).

In (10), use of the active is probably stylistic, to avoid an awkward passive, such as "Data from a standard 12-lead electrocardiogram (ECG) were also collected"; here a lengthy informative subject, or unmarked theme is followed by a short uninformative verb in the rheme (Halliday 2005: 75), resulting in an unbalanced sentence.

A second important associated function of these first-person forms was to describe the total or initial study population or to define inclusion or exclusion criteria (M1 and M1a). These sequences appeared as section-initial sentences and respond to theme-rheme patterns and the principles of end focus and end weight (Quirk et al. 1985: 1361). Since the last rhetorical move in the Introduction serves to present the current study and often involves a switch to the first person (Swales 1990: 166), this is picked up at the start of the Methods, as in (11):

(11)   For these reasons **we performed** a randomised controlled trial to investigate whether one week of treatment is sufficient to eradicate *H. pylori*.
       Patients and Methods
       We performed antral biopsies on all patients undergoing oesophagogastro-duodenoscopy during a four month period at this hospital and found to have an active duodenal ulcer. **We included** patients with dyspeptic symptoms and also those with gastrointestinal bleeding from their duodenal ulcer.

Here, continuation of the first-person thematic pattern allows the author to place the most informative content in the rheme; he is thus able not only to define the target population, but also to draw the reader's attention to two distinct patient groups, the significance of which he will reveal in the Discussion section. When not section- or paragraph-initial, these presentational sentences avoid the cumbersome use of passives and allow better information flow, as with the list in (12):

(12)   Thus, for each iron-status class separately, **we tested** for: (1) differences between treatment groups (i.e., ferrous sulphate and placebo) in changes

over the period of intervention, and (2) post-treatment differences between treatment groups after controlling for possible pretreatment differences.

Thus, the main characteristic of first-person use in the English texts is the expression of non-standard methods and of personal choices and decisions. The authors assume responsibility for their actions, and so leave readers free to decide whether to accept or reject the validity of the results, in what Hyland (1998: 181) has identified as a reader-oriented hedging strategy.

In the linguistic profile for the Spanish texts (Table 5), the outstanding verb collocate was *realizar* "perform" (14 tokens), followed by *comparar* "compare", *estudiar* "study", and *utilizar* "use", each used 6 times. The only non-procedural verb used more than once was the cognitive *considerar* "consider". For colligation, the past tense also predominated (34 of 70 instances, 49%), but a good many verbs appeared in the present perfect (20 tokens, 29%) and the present (15 tokens, 21%).

Table 5. Linguistic profile of first-person use in the Spanish NL texts

Collocation		Colligation		Semantic Preference		Semantic Prosody	
Verb		**Tense**		**Verb Type**		**Functions and Features**	
realizar	14	Past	34	Procedural	54	To state a standard method	
comparar	6	Pres. perfect	20	Speech Act	7		26
estudiar	6	Present	15	Cognitive	4		
utilizar	6			Desiderative	3	To state a non-standard	
aplicar	3	**Syntax**				procedure	25
administrar	2	Fronted				– linked to rationale (16)	
considerar	2	adjunct	27			– based on choice (6)	
incluir	2	– spatial (10)				– related to study design (6)	
revisar	2	– temporal (6)					
		– purposive (4)				To present subjects/methods	13
		Adverb					
		subclause	7			To make a comment	3
		– preceding (7)					
						To refer to current text	3

Syntactically, Spanish first-person forms were associated with a fronted adjunct in 27 contexts, with a preference for spatial adjuncts (10 instances):

(13) *En nuestro estudio* **comparamos** *el número de partos en adolescentes y su forma de finalización con el total de partos.*
      "In our study **we compared** the number of adolescent deliveries and final delivery type with the total number of deliveries."

However, there were also temporal adjuncts (6 cases):

(14) _Desde abril de 1988 a marzo de 1992_ **hemos realizado** 100 toracoscopias a 60
      hombres y 40 mujeres.
      "From April 1988 to March 1992 **we performed** 100 thoracoscopies on 60
      men and 40 women."

and purposive adjuncts (4 cases):

(15) _Para la realización de ambas técnicas_ **seguimos** las indicaciones de los
      fabricantes: Abbot para la prueba de EIA y Gen Probe para la sonda ADN.
      "To carry out both techniques, **we followed** the manufacturers' instructions:
      Abbot for the enzyme immunoassay and Gen Probe for the DNA probe."

First-person forms had related adverbial clauses in 7 contexts, all of which were
non-finite and appeared before the main first-person verb:

(16) _Para aliviar el síndrome gripal agudo que suele producirse tras la
      administración del interferón_, **pautábamos** de forma sistemática paracetamol,
      a dosis de 1200 mg dos horas antes y 600 mg una hora después de la inyección.
      "To alleviate the acute flu-like symptoms that usually develop after interferon
      administration, **we** systematically **prescribed** paracetamol at a dose of 1200
      mg two hours before and 600 mg one hour after the injection."

As in the English profile, there was also a clear semantic preference for procedural
verbs (54 of 70 tokens, 77%), with small contributions from communicative verbs
(7 tokens) and cognitive ones (4 instances).

   In contrast to the English texts, the number of contexts expressing standard
and non-standard procedures was almost identical (26 and 25, respectively). For
non-standard methods, the distribution of instances supported by rationale, based
on choice or related to the specific study design was similar to that of the English
text profile, but there were no contexts expressing novelty in this subcorpus. The
Spanish texts also included 13 instances of the presentational function, a figure
comparable to that of the English profile:

(17) **Hemos revisado** las historias de 144 pacientes con tumores orbitarios que
      fueron en algún momento examinados por el Servicio de Oftalmología entre
      1972 y 1992.
      "**We reviewed** the case notes of 144 patients with orbital tumours who had at
      some time been examined in the Ophthalmology Department between 1972
      and 1992."

Comments and metatextual references were minor functions associated with first-
person use. As in the English subcorpus, the comments justify a methodological
choice. In (18) the authors mention a technical failure when a stapler was used,
adding that this offers no advantage over the hand-stitching method they use:

(18) *Realizamos un intento de anastomosis mecánica con stapler circular por vía
oral, pero tras superar las grandes dificultades de introducción del aparato, se
acabó desgarrando el muñón del esófago y hubo que realizar la sutura a mano.
Pensamos que dada la buena exposición a ese nivel, no merece la pena el
empleo del stapler.*

"**We attempted** mechanical anastomosis in one patient using a transoral
circular stapler, but when the difficulty of introducing the device into the
oral cavity had been overcome, the oesophageal stump tore and suturing had
to be performed by hand. Given the good exposure at this level, **we do not
consider** it worthwhile using the stapler."

In view of the similar number of first-person forms describing standard and non-
standard methods, Spanish authors do not appear to be consciously drawing attention to the choice of an unconventional procedure, but rather — and especially
in those texts with a relatively high proportion of these forms — to make the readers participants in the overall decision-making process and thus persuade them
that they would have proceeded in the same way if they had been involved in the
study. In addition, these verbs, together with occasional use of the related possessives and object pronoun, form referential chains, making the discourse strongly
cohesive.

Table 6 shows a complete Spanish Methods section with a high proportion
of first-person verbs, illustrating the cohesive function of the first-person (the
English literal gloss is mine). This text contains four paragraphs (indicated by the
symbol #) and 10 sentences, 9 of which have first-person forms (9 verbs plus 2
related possessives), the exception being sentence 3 (S3). The high frequency of
this verb form indicates use as a cohesive device and one that maintains a fairly
constant perspective, although seven of the nine first-person forms are preceded
by some other thematic material.

Rhetorically, the text opens by characterising the study population in S1 and
this is followed by a numerical procedural statement that will allow calculation of
the incidence of the phenomenon under study. The two sentences in paragraph 2
concern patient selection, the first is a simple procedure (M2), but the second asserts the uniformity of the selected sample, which is justified by the study protocol
presented in the appendices (M1a). Paragraph 3 contains five sentences, the first
four of which are plain statements of procedures (M2) detailing what is analysed
in the protocol but including nothing exceptional for this type of retrospective
study. Then, S9 returns us to the study sample and gives the exclusion criteria that
justify the final adjustment of the study sample (M1a). The final single-sentence
paragraph is a plain procedural statement (M2) describing the ultrasound equip-
ment used.

Table 6. Spanish text with a high proportion of first-person verbs

	Spanish Text	Gloss
# S1	**Estudiamos** 30 pacientes que presentan una tumoración ovárica coincidente con la gestación en el período de tiempo comprendido entre enero de 1989 y junio de 1991.	**We studied** 30 patients who presented an ovarian tumour coinciding with pregnancy in the period between January 1989 and June 1991.
S2	En este espacio de tiempo **realizamos** un total de 8.959 ecografías obstétricas (Tabla 1).	In this period **we performed** a total of 8,959 obstetric ultrasound scans (Table 1).
# S3	Las pacientes fueron seleccionadas partiendo de la ecografía como primer diagnóstico.	Patients were selected based on the ultrasound scan that established the initial diagnosis.
S4	Del total **seleccionamos** nueve casos, únicos que cumplían todos los requisitos de nuestro protocolo (Anexos 1 y 2).	From the total **we selected** the nine cases that met all the requirements of our protocol (Appendices 1 and 2).
# S5	En el protocolo **destacamos** los datos de afiliación, la exploración clínica y el estudio ecográfico.	In the protocol **we emphasise** demographic data, clinical examination and the ultrasound study.
S6	**Estudiamos** el parto y al recién nacido.	**We studied** the delivery and the newborn.
S7	Finalmente **incluimos** el momento de la exéresis del tumor, su estudio anatomopatológico y el diagnóstico al alta clínica.	Finally, **we included** the time of tumour excision, the pathological study and the diagnosis on clinical discharge.
S8	En el estudio ecográfico **describimos** la imagen, su localización, semanas de gestación en que se hace el diagnóstico y el tamaño de la tumoración.	In the ultrasound study **we describe** the image, site, gestation week when the diagnosis was made, and tumour size.
S9	Por ello **hemos desechado** todas aquellas pacientes en donde el tamaño de la tumoración era inferior a 80 mm de diámetro o que no tuvieron estudio anatomopatológico.	Therefore, **we excluded** patients if the tumour was less than 80 mm in diameter and if no pathological study was available.
# S10	En todas nuestras exploraciones **hemos utilizado** el ecógrafo Sonoline SL de la casa Siemens, con un transductor lineal de 5 MHz y otro sectorial mecánico de 3,5 MHz.	In all our ultrasound studies **we used** a Sonoline SL ultrasound system (Siemens) with a 5 MHz linear transducer and 3.5 MHz mechanical sector transducer.

3.3 Translation behaviour

Having established the reference values and linguistic profiles for first-person use in the SL and NL texts, we now examine what the translators did when transferring the SL Methods sections into Spanish. Of the 58 SL first-person verbs, 46 became TL first-person forms. The 12 rendered by other means were 3 in category M1a, 2 in M2, 5 in M2a, and 2 in M3a. The form preferred to the first person was the *se* reflexive passive in 10 contexts. This is a valid option in most cases because, as a "pseudoactive" form, its use does not entail changing the order of sentence elements. However, in the translation of example (6), repeated here as example (19), one might expect consistency of verb form between the methodological decision and the underlying rationale rather than the impersonal opening "It was decided to use …":

(19) **We decided** to use a 90% threshold to define desaturation because pilot data had shown that episodic fills in SaO_2 to <80%, the definition chosen in our studies on infants, are so rare in children that **we would not have obtained** informative results if **we had used** the same definition in the present study.
> *Se decidió utilizar el umbral del 90% para definir la desaturación porque los datos piloto habían demostrado que las disminuciones episódicas de la SaO₂ a <80%, definición escogida en nuestros estudios en lactantes, son tan escasas en los niños que **podríamos no haber obtenido** resultados informativos si **hubiésemos utilizado** la misma definición en el presente estudio.*

Of the other two instances of the 12 expressed by other means, one defined a target population through a standard impersonal formula with the verb *aim* replaced by the synonymous noun *objetivo* linked to an infinitive:

(20) **We aimed to recruit** 50 males and 50 females in each of the two age-groups 25–34 years and 55–64 years.
> *El objetivo era reclutar a 50 varones y 50 mujeres en cada uno de los dos grupos de edad, 25–34 y 55–64 años.*

The final context involved a transposition from first-person verb to possessive adjective to express a hypothesis:

(21) **We hypothesised** that 20–30% of the patients treated with heparin alone and 55–60% of rt-PA treated patients would improve when qualitative right-ventricular wall motion on the 24 h echocardiogram was compared with baseline.
> *Nuestra hipótesis fue que un 20–30% de los pacientes tratados con heparina sola y un 55–60% de los tratados con rt-PA presentarían una mejoría al comparar la motilidad cualitativa de la pared del ventrículo derecho en la ecocardiografía obtenida a las 24 h con la basal.*

In contrast, in 6 contexts a first-person form was added to the TL texts. Four of these involved raising non-finite past participles of communicative verbs to full finite status in the metatextual function: e.g. the definition of cardiogenic shock **as described** > *la definición de shock cardiogénico **tal y como la hemos descrito*** ("as **we have described** it"). Another addition rendered the English adjective *available* by the semantically related Spanish verb *disponer* "have at one's disposal":

(22)   For the Algerian centre, mortality data **were not available**.
       > *No dispusimos de datos sobre mortalidad del centro de Algeria* (sic).

The final addition was due to an error in interpreting a SL text.

As a result, the TL texts have a total of 50 first-person verbs with the following distribution by move categories: M1: 9; M1a: 5; M2: 11; M2a: 22; M3: 1; M3a: 2. When compared with the data in Table 3, the TL move distribution is seen to conform to the SL rather than the NL profile. Although the difference between the TL and NL subcorpora does not quite reach the level of significance ($\chi^2 = 9.305$, 4 df, $p = 0.054$), the total number of first-person verbs is low because the TL subcorpus is larger than the NL subcorpus. In fact, the Spanish NL reference value of 70 (59 per 10,000 words) predicts a figure around 105 for the TL texts, and the largest deficit is for plain statements of methods (M2) and, to a lesser degree, of statistical methods (M3).

4.   Discussion and applications

The quantitative results showed that writers publishing in English and Spanish journals make a similar two-way choice for the Methods section. In approximately two thirds of the texts they used an impersonal style with no intervention from the authors in the form of first-person verbs. In contrast, in the remaining one third, the authors' presence was manifested to a greater or lesser extent through these verb forms. This division may well reflect what Swales (2004) has noted in Methods sections across a number of disciplines, and refers to as 'clipped' and 'elaborated' texts. Of nine contrasting features pointed out by Swales, two are relevant here. Firstly, 'clipped' texts provide few justifications for methodological choices whereas 'elaborated' texts "include justifications and rationales for details of the procedures adopted, sometimes placed in the marked presubject position via a purpose clause" (Swales 2004: 220). Second, 'clipped' texts use very few 'volitional' verbs whereas 'elaborated' texts can contain one or more verbs of this type.

This does not mean that the Methods sections in the present corpus with no first-person verbs all lack the expression of justification, rationale and volition, that there are no choices made or deviations from conventional methodology, but that the authors have opted to convey them impersonally. In some cases, they may delay intervention and justification of methodological choices until the Discussion section, where first-person verbs are more frequent and appear in a variety of communicative situations (Williams 2005: 140); these include the explanation of relevant decisions before a discussion of the significance of the results, and in replies to limitations of the methods used in order to minimise the impact of selection bias or failure to follow procedures that would guarantee the validity of the results, as shown in (23):

(23)   **We believe** that the most reliable analysis is for cumulative cancer mortality from 0–74 years (a coefficient of 1.79 [$p = 0.002$]). Although there are theoretical reasons to favour analyses based on registration data or on cancer rates accumulated to 54 years, **we prefer** to emphasise the estimate based on the maximum data available using all the study populations to minimise random errors introduced by small numbers.

In the texts containing first-person forms, both the quantitative data and the qualitative evidence obtained in the profiles indicate that writers publishing in English-language journals and Spanish authors publishing in their national journals use different discourse strategies with regard to making their presence felt in the Methods section. In the English SL subcorpus, first-person forms appear sporadically through the text, rarely appearing in successive sentences (3 occurrences) and with isolated cases of inclusion of two or more forms in the same clause complex (3 occurrences). This sporadic use of the first person will draw the reader's attention to itself, signalling that something discoursally significant is taking place at the point of occurrence.

In contrast, in the Spanish NL subcorpus, first-person verbs appeared in successive sentences more frequently (8 texts) and also in longer chains of 3, 4, 5 and even a chain of 7 sentences (see Table 6), while one further text had two forms in a single clause complex. It seems clear that the strategy underlying this use is different; it provides cohesion and a consistent perspective to the text segments involved.

These contrasting discourse functions are supported and strengthened by evidence from our previous study on the Results section (Williams 2010). In the English subcorpus only seven of the 22 texts with first-person forms in the Methods also contained one or more of these verb forms in the Results section, whereas the corresponding figure in the Spanish subcorpus was 20 out of the 24 texts. Interestingly, the preferred function of statements containing first-person verbs in the English Results sections was to describe a non-conventional procedure, again drawing attention to this "displaced" methodological element, whereas in the Spanish texts the preferred associated function was to present a result.

It can be claimed, therefore, that the semantic prosody conferred on the first-person in the English texts is that of an individualised or even "deviant" procedure. This derives in part from the associated features of explicit rationale in non-finite purpose clauses or full subordinate clauses expressing the conditions under which the methodological choice was made (see examples (2) and (3) above). Of the 10 tokens of the verb *use*, nine had some fronted material, usually justifying the method employed. However, even when there was no explicit rationale in the thematised element, as in example (24), or in the single instance of a thematic pronoun, shown in (25), the first person plus procedural verb combination took on the "aura" of implicit personal choice:

(24)   For this survey, as outlined in Table 2, **we used** specimens from 24 patients, including four with PG, two with PDS, 11 with POAG, and seven with NL.

(25)   **We used** the Microlase laser (Keeler Corp, Broomall, Pa) for this study, which incorporates two infrared laser diodes with a wavelength of 780 and 830 nm and is used as a slit-lamp attachment.

Given the small number of instances of description of standard methods with first-person forms, it could be argued that this 'aura' of meaning would apply in all such cases (Louw 1993: 157), since even these cases stand out against the characteristic use of the past passive for the description of methods (Swales 1990: 120).

The strong correlation in the English texts between tense (past), verb type (procedural) and discourse function (state a method) should also be noted, since any deviation from this pattern immediately indicates a different function. Thus, in (26) the association of the present perfect with *use* is indicative of a comment even before the reader reaches the second part of the sentence:

(26)   **We have not used** phacoemulsification in these eyes, but if the surgeon prefers phacoemulsification to ECCE, it is possible to aspirate the cortex and nucleus with the phacoemulsification probe.

In the Spanish subcorpus, however, the similar frequency of descriptions of standard and non-standard procedures via first-person verbs means that this grammatical form does not acquire the distinctive aura of the English texts. Nevertheless, this personalised use does contrast with the neutral descriptive style typically realised through *se* reflexive passive verbs with which it alternates. It appears, therefore, that the authors of these texts are employing a strategy that confers a more personal perspective on the discourse, appealing to readers and drawing them into the line of reasoning. Although there were no instances of inclusive first-person use in the Methods section, a number of authors make use of inclusive forms in the Results section, making the readers participants in the ongoing description and rationale (Williams 2010):

(27)   *En relación con las complicaciones, **podemos dividirlas** en precoces y tardías.*
"With regard to complications, **we can divide** them into early and late."

(28)   *Si **comparamos** estos datos con el global de partos, **observamos** que entre ambos grupos no existen diferencias estadísticamente significativas (p > 0,05).*

"If **we compare** these data with the overall figures for deliveries, **we see** that there are no statistically significant differences between the two groups ($p > 0.05$)."

Fronted sentence constituents were present in approximately half of the Spanish clauses with first-person forms. In contrast to the English texts, the predominant thematised elements were descriptive spatio-temporal adjuncts as opposed to sub-clauses expressing rationale. In addition, although the past tense was the most frequent choice, selection of the present perfect did not appear to signal any special effect. It was particularly associated with the characterisation of the study population, as in example (29), but was also used to describe standard and non-standard methods, as in (30), which presents a rationalised choice:

(29)   *Entre 1983 y 1991 **hemos realizado** 5.221 estudios ecocardiográficos en pacientes afectados de cardiopatía congénita.*
"Between 1983 and 1991 **we [have] carried** out 5,221 echocardiographic studies on patients with congenital heart disease."

(30)   *A partir de entonces, y debido a su mayor simplicidad con resultados similares, **hemos realizado** todas las VMP con el balón de Inoue.*
"Thereafter, because of its greater simplicity and similar results, **we [have] performed** all percutaneous mitral valvuloplasties with the Inoue balloon."

The differences in discourse strategies observed have implications both for translation and for the writing of research articles in cross-cultural contexts. For texts written in an impersonal style with no first-person forms, transfer from Spanish to English and vice versa should present no difficulty. For Spanish authors writing in English, one strategy could be to write the Methods in the impersonal, possibly 'clipped' style (Swales 2004), and present any methodological issues either in the Introduction or Discussion. However, for texts containing first-person forms, direct transfer between the two languages cannot be expected to achieve the same pragmatic effects as when the discourse is addressed to a native speaker audience. As seen in Section 3.3, practising translators tend to transfer English texts directly in Spanish, but with no guarantee that the impact of the first-person will be carried over, and the TL texts may appear unnatural. An awareness of the functions of the rhetorical moves in the Methods section together with the quantitative and qualitative data derived from the contrastive analysis could prove useful in translator training, translation practice and as pedagogical input for academic writing in cross-cultural contexts. The remainder of this section will be used to outline and illustrate strategies that could be used in these contexts.

For Spanish-English transfer one basic strategy would be direct translation of first-person verbs in those communicative contexts in which the profiles showed roughly equivalent frequencies: namely, characterisation of the study population (M1) and adjustments to it (M1a), plus any descriptions of procedures and statistical methods that are justified by rationale, novelty and volition (M2a and M3a). This transfer option would apply in all cases unless overridden by local factors. An impersonal formula could be preferred to characterise the patients, e.g. "The study population consisted of…". For descriptions of non-standard choices, Spanish sequences with an adjunct containing *paciente/s* or *caso/s* plus an empty verb like *realizar* "perform" and a technique or treatment, a change of perspective may be indicated to the typical English S + V + DO sequence with *patient/s* as subject of *undergo, have* or *receive* as shown in (31):

> (31)   *Solamente en el caso de CAS **realizamos** la EO asociándola a una etmoidectomía, ya que el tumor había invadido el seno etmoidal.*
> **"Only the patient with the sebaceous carcinoma underwent** orbital exenteration in association with an etmoidectomy, since the tumour had invaded the etmoidal sinus."

The second strategy, which applies to plain description of methods, aims at reducing the M2 and M3 categories in English: first-person forms are candidates for transfer by other means unless specifically indicated for first-person expression. Justification for maintaining the first-person could be thematic continuity in co-ordinated sentences expressing different moves, as in (32):

> (32)   ***Hemos revisado** 100 tumores extirpados a lo largo de un período de 13 años y **estudiamos** los siguientes parámetros clínicos: edad, sexo, localización, tiempo de evolución, tamaño, color, consistencia y diagnóstico clínico.*
> **"We retrospectively reviewed** 100 tumours excised over a period of 13 years and **studied** the following clinical variables: age, sex, site, evolution time, size, colour, consistency and clinical diagnosis."

The other means to express procedures impersonally include (i) making a technique or analytical method the grammatical subject of an active verb (e.g. *include, assess, compare*) so that the procedure is often vested with agentivity via anthropomorphic metonymy (Williams 2005: 140); (ii) active to passive transformation with the same or a different verb; (iii) use of non-finite forms. Table 7 shows the results of the application of these transfer options to the 70 Spanish NL contexts, of which 38 were deemed appropriate for direct transfer into English. A further four first-person forms were added in associated coordinate and subordinate clauses.

The main alternatives were passives, active structures with a variety of verbs (*compare, describe, include, undergo, cover* and *have*). A minor option was the use of a non-finite form, two with metatextual references (*los resultados que **presentamos***

Table 7. Application of Spanish-English translation options to Spanish NL first-person forms

Transfer Procedure	No.	No. by Rhetorical Category	
First person	38 *	Move 1	9
		Move 1a	2
		Move 2	8
		Move 2a	17
		Move 3a	6
Passive	19	Move 2	13
		Move 3	5
		Move 3a	1
Active verbs	10	Move 1a	1
		Move 2	6
		Move 2a	3
Non-Finite form	3	Move 1a	1
		Move 2	2

Note. * Four first-person forms were added in the application: 2 in Move 2a and 2 in Move 3a

ahora > "the results **presented** here"; and *como **hemos explicado** antes* > "as explained above").

Although all rhetorical move categories were affected, the changes mainly reduced the plain description of procedures (21 instances) and statistical methods (all 5 cases). The resulting distribution of the 42 first-person forms shown in Table 7 corresponds very closely to that of the SL subcorpus given in Table 3 ($\chi^2 = 2.559$, 4 df, $p = 0.634$).

Table 8 illustrates how the options were applied to the Spanish text presented in Table 6. In addition to the main Spanish sentence components and the literal gloss, the table outlines the proposed sentence structure based on the strategic choices, and shows the moves and transfer options involved. Three sequences (S1, S4 and S9) were considered suitable for first-person use, with the other seven sentences expressed impersonally. Of greatest interest are the four consecutive sentences (S5-S8) in the third paragraph, where a consistent thematic viewpoint has been constructed with the concepts of study and analysis either as subjects of active verbs (Johns 1992: 28; Baker 1992: 168) or by thematising the verb to allow inversion and location of the focus in the postposed subject (S6).

For English-Spanish transfer, the basic strategy, as seen in Section 3.3, is direct transfer of first-person forms into Spanish. However, the quantitative analysis and the linguistic profiles show that this is not sufficient to bring the TL texts into line

Table 8. Application of strategic choices to a Spanish NL text

	Spanish	Gloss	Proposed structure	Move + Option
# S1	**Estudiamos** 30 pacientes…	**We studied** 30 patients…	**We studied** 30 patients…	M1: 1st person direct transfer
S2	En este espacio de tiempo **realizamos** un total de … eco-grafías	In this period **we performed** a total of … scans.	In this period a total of … scans **were performed**.	M2: Active — passive
# S3	Las pacientes fueran seleccionadas …	Patients were selected …	Patients were selected …	(not applicable)
S4	Del total **selecciona-mos** 9 casos únicos que…	From the total **we selected** the 9 cases…	From the total **we selected** the 9 cases…	M1a: 1st person direct transfer
# S5	En el protocolo **destacamos** los datos de afiliación…	In the protocol **we emphasise** demographic data…	The protocol **covered** demographic data…	M2: Inanimate + active verb
S6	**Estudiamos** el parto …	**We studied** the delivery…	**Also studied** were the delivery…	M2: Thematised verb
S7	Finalmente **inclui-mos** el momento…	Finally, **we included** the time…	Finally, the analysis **included** the time…	M2: Inanimate + active verb
S8	En el estudio ecográfico **describi-mos** la imagen…	In the ultrasound study **we describe** the image…	The ultrasound study **describes** the image…	M2: Inanimate + active verb
S9	Por ello **hemos desechado** todas aquellas pacientes…	Therefore, **we excluded** patients if…	Therefore, **we excluded** patients if…	M1a: 1st person direct transfer
# S10	En todas nuestras exploraciones **hemos utilizado** el ecógrafo Sonoline…	In all our ultrasound studies **we used** a Sonoline… system…	All ultrasound studies **were performed** with a Sonoline… system…	M2: Active — passive

with the Spanish discourse style due to the deficit of first-person forms in descriptions of conventional procedures and statistical methods.

According to the corpus data (Table 2), we can expect about 24 TL texts to contain first-person forms. In addition, the expected first-person frequency will be between 100 and 110, almost twice the number in the English SL texts, with most of the required additions corresponding to the M2 and M3 categories.[4] Therefore, for the TL texts to conform to the Spanish profile, it is first necessary to identify English SL texts suitable for amplification and inclusion of first-person verbs. The most likely candidate texts will be (i) those already containing first-person forms in the Methods section; and (ii) those with other related forms such as the object pronoun *us* and the possessive *our* in the Methods section.

The transfer options required are the inverse procedures to those in the previous section: (i) English SVO structures with *patient/s* as subject of verbs such as *undergo, receive* or *have* plus some kind of diagnostic technique or medical treatment can be transformed into the Adjunct + procedural verb (e.g. *realizamos, aplicamos, efectuamos, practicamos,* etc.) + DO pattern with *paciente/s, enfermo/s, caso/s* etc. as headnoun in the adjunct; (ii) abstractions representing techniques and investigational procedures as grammatical subjects of active verbs (e.g. *analyse, assess, compare, evaluate*) can be represented in Spanish instrumental adjuncts introduced by *mediante* "by means of" or *con* "with", or in non-finite clauses, especially with infinitives, plus a suitable Spanish first-person procedural verb; (iii) passive-active transpositions both with and without a change of verb; (iv) raising of non-finite forms, particularly past participles of communicative verbs, to full finite status in defining relatives or subclauses with *tal y como* "as".

Table 9. Application of transfer options to an English SL text

	English SL Text	Structure of Spanish TL Text	Transfer option
# S1	**We** retrospectively **studied** 56 cases…	**We have** retrospectively **reviewed** 56 cases…	M1: First-person direct transfer
S2	… the total population of… **is not known to us**	… **we do not know** the total population of…	M1a: object-to-subject shift
# S3	In patients in stage I…, whether **they received** only vaginal contact radiation or additional percutaneous pelvic lymph node radiation depended on risk factors…	In cases in stage I…, **we performed** vaginal contact radiation alone or additional percutaneous pelvic lymph node radiation according to risk factors…	M2: option 1
S4	All patients in advanced stages **received** both local and percutaneous radiation treatment.	In all cases of advanced disease **we applied** both local and percutaneous treatment.	M2: option 1
S5	Till 1980 radium **was used** in …; thereafter iridium-192 **was used** in …	Till 1980 **we employed** radium in…; after that date, **we used** iridium-192 in…	M2: option 3
S6	Where post-surgical external radiation was incorporated using cobalt-60, **we tried to achieve** doses of 56 Gy…	When incorporating post-surgical external radiation with cobalt-60, **we tried to achieve** doses of 56 Gy…	M2a: first-person direct transfer
# S7	All local recurrences **were** histologically **verified**.	In all cases of local recurrence **we obtained** histological verification…	M2: option 3

Table 9. *(continued)*

	English SL Text	Structure of Spanish TL Text	Transfer option
S8	Extravaginal recurrences **were** only **examined** histologically if…	In extravaginal recurrences we only **performed** the histological study if…	M2: option 3
# S9	In 25% of all cases only contact radiation therapy **was applied**.	In 25% of our cases **we performed** only contact radiation.	M2: option 3
S10	In 46.4% application of contact radiation **was combined** with percutaneous radiation and 16.1% **received** only teletherapy.	In 46.4% **we combined** contact and percutaneous radiation and in 16.1% **we** only **applied** teletherapy.	M2: option 3
# S11	Figures **given** on survival periods begin with recurrence diagnosis…	The survival figures that **we present** were calculated from the time of diagnosis of recurrence…	M2: option 4
S12	In the case of simultaneous diagnosis of local and extravaginal recurrence, the patient **was included** in the extravaginal category.	In the case of simultaneous diagnosis of local and extravaginal recurrence, **we classified** the patient in the extravaginal category.	M2: option 3
S13	Statistical evaluation of survival rates **was carried out using** the Kaplan-Meier method.	For statistical evaluation of survival rates **we used** the Kaplan-Meier method.	M3: option 3
S14	Statistical comparisons of differences… **were calculated using** the Mantel-Test.	For statistical comparison of differences… **we used** the Mantel-Test.	M3: option 3

Table 9 illustrates the amplification of first-person use in a text describing a personal series of cancer patients treated over a period of 14 years (1973–1987). The SL text, which consists of six paragraphs and 28 sentences, contains two first-person verbs, plus an object pronoun (*is unknown to us*) and five tokens of the possessive *our* (three tokens with *department* and one each with *patients* and *patient population*). The table shows only those sentences in which the SL forms have given rise to TL first-person verbs when the proposed strategies were applied. For the sake of brevity, the table reflects only the main components of the sentence structure, and gives the English gloss of the proposed Spanish TL text. The two SL first-person verbs (S1 and S6) were transferred directly, as they were in the published translation, and the object pronoun (S2) became a Spanish first-person form *desconocemos*. The most frequent transfer option was passive-active transposition (option 3) both in its simple form (e.g. S5) or with additional changes in syntax and perspective (S7, S8, S13 and S14). The switch from unmarked *patient* theme to marked *patient* adjunct (option 1) was used twice (S3 and S4). There is also one instance of non-finite raising (S11), but none of transfer option 2.

The proposed TL text now includes 16 first-person verbs in a total of 28 sentences. The revised text also contains six instances of the possessive *nuestro/a(s)*, some of which appear in sentences with no associated first-person verb. Therefore, the text now reflects the cohesive function observed in the Spanish NL texts. In the proposed version, only the text-initial verb (S1) and the metatextual reference in S11 are thematic. All the remaining verbs are preceded and covered by other thematic material in the shape of spatial (7 instances), time (2), purpose (2) or conditional (1) adjuncts or a non-finite infinitive clause (1), the remaining instance being the verb in S2, which is embedded in a subclause. Thus, these forms do not display the orienting function of theme, i.e. do not provide the framework in which the new message can be interpreted (Fries 1995: 318). Instead, the first person constitutes an extensive referential chain, a feature congruent with the description of a personal case series stressing the need for individualised treatment for this type of cancer patient. The first person does not stand out to signal a rationalised decision-making process, as suggested by the English profile, but rather reflects the constant personal concern for tailoring treatment and providing the most appropriate therapy for the patient. The function is less the assumption of responsibility by the writer in order to free the readers so that they can assess the validity of the methods used, and more a means of creating empathy with the readers so that they are drawn into the human side of the doctor-patient relationship in the oncological setting.

5.   Conclusions

The study has shown that the distribution of first-person verbs in English and Spanish Methods sections reflects a two-way choice on the part of the authors. For about 60% of texts, the objective description of material and narrative of procedures in a neutral, impersonal style will be appropriate both in English and in Spanish. In the remaining texts, move analysis proved a useful tool to reveal the presence of a subjective element in the Methods section. This knowledge, together with the information provided by a deeper analysis of linguistic profiles of first-person use, indicates where a more personal style is suitable. In the English texts that include first-person verb forms, these are mainly selected to signal and emphasise those methodological approaches and options in which the author has chosen to implement a non-standard procedure, and only rarely to describe conventional techniques. In contrast, in the Spanish NL texts, first-person forms were used equally to express both standard and non-standard methods. In studies in which a personal or individualised component is present, first-person verbs appear in cohesive referential chains that confer a consistent perspective on the discourse, making it more strongly coherent. The quantitative and qualitative data derived from the study serve as a solid empirical basis for strategic options that should prove useful both in translation practice and as pedagogical input for academic writing in cross-cultural contexts.

The study has revealed two different discourse strategies involved in first-person use: one preferred by authors publishing in Anglo-American journals whereby readers are released from any commitment to the content of the statement involved so that they can judge for themselves the potential implications on the study, and the other, employed by Spanish writers, in which they establish empathy with their readers, making them feel they are participants in the narrative and methodological choices.

Notes

1. The examples selected for inclusion in Table 1 contain no first-person forms to illustrate the point that this form represents a systemic choice on the part of the author.

2. Louw (1993: 157) refers to semantic prosody — often positive or negative implication — as "a consistent aura of meaning with which a form is imbued by its collocates".

3. In the tables giving the profiles (Tables 4 and 5) the column for collocations shows only the verbs with two or more tokens; those for colligation and semantic preference show the most significant categories; and for semantic prosody, the subcategories of non-standard procedure add up to more than the total as this function may exhibit more than one of the features.

4. The estimate is based on the relative size of the subcorpora. Any English methods section will yield a Spanish target text up to 18% longer mainly because of the higher proportion of grammatical to lexical items in Spanish than in English (Williams 2006: 37). I took the size of the English SL subcorpus (41,850) as the minimum, and that of the Spanish TL subcorpus (49,570) as a figure close to the maximum, and obtained the mean as an intermediate figure (45,710). Taking as a reference the 30,265 of the Spanish NL subcorpus, which contains 70 instances, the hypothetical intermediate subcorpus will have 105 instances, plus or minus 5, which is the 5% confidence margin.

References

Baker, M. 1992. *In Other Words*. London/New York: Routledge.
Firth, J. R. 1968. "A synopsis of linguistic theory 1930–1955". In F. R. Palmer (Ed.), *Selected Papers of J. R.Firth 1952–59*. London and Harlow: Longman Linguistic Library, 168–205.

Fries, P. H. 1995. "Themes, methods of development, and texts". In R. Hasan & P. H. Fries (Eds.), *On Subject and Theme*. Amsterdam/Philadelphia: John Benjamins, 317–359.

Halliday, M. A. K. 2005. *An Introduction to Functional Grammar*. London: Arnold.

Harwood, N. 2005a. "'We do not seem to have a theory… The theory I present here attempts to fill this gap': Inclusive and exclusive pronouns in academic writing". *Applied Linguistics*, 26 (3), 343–375.

Harwood, N. 2005b. "'Nowhere has anyone attempted…. In this article I aim to do just that': A corpus-based study of self-promotional *I* and *we* in academic writing across four disciplines". *Journal of Pragmatics*, 37 (8), 1207–1231.

Hyland, K. 1998. *Hedging in Scientific Research Articles*. Amsterdam/Philadelphia: John Benjamins.

Hyland, K. 2001. "Humble servants of the discipline? Self-mention in research articles". *English for Specific Purposes*, 20 (3), 207–226.

Hyland, K. 2002. "Authority and invisibility: Authorial identity in academic writing". *Journal of Pragmatics*, 34 (8), 1091–1112.

Johns, T. F. 1992. "It is presented initially: Linear dislocation and interlanguage strategies in Brazilian academic abstracts in English and Portuguese". *Ilha do Desterro*, 21 (1), 9–32.

Kuo, C.-H. 1999. "The use of personal pronouns: Role relationships in scientific journal articles". *English for Specific Purposes*, 18 (2), 121–138.

Louw, W. E. 1993. "Irony in the text or insincerity in the writer? The diagnostic potential of semantic prosodies". In M. Baker, G. Francis & E. Tognini-Bonelli (Eds.), *Text and Technology: In Honour of John Sinclair*. Amsterdam/Philidelphia: John Benjamins, 157–174.

Paton, A. 1976. "How I write a paper". *British Medical Journal*, 2 (6044), 1115–1116.

Quirk, R, Greenbaum, S., Leech, G. & Svartvik, J. 1985. *A Comprehensive Grammar of the English Language*. London: Longman.

Scott, M. 1998. *WordSmith Tools*. Oxford: Oxford University Press.

Sinclair, J. 1991. *Corpus, Concordance, Collocation*. Oxford: Oxford University Press.

Sinclair, J. 1996. "The search for units of meaning". *TEXTUS*, 9 (1), 75–106.

Skelton, J. 1994. "Analysis of the structure of original research papers: An aid to writing original papers for publication." *British Journal of General Practice*, 44 (387), 455–459.

Swales, J. M. 1990. *Genre Analysis*. Cambridge: Cambridge University Press.

Swales, J. M. 2004. *Research Genres: Exploration and Applications*. Cambridge: Cambridge University Press.

Tang, R. & John, S. 1999. "The 'I' in identity: Exploring writer identity in student academic writing through the first person pronoun". *English for Specific Purposes*, 18, S23-S39.

Tognini-Bonelli, E. 2001. *Corpus Linguistics at Work*. Amsterdam/Philadelphia: John Benjamins.

Vassileva, I. 1998. "Who am I/who are we in academic writing? A contrastive analysis of authorial presence in English, German, French, Russian and Bulgarian". *International Journal of Applied Linguistics*, 8 (2), 163–190.

Williams, I. A. 2005. "Thematic items referring to research and researchers in the discussion section of Spanish biomedical articles and English-Spanish translations". *Babel*, 51 (2), 124–160.

Williams, I. A. 2006. "Towards a target-oriented model for quantitative contrastive analysis in translation studies: An exploratory study of theme–rheme structure in Spanish-English biomedical research articles". *Languages in Contrast*, 6 (1), 1–45.

Williams, I. A. 2010. "Getting the ACCENT right in Translation Studies". In D. Gile, G. Hansen & N. K. Pokorn (Eds.), *Why Translation Studies Matters*. Amsterdam/Philadelphia: John Benjamins, 137–152.

Appendix

List of journals included in the corpus
1. English Source Language Subcorpus
>   *The Lancet* (8 articles)
>   *British Medical Journal* (8 articles)
>   *Journal of the American College of Cardiology* (8 articles)
>   *British Journal of Surgery* (8 articles)
>   *Archives of Dermatology* (8 articles)
>   *Acta Obstetrica Gynecologica Scandinavica* (8 articles)
>   *Archives of Ophthalmology* (8 articles)
>   *Pediatrics* (8 articles)
2. The Spanish Target Language Subcorpus consisted of the 64 TL texts published in the Spanish editions of the above journals.
3. Spanish Native Language Subcorpus
>   *Medicina Clínica* (8 articles)
>   *Revista Clínica Española* (8 articles)
>   *Revista Española de Cardiología* (8 articles)
>   *Cirugía Española* (8 articles)
>   *Actas Dermo-Sifiliográficas* (8 articles)
>   *Actualidad Obstétrico-Ginecológica* (2 articles)
>   *Clínica e Investigación en Ginecología y Obstetricia* (4 articles)
>   *Progresos de Obstricia y Ginecología* (2 articles)
>   *Archivos de la Sociedad Española de Oftalmología* (8 articles)
>   *Anales Españoles de Pediatría* (7 articles)
>   *Archivos de Pediatría* (1 article)

Cognitive verbs in context

A contrastive analysis of English and French argumentative discourse*

Anita Fetzer and Marjut Johansson
University of Würzburg / University of Turku

This paper examines the frequency, distribution and function of 1st person self-references with the cognitive verbs *think* and *believe*, and *penser* and *croire* in British English and French argumentative discourse comprising 29 British political interviews (178,712 words) and 26 French political interviews (118,825 words). It employs quantity-based methodology supplemented by insights from a context-dependent qualitative analysis, considering explicitly the co-occurrence of these cognitive verbs with discourse connectives. It argues for these 1st person self-references to be assigned not only a subjectivising function, but also one of expressing intersubjectivity.

In the two sets of data, the parenthetical constructions signify that the status of a particular piece of information encoded in a proposition is open for negotiation. Depending on their co-occurrences with discourse connectives they may boost or attenuate the pragmatic force of the contribution which they qualify.

1. Introduction

In contrastive analysis "any two objects can be compared with respect to various features and they may turn out to be similar in some respects but different in others" (Krzeszowski 1989:60). For instance, cognitive-verb-anchored parentheticals may have a similar structure in English and French realised as the indicative non-progressive forms *I think* and *je pense*, but they may be different in their distribution within a conversational contribution. To be compared in a felicitous manner, the phenomena at hand need to have at least some features of similarity (Chesterman 1998).

Contrastive analysis has traditionally concentrated on syntactic and lexical phenomena. More recently, sociolinguistic and pragmatic equivalence, and functional and relational properties of language use have been examined (Aijmer

2009). While the more traditional contrastive approaches are form-based and have favoured quantitative methodologies in the field of corpus linguistics, sociolinguistic and pragmatic analyses account for both form and function. This is due to the fact that there are no fixed form-function and function-form relationships in natural-language communication (Verschueren 1996). Hence, a corpus-based analysis of linguistic devices within the research domain of functional linguistics needs to consider both quantitative and qualitative methodologies, accounting explicitly for co-occurrence, frequency and context.

This study of 1st person self-references with the cognitive verbs *think* and *believe* in English, and *penser* and *croire* in French starts off with the analysis of a linguistic form and its semantic and morpho-syntactic equivalents in two languages.[1] Adopting the three classical steps of description, juxtaposition and comparison (Krzeszowski 1989: 57) to identify cross-linguistic similarities and differences, we additionally examine the parentheticals' embeddedness in local linguistic context with respect to patterned co-occurrences with discourse connectives, and in social context with respect to their pragmatic function as booster or attenuation devices indicating the participants' intersubjective positioning.[2]

The two sets of data share similar contextual features: they are instances of mediated argumentative discourse, and in both sets the speakers have the same communicative goals. They want to win the argumentative battle by persuading their communication partners of their position. In argumentation theory, argumentation is assigned a dual status. It refers to the process of calculating intra-subjective meaning (Anscombe & Ducrot 1983, Ducrot 1984), and it refers to an intersubjective activity, in and through which situated communicative meaning is negotiated. Argumentation is thus assigned a key function in the internal and external relationships between premises and conclusions. Because of that, it is not only discourse connectives which are of relevance in those contexts, but also self-references with the cognitive verbs *think* and *believe*, and *penser* and *croire*, as they make the intra-subjective processes of reasoning explicit, signalling how the speaker intends her/his conversational contribution to be taken and how the hearer is intended to interpret it. Argumentative strategies and references to intra- and intersubjective processes of reasoning are of particular importance in argumentative media discourse in which not only the direct communication partners need to be persuaded but also — if not primarily — the indirect communication partner, viz. the audience.

Self-references with cognitive verbs with the overt and non-overt realization of a complementizer have been assigned the status of parenthetical, which Bußmann (1996: 349) defines as an "[e]xpression (word, phrase, clause) inserted into a sentence from which it is structurally independent". According to Urmson (1952), parentheticals perform a further speech act, viz. a secondary speech act, which fine-tunes the interpretation of the primary speech act. Relevance theory sees parentheticals as higher-level explicatures (Ifantidou 2001), and pragmatics and discourse analysis assign them the status of a metapragmatic comment which intensifies the pragmatic force of a conversational contribution (e.g. Aijmer 1997, Simon-Vandenbergen 2000).

The methodological framework of this contrastive discourse-based corpus analysis is an integrated one, supplementing quantitative methodology with qualitatively oriented sociopragmatics and cognitive pragmatics. Context is accommodated explicitly in the analysis: social context is accounted for through the speech activity of argumentative political media discourse, linguistic context is accounted for through co-occurrence, and cognitive context is accounted for through intersubjective positioning and manoeuvring. Supplementing frequency and distribution of linguistic form with co-occurrence and pragmatic function allows for a fine-grained contrastive analysis of emergent, context-based patterns. In line with Hunston (2007), this analysis is based on the premise that

> quantitative methods are not irrelevant to discourse studies, in the sense that recurring instances of a phenomenon are noted, the explication of a single instance normally implies that a pattern has been identified, and that the explanation would hold true for similar instances. This is the case even when the amount of data collected is relatively small; *quantitative* does not mean *huge*, but simply that statements of the type 'this is a demonstrably typical occurrence' are worth making. The second assumption is that, on the other hand, research in the area of discourse will never be wholly quantitative.
>
> (Hunston 2007:28)

In spite of the two sets of data under investigation being not excessively "huge", we do not only expect patterned co-occurrences anchored to *I think* and *I believe*, and *je pense* and *je crois* signifying the intensification of pragmatic force within the particularized context of dyadic argumentative media discourse but we also expect similar co-occurrence patterns in the two languages. These similarities are not only due to the semantics of the cognitive verbs under investigation and to their status as parentheticals, but also, if not primarily, to their co-occurrence with discourse connectives of similar classes, such as the contrastive connectives *but* and *mais*. We intend to show that *I think*, *je pense* and *je crois*, which have been classified as attenuating devices (e.g. Apothéloz 2003, Jucker 1986, Kärkkäinen 2003), may also function as a booster in the local context of discourse connectives with a boosting force, e.g. *of course*, thus corroborating Aijmer (1997) and Simon-Vandenbergen (2000), who assign the parenthetical *I think* a both mitigating and deliberative function. This study is intended to contribute to the contrastive study of pragmatic markers (Aijmer & Simon-Vandenbergen 2006), shedding more light on context-specific use of discourse connectives.

The paper is organised as follows. The next section introduces the data. Section 3 discusses cognitive verbs, giving particular attention to their form and function. Section 4 presents the contrastive analyses, discussing quantitative results and qualitative context-based co-occurrences and their pragmatic function. Section 5 concludes.

2. Data

The data under investigation comprise a corpus of spoken political discourse, which contains two sets of data: 29 British interviews with 178,712 words and 26 French interviews and debates with 118,825 words. Both sets contain interviews with ministers, leaders of political parties and other prominent politicians. The data have been recorded by the authors and their colleagues, and they have been transcribed according to interactional principles, adhering as closely as possible to the speakers' wording of their conversational contributions.[3] The data have been manually tagged with regard to the relevant linguistic structures and then have been hand-counted in order to capture subtle aspects of analysis. As the focus of this investigation lies on the distribution of cognitive verbs in their local linguistic context, and to facilitate readability, the transcription presented here adheres to orthographical standards.

The British interviews were recorded at the beginning of 1990, and in 1997 and 2001 from the programme *On the record* (OTR) and from several pre-election interviews (PEI) with the leaders of the major British political parties. The French interviews and debates were recorded at the beginning of the 1990s, in 2002, 2003 and 2007 from the programmes *7 sur 7* (7sur7), *L'heure de vérité* (HDV), *France2 Elections* (FR2E) and *Question ouverte* (QO). The data are listed in Tables 4 and 5 in the appendix.

In the following section the semantic class of cognitive verbs is examined, considering both its subjectivising and intersubjectivising functions.

3. Cognitive verbs

The category of cognitive verb is based on the semantics of its members focussing on the verb's private domain of reference, which may denote the speaker's psychological disposition or the psychological disposition of other discourse identities or other objects of talk. In contemporary English grammar, cognitive verbs are classified as 'private verbs' (Biber 1988), 'psychological verbs' and 'psychological predicates' (Leech 1983). Prototypical representatives are, for instance, *think*, *believe, assume, guess* or *suppose*. In systemic functional grammar, they are classified as mental processes and assigned the status of grammatical metaphor when used with 1st person self-reference in the simple present, expressing epistemic modality (Halliday 1994). Cognitive verbs, as they are referred to in this paper, have attracted a lot of attention in formal and functional linguistics (Brinton 2001, Givón 1993, Horn 1989, Kärkkäinen 2003). This is particularly true of *I think* representing a polysemic construction par excellence (Aijmer 1997, Van Bogaert 2006, Simon-Vandenbergen 2000, Thompson & Mulac 1991).

In French grammar and in enunciation theory, the cognitive verbs *penser* and *croire* are seen as subjectification and distancing devices. Benveniste (1966:264) claims that *je crois que* does not denote a process of thinking but rather indicates a mitigated assertion in the 'enunciation', viz. subjective production, of an utterance. Semantically, cognitive verbs express epistemic modality, and pragmatically, they signal a subjective standpoint (Andersen 1996:313–314). From an intersubjective viewpoint, cognitive-verb-anchored parentheticals are seen as a contextualization device informing the addressee(s) how a conversational contribution qualified by the devices is to be interpreted. Recently, cognitive verbs and discourse markers have received more attention from cross-linguistic and pragmaticalization perspectives (Dostie 2004, Schneider 2007). Assigning cognitive-verb-anchored self-references the status of parentheticals with an attenuating function is also supported by Apothéloz (2003), and Blanche-Benveniste & Willems (2007). While the former argues for the parentheticals to have become weaker in their semantic meaning and to have obtained a strong adverbial character, the latter argue for their classification as polysemic parentheticals.

Complementizer dropping in the context of cognitive-verb-anchored parentheticals is very frequent in English when used with a self-referencing intentional agent. This is also possible in French (Schneider 2007), but the parentheticals display less syntactic detachability and mobility than in English.

Cognitive verbs are also considered from an intersubjective perspective. Givón (1993) categorises perception verbs (P), cognition verbs (C) and utterance verbs (U) into a single class of PCU-verbs. Kerbrat-Orecchioni (1997:117–119) postulates a category of opinion verbs which relate the private act of cognition with the public act of communication. This view is based on Ducrot (1980:266) who states that opinion verbs like *penser, croire, considérer, trouver, se douter* in a linguistic context of "X — que p" give information about the opinion of a person to the addressee.

There are currently two dominant views of (inter)subjectivity in language: the sentence-based approach by Verhagen (2005) and the semantics-pragmatics anchored paradigm by Traugott (1995), and Stein & Wright (1995). In the latter approach, context and meaning are assigned a key role in the construal of subjectivity. Nuyts (2001) takes the argument one step further by examining the function of cognitive verbs in interaction. He claims that these verbs do not only signify subjectivity, but rather intersubjectivity, which he defines as follows: "Intersubjectivity means that the information (and the epistemic evaluation of it) is generally known, and hence is not new (or surprising) to the speaker and hearer(s)" (Nuyts 2001: 396).

In his work on constructions of intersubjectivity, Verhagen (2005) examines the connectedness between cognitive verbs and finite complements with respect to the coordination of communicative action. He comes to the conclusion that in "a complementation sentence the addressee is invited to adopt the perspective of the onstage conceptualizer. When this is a third person the utterance exhibits the same argumentative orientation as when it is a first-person" (Verhagen 2005: 106). That is to say, by using the *I think/I believe* or *je pense/je crois* parenthetical the speaker invites the hearer to adopt her/his perspective, and that is why a 1st person-cognitive-verb parenthetical is assigned the status of a construction of intersubjectivity operating

> in the dimension of intersubjective coordination [...]. It consists of instructions to perform inferential operations of a certain type, independently of the 'objective' content of the utterances. The accessibility of certain cultural models (topoi) to provide material for these inferential processes is presupposed, but nothing about their content is itself coded in the conventional meaning of the elements of the system.   (Verhagen 2005: 76).

Hence, the primary function of cognitive-verb-anchored parentheticals is not to represent but to instruct the addressee how to interpret a conceptualization. This sort of instruction, we claim, is further refined by the local context in which the parenthetical is embedded. It is the parenthetical's co-occurrence with other discourse connectives which fine-tunes the instruction with respect to speaker-intended meaning and speaker-intended hearer interpretation. It is that extension of frame from the individual speaker to the dyad of speaker and addressee which assigns the 1st person self-reference the status of a construction of intersubjectivity.

However, intersubjectivity is not only a matter of how the speaker conceptualizes her/his assessment as regards the status of information s/he intends to communicate. It is also a matter of how the speaker aligns with her/his interlocutors. This is of even greater importance in our data; in political discourse, which is media discourse par excellence, it is not only the direct interlocutors, i.e. the first-frame participants of interviewer and interviewee (Fetzer 2000), who negotiate the communicative status of a conversational contribution, but also the second-frame participant of audience. In that particularized setting, the first-frame participants intend to align with the audience, guiding them in their construal of communicative meaning.

In the following section a corpus-based examination of 1st person self-references with *think/believe* and *penser/croire* is presented, considering frequency and co-occurrence.

4. Contrastive analysis

This contrastive analysis of the distribution, co-occurrences and function of the cognitive verbs in question is based on a corpus of spoken standard British English and French political discourse, which has been introduced in Section 2. It employs quantitative methodology, accounting for frequency and distribution, supplemented by qualitative microanalysis, accounting for emergent co-occurrence patterns and function.

In the following subsection, the British and French data are analysed from a quantitative perspective.

4.1 Quantitative contrastive analysis

The British and French data have been analysed with respect to the occurrence of the tokens *I/we think* and *I/we believe*, and *je crois/nous croyons* and *je pense/nous pensons* in their affirmative and negated forms. First person plural self-references have been included in the analysis because of social-context constraints. In the particularized context of mediated political discourse, politicians do not only speak on behalf of themselves as individual agents, but also, if not primarily, on behalf of the political party (or government) they are affiliated with and which they represent.[4] The results of the quantitative contrastive analysis are summarised in Table 1; the frequency is given in absolute figures as well as in instances per 10,000 words.

Table 1. Quantitative analysis of the British and French data

British data (178,712 words)		French data (118,825 words)	
I think	516 (28.87‰)	102 (8.58‰)	*je pense*
we think	18 (1.00‰)	3 (0.25‰)	*nous pensons*
I believe	88 (4.95‰)	195 (16.41‰)	*je crois*
we believe	21 (1.18‰)	0	*nous croyons*
I don't think	64 (3.58‰)	6 (0.5‰)	*je ne pense pas*
we don't think	2 (0.11‰)	0	*nous ne pensons pas*
I don't believe	21 (1.18‰)	7 (0.59‰)	*je ne crois pas*
we don't believe	3 (0.16‰)	0	*nous ne croyons pas*

I think is the most frequent parenthetical in the British data, occurring 28.87 times per 10,000 words. Its first-person plural counterpart is significantly less frequent with only one instance per 10,000 words. In the French data, *je crois* is the most frequent construction with 16.41 occurrences per 10,000 words. Contrary to its plural-based British counterpart *we believe, nous croyons* does not occur at all. Another difference between the two sets of data is the rather high frequency of the negated parenthetical *I don't think* in the British corpus, occurring with singular self-reference (3.58 instances per 10,000 words) and with plural self-reference (0.11 instances per 10,000 words). In the French data, there are only 8.58 instances per 10,000 words for the singular self-reference *je pense*, 0.5 instances per 10,000 words for its negated counterpart, and 0.25 instances for the plural self-reference. *I believe* occurs 4.95 times per 10,000 words with its negated counterpart occurring 1.18 times. The plural self-reference occurs 1.18 times per 10,000 words with its negated counterpart occurring 0.16 times. In the French data, *je ne crois pas* occurs 0.59 times per 10,000 words with no occurrences for its plural-based negated counterpart.

As regards frequency, *think-* and *believe*-anchored singular self-references differ significantly, which is not the case with their plural-based forms. In the French data, *je crois* and *je pense* do not differ to that extent in frequency, with *je crois* being twice as frequent as *je pense*, relatively speaking. Negated parentheticals only occur with singular self-references (0.59 instances per 10,000 words for *je ne crois pas* and 0.5 instances for *je ne pense pas*).

The parenthetical *je crois* (16.41) is significantly more frequent than *I believe* (4.95). From a quantitative perspective, it would have been more appropriate to compare and contrast it with *I think* (28.87), which is the most frequent parenthetical in the British data. From a qualitative viewpoint, however, *I believe* shares more co-occurrence patterns with *je crois* than with *je pense*.

The high frequency of the *I think* parenthetical corroborates the results obtained in the research on grammaticalization and pragmaticalization (Aijmer 1997, Thompson & Mulac 1991). The results obtained from our contrastive analysis indicate that the two cognitive-verb-anchored parentheticals *je crois* and *je pense* seem to have undergone a process of grammaticalization. As regards pragmaticalization, that process may be emergent.

In the following, the results obtained from the quantitative analysis of the parentheticals will be refined by the explicit accommodation of their co-occurrence with discourse connectives and other relevant contextualization devices. Particular attention will be given to the emergence of co-occurrence patterns.

4.2 Qualitative analysis

The quantitative analysis of self-references with the cognitive verbs *think* and *believe*, and *penser* and *croire* has shown interesting results for language-specific preferences, with a clear preference for *I think* in English and a less-clear preference for *je crois* in French — less clear, as *je crois* is only 1.89 times as frequent as *je pense*. While *I think* has generally been assigned the status of expressing epistemic modality attenuating pragmatic force, *I believe* is looked upon as a marker of belief, boosting the pragmatic force of a conversational contribution (Berlin 2008). However, that differentiation between *I think* as an attenuation device and *I believe* as a booster is not that simple, as has been shown by Aijmer (1997), Fetzer (2008) and Simon-Vandenbergen (2000), who distinguish between a probability-based mitigating function of *I think* and a certainty-based boosting (or deliberative) function. In French, Ducrot (1980) classifies cognitive verbs like *je pense* and *je crois* as opinion verbs with an effect on modality. Vet (1994) considers *je crois* as a device for attenuating knowledge.

   In the following, the results of the quantitative analysis presented above will be refined by the explicit accommodation of local linguistic context and co-occurrence, showing that adjacent discourse connectives make the pragmatic function of the parenthetical they co-occur with, more determinate as regards their status as a booster or attenuation device.

4.2.1   I think *and* je pense *in context*
A qualitative analysis of linguistic corpora cannot but consider quantitative aspects. This is particularly true if emergent co-occurrence patterns are under investigation. Against that background, the frequencies of co-occurring discourse connectives and other cognitive-verb-anchored parentheticals are accommodated explicitly in the analysis.

   The parentheticals under investigation co-occur with discourse connectives expressing an additive connection or continuation (*and*), cause (*because*), concession (*of course*), result (*so, then*) and contrast (*but, no, well*) with different degrees of frequency. These may be looked upon as emergent patterns and are referred to as syntagmatic configurations in this contribution. Furthermore, there are idiosyncratic co-occurrences with diverse conjuncts and disjuncts (Quirk et al. 1985), such as *and in addition, in the end, also, absolutely* and *quite frankly*. However, *I think* and *I believe* do not only co-occur with discourse connectives. There are also patterned clusters of two cognitive-verb-based parentheticals (*I mean **I think** (0.33)*), and less frequently two cognitive-verb-based parentheticals co-occurring with a discourse connective (*no I mean **I think***; *but I mean **I think***) and two discourse connectives co-occurring with *I think* (*but because **I think***; *well no you see **I don't think***) and *I think* co-occurring with *you know* and *you see*.

In the French data, there is also a lot of variation in discourse-connective-anchored co-occurrences of *je crois* and *je pense*. They co-occur with the discourse connective *et* expressing an additive connectedness. The syntagmatic configuration *et je pense/et je crois* is also found in the initial position of an utterance with emphatic *moi* or a fronted adverbial, e.g. *et moi je crois* or *et aujourd'hui je crois*. They also co-occur with discourse connectives expressing cause (*parce que*), result and consequence (*alors, donc*), contrast (*mais, non, ben, bon*), acceptance (*oui*), and with conjuncts (*d'abord*). Furthermore, there are idiosyncratic co-occurrences with various discourse connectives and adverbs (*hein je pense*), other-oriented devices (*écoutez moi je pense*) and some rare cases where they co-occur together with *et* (*je crois et je pense*) or with other parentheticals like *j'espère, je trouve*.

The results of the British and French co-occurrences for *I think* and *je pense* with more than one occurrence are juxtaposed in Table 2. To show possible co-occurrence patterns, the rows of the British data are organised according to frequency. The column of the juxtaposed French data is organised according to semantic-pragmatic equivalence, as they do not display such frequency-based emergent patterns. The figures given denote absolute frequency as well as frequency per 10,000 words.

The most frequent co-occurrence for *I (don't) think* and *je pense* is the discourse connective *and* (4.42 occurrences per 10,000 words) and *et* (1.01 occurrences per 10,000 words). The difference in frequency seems to indicate that there is an emergent co-occurrence pattern for *and I think*, which is not — or at least not yet — the case with *et je pense*. Analogously to the polysemic status of *I think* expressing a cognitive action, the epistemic modalities of probability, certainty and evidence — to name but the most prominent ones —, the discourse connective *and* may also fulfil a number of discourse-semantic and interpersonal functions, such as signifying an additive relation, a contrastive relation, or continuation (Schiffrin 1987).

The emergent co-occurrence pattern of *and I think* and the co-occurrence of *et je pense* are illustrated by excerpts (1) to (3):[5]

(1) *Well* we had all that, *didn't we*, last November when people were looking around and *one or two people* did ask me what my position was. *And* I think the words I used which were absolutely accurate: "I'll take no part in this".

[1990a OTR]

(2) *So I said well now* you *must* otherwise shut up and apologise or get out of the party. *And* I think that is a very straightforward way of dealing with it.

[2001d PEI]

Table 2. Patterned co-occurrences of *I think* and *je pense*

British data (178,712 words)		French data (118,825 words)	
Discourse connective [I think] [[+/−that] [complement]]		Discourse connective [je pense] [[+/−que] [complement]]	
and I think	79 (4.42‰)	12 (1.01‰)	*et je pense*
and I don't think	7 (0.39‰)	0	*et je ne pense pas*
well I think	29 (1.62‰)	1 (0.08‰)	*ben je pense*
well I don't think	2 (0.11‰)	0	*bon je pense*
		0	*bon je ne pense pas*
but I think	20 (1.11‰)	2 (0.17‰)	*mais je pense*
but I don't think	6 (0.33‰)	0	*mais je ne pense pas*
now I think	12 (0.67‰)		
now I don't think	2 (0.11‰)		
because I think	8 (0.44‰)	4 (0.34‰)	*parce que je pense*
because I don't think	2 (0.11‰)	0	*parce que je ne pense pas*
no I think	6 (0.33‰)	3 (0.25‰)	*non je pense*
no I don't think	6 (0.33‰)	0	*non je ne pense pas*
so I think	6 (0.33‰)	2 (0.17‰)	*alors je pense*
		0	*alors je ne pense pas*
		2 (0.17‰)	*donc je pense*
		0	*donc je ne pense pas*
yeah I think	5 (0.27‰)	2 (0.17‰)	*oui je pense*
yes I think	4 (0.22‰)	0	*oui je ne pense pas*
of course I (don't) think	2 (0.11‰)		
then I think	2 (0.11‰)		
		3 (0.25‰)	*d'abord je pense*
		0	*d'abord je ne pense pas*

(3) **Oui** *c'est* la vie, *c'est* l'identité, *c'est* l'affiliation, *c'est c'est* l'alliance. Et **donc** *c'est* ça une espèce de valeur symbolique **très très** forte. *Et* **je pense que** on a parlé de la génération de la crise économique et du sida chacun à leur façon…

[1994 7sur7]

In (1)–(3), the syntagmatic configuration *and I think/et je pense* occurs in the initial position of an utterance.[6] In Halliday's systemic functional grammar, it would be classified as a constitutive part of a multiple theme composed of a textual theme (*and/et*) and an interpersonal theme (*I think/je pense*). In that frame of reference, these two parts and the topical theme form a whole unit: the theme. Looked upon from a discourse-analytic perspective, the syntagmatic configurations *and I think/*

et je pense are a constitutive part of an argumentative sequence, introducing some backing in (1), and a necessary consequence, result or conclusive statement in (2) and (3). The local linguistic context of the syntagmatic configuration *and I think* comprises the negative discourse connective *well*, indicating some upcoming disagreement (Schiffrin 1987), the interaction-based device of reversed polarity question tag, and the vagueness marker *one or two people* in (1). All of these devices express the epistemic modality of probability. That probability-coloured context affects the communicative meaning of both the discourse connective *and* and the parenthetical *I think*, attributing an attenuating function to the syntagmatic configuration. To employ discourse-pragmatic terminology, the syntagmatic configuration *and I think* is assigned the status of a metapragmatic comment which attenuates the pragmatic force of the utterance it qualifies if it occurs in a local context coloured by epistemic probability. In (2), by contrast, *and I think* occurs in a local context coloured by epistemic necessity (*must*), a public verb (*say*) realised in indicative mood, indicating factivity, and the discourse connectives *so, now* and *well*: *so* signals an upcoming conclusive statement, *now* focuses the participant's attention on the here-and-now, and *well* signifies an upcoming disagreement. Almost all of those devices, except for *well*, express epistemic certainty, and it is that certainty-coloured context which assigns the metapragmatic device the status of a booster. Looked upon from a dialogic perspective, *and I think* fulfils an important intersubjective function in argumentative discourse, instructing the addressee(s) how the speaker intends them to interpret a particular piece of discourse. In (3), the argument begins with an acceptance expressed by a discourse connective (*oui*), the repetition of a presentational form with a copula (*c'est*) and a conclusive statement introduced by the discourse connective *donc* containing an adverb *très* which has a boosting function. This is followed by the syntagmatic configuration *et je pense que* and additional information supporting the argument, thus boosting the pragmatic force.

In (4), *I think* co-occurs with the discourse connective *well*, which is classified as a negative discourse marker, whose function it is to attenuate the pragmatic force of a conversational contribution (Schiffrin 1987). Looked upon from an intersubjective perspective, *well* is seen as a heteroglossic device (Simon-Vandenbergen et al. 2007). The syntagmatic configuration *well I think* occurs in the local context of another cognitive verb attributed to a 3rd person plural subject and weak epistemic prediction (*was bound to be*). In that weak epistemic-modality coloured context, *well I think* attenuates the pragmatic force. In (5), the initial discourse connective *ben* expresses a certain reservation on the side of the speaker as regards a previous utterance while at the same time boosting the force of his own. In the local context of *ben je pense que,* there are several presentational forms (*c'est*) introducing certainty and boosting devices, like the adverb *très* and the contrastive discourse connective *mais*.

(4) *Well* I **think** all the party from the prime minister downwards *recognise* that there *was bound* to be teething troubles …   [1990a OTR]

(5) *Ben* je **pense** que *c'est très* compliqué de se débrouiller avec ça, *mais c'est* une *vraie* question et *c'est* une question aussi de de grandeur et de dignité de notre pays.   [1994 7sur7]

(6) *Well yes* it is expensive. *But* I **think** *erm* you'*ve got to recognize* that these solutions have been adopted in Europe…   [1990b OTR]

(7) *Je ne vais pas me mettre* à faire du Kriegspiel, *mais* je **pense** qu'*il faut* étudier toutes les options…   [2002d QO]

In (6) and (7), the syntagmatic configurations *but I think* and *mais je pense* occur in a local context coloured by epistemic necessity (*have got to, il faut*). In (6), *but I think* introduces a counter in the politician's argumentation, which is realised after an unavoidable acknowledgment of the interviewer's valid refutation (*well yes it is expensive*). In (7), *mais je pense* is preceded by a negative context (*ne-pas*) with a prediction (*va me mettre*). In these local contexts, the *but I think/mais je pense* configuration functions as a booster, intensifying the degree of epistemic necessity contained in the proposition. Looked upon from an intersubjective angle, the contrast-anchored configuration indicates the speaker's preference towards her/his addressee adopting their stance.

The semantic-pragmatic equivalent of the English syntagmatic configuration *now I think* does not occur in the French data. In (8), it occurs in a linguistic context coloured by the evidentiality-anchored expression *obviously* and emphatic *do*, which both are boosting devices. The discourse connective *now* has been classified as anchoring a conversational contribution to the here-and-now, thus focussing the participants' attention to upcoming talk (Schiffrin 1987). This attention-focussing force, which is intensified by *obviously* and emphatic *do*, assigns the syntagmatic configuration the function of a booster. Considered from an intersubjective perspective, it indicates situation-anchored intersubjective positioning:

(8) And it reflects the very proper conservative or conservative party to make what adjustments may be appropriate. *Now* I **think** that there are problems that *obviously do* exist and I've mentioned them in the article that I wrote…   [1990a OTR]

The syntagmatic configuration *because I think* in (9) occurs in the local context of the account *this is actually very very important*, which is intensified by the modal adverb *actually* and the reduplicated adverb *very*, and in (10), the local context of *parce que je pense* contains the reduplicated negative discourse connective *non*, the adverb *effectivement*, boosting the force, and the epistemic modality of necessity (*il faut*). In (11) and (12), the syntagmatic configuration *no I think/non je pense* occurs in a linguistic context containing morphosyntactic negation (*n't*) and the cognitive-verb-anchored parenthetical *I think* in (11), and the discourse connective *mais* expressing contrast and the boosters *en tout cas* and *sans doute* in (12). All of those local contexts are coloured by epistemic certainty, and in all of those excerpts the *I-think/je-pense*-based configuration introduces a counter move boosted by the metapragmatic device in question:

(9)   *And if I might if I might* just make this point to you. *Because* I **think** this is *actually very very important.* What you are really trying to say to me is this...
[1990g OTR]

(10) *Non non parce que* je **pense** *ça* peut pas se faire du jour au lendemain **et que** *effectivement il faut* amener des femmes à être formées et avoir le désir profond la capacité etcetera...
[1994 7sur7]

(11) *No* I **think** millions of people have*n't* decided how to vote. *I think* millions have*n't* decided whether to vote...
[2001d PEI]

(12) *Non* je **pense** que c'était *en tout cas* déjà engagé par le gouvernement précédent, *mais* il y a eu une poursuite qui a pu mettre *sans doute* l'entreprise au niveau international, elle l'est, *mais* qui a effacé le service public.
[2002c QO]

The syntagmatic configurations *so I think/alors je pense/donc je pense* occur in the local context of epistemic necessity (*should*) and evaluation (*ont droit à...un veritable débat; un élément des libertés fondamental*) in (13), (14) and (15). Introducing a logical consequence, the metapragmatic devices boost the pragmatic force of the propositions they qualify:

(13) Now if I if I may. Now you've asked me the question. *So* I **think** I *should* complete the answer. The plain fact is ...
[1997g PEI]

(14) *Alors* je **pense** que les Français *ont droit à* autre chose, à *un véritable débat* digne d'une démocratie...
[2002b FR2E]

(15) Nous considérons dans tous les pays démocratiques que ce qui est très important c'est qu'il y ait des possibilités d'appel pour les choses importantes pour les choses graves *donc* je **pense** que c'est *un élément des libertés fondamental*...
[2003e QO]

In (16), the syntagmatic configuration *yeah (yes) I think* occurs in a local context coloured by hypothetical meaning (*if we had*) and another cognitive verb *I mean*, which introduces a self-reformulation. In (17), the local context of the configuration *oui je pense* contains epistemic probability (*peut-être*). In the probability-coloured contexts, the metapragmatic devices attenuate the pragmatic force of the propositions they qualify, fulfilling an important intersubjective function by signalling that information encoded in a proposition is open for negotiation:

(16) *Yeah*, **I think** that if we had a referendum that the British would just vote against the pound. Because *I mean*, for the for the pound, because we've got an aging population, they're so opposed to change, but I'm I'm for Europe.
[2001f PEI]

(17) *Oui* **je pense** qu'il *n*'était *pas peut-être* en bonne situation pour faire ce genre de manifestation lui-même...
[2002g FR2E]

In (18) and (19), the syntagmatic configurations *of course I think* and *then I think* occur in a local context coloured by epistemic modality (*wouldn't be right*) mitigating the force of the negated proposition, and by an unmitigated predication (*is in a different dimension*). In (18), the qualified proposition serves as a counter in an argumentative exchange. In spite of the conventional politeness-based degree of attenuation, the metapragmatic device boosts the force of the counter. In (19), the metapragmatic device *then I think* introduces the concluding statement in an argumentative sequence and is for that reason also assigned a boosting function. The syntagmatic configuration *d'abord je pense* in (20) introduces an utterance commenting on the previous question, thus referring to its appropriateness conditions. Since it co-occurs with the hesitation marker (*euh*) and a public verb in future tense (*dirai*), the syntagmatic configuration *d'abord je pense* attenuates the pragmatic force.

(18) *Of course* **I think** it is *wouldn't be right* to change the forecast. All sorts of things can happen and we are sticking to that forecast... [1990i OTR]

(19) But when you actually produce a charge like that, that will frighten and worry many vulnerable people. *Then* **I think** that *is in a different dimension*...
[1997a PEI]

(20) *D'abord* **je pense** que *euh* en préambule *je dirai* deux choses un c'est utile c'est deux et deux c'est normal... [1994 7sur7]

In grammaticalization and pragmaticalization research, *I think* is described as having undergone a process of semantic bleaching and subjectification, resulting in its status as a grammaticalized parenthetical construction (Thompson & Mulac 1991) and as a pragmatic marker (Aijmer 1997). These results are corroborated in our data. However, the claim that *I think* has the function of mitigating pragmatic force could not be confirmed by our analysis. In argumentative discourse,

I think tends to co-occur with argumentative discourse connectives. If realised in the initial position of an utterance, the corresponding syntagmatic configurations form a unit composed of textual and interpersonal themes (in Hallidayean terms) and function accordingly. In speech-act-theoretic terms, they are assigned the function of a metapragmatic device. It is at that stage that the status of *I think* as a pragmaticalized construction surfaces best, colouring the argumentative force of the connectives accordingly. Except for *well* and *yeah*, the discourse connectives have a boosting function in the argumentation, introducing further arguments (*and, now*), providing reasons (*because*), and introducing counterarguments (*but, no*) and acceptance (*of course*), thus boosting the pragmatic force.

The syntagmatic configuration *je pense* and its co-occurrence with discourse connectives has similar functions. It occurs most often in the initial position of an utterance, also forming a whole and functioning as a metapragmatic device. Analogously to *I think,* it may also attenuate and boost the pragmatic force. If it co-occurs with a discourse connective expressing acceptance (*oui*), and with a discourse conjunct (*d'abord*), it has an attenuating function. In cases where it co-occurs with discourse connectives that introduce a further argument (*et*), express cause (*parce que*), result and consequence (*alors, donc*) or contrast (*mais, non, ben, bon*), it boosts the pragmatic force of the contribution.

4.2.2   I believe *and* je crois *in context*

The parentheticals under investigation co-occur with discourse connectives expressing an additive relation or continuation (*and/et*), acceptance or agreement (*yes/oui*), contrast (*but, well/mais, bon*), and cause (*because/parce que*). Analogously to *I think, I believe* also co-occurs with the discourse connective *now*, while this does not take place in French. However, *je crois* displays more co-occurrences than *I believe*, additionally co-occurring with *alors* and *donc* expressing result and consequence, and with the conjunct *d'abord* indicating the first position in a sequence. The frequency of the co-occurring discourse connectives — except for *and/et* — is significantly lower with the other parentheticals than with *I think*, and that is why it would not be appropriate to interpret the results as emergent co-occurrence patterns. As has been explicated above, there are clusters of two cognitive-verb-based parentheticals (*I mean **I believe** (0.11)*), and *I believe* co-occurring with *you know* and *you see*. In the French data, the syntagmatic configuration *et je crois* is also found in the initial position of an utterance with emphatic *moi* or a fronted adverbial, e.g. *et moi je crois* or *et aujourd'hui je crois*. Furthermore, there are idiosyncratic co-occurrences with various discourse connectives and adverbs (*euh je crois, non bien sûr non je crois, parce que effectivement je crois*), and some rare cases where they co-occur together.

Table 3. Patterned co-occurrences of *I believe* and *je crois*

British data (178,712 words)		French data (118,825 words)	
Discourse connective [I believe] [[+/−que] [complement]]		Discourse connective [je crois] [[+/−que] [complement]]	
and I believe	13 (0.72‰)	32 (2.67‰)	*et je crois*
and I don't believe	2 (0.11‰)	0	*et je ne crois pas*
yes I believe	4 (0.22‰)	1 (0.08‰)	*oui je crois*
		0	*oui je ne crois pas*
but I believe	3 (0.16‰)	5 (0.42‰)	*mais je crois*
		1 (0.08‰)	*mais je ne crois pas*
now I believe	3 (0.16‰)		
because I believe	2 (0.11‰)	9 (0.76‰)	*parce que je crois*
because we believe	2 (0.11‰)	0	*parce que je ne crois pas*
no I do not (don't) believe	2 (0.11‰)	3 (0.25‰)	*non je crois*
		0	*non je ne crois pas*
well I don't believe	2 (0.11‰)	1 (0.08‰)	*ben je crois*
		4 (0.34‰)	*bon je crois*
		0	*bon je ne crois pas*
		8 (0.67‰)	*alors je crois*
		0	*alors je ne crois pas*
		7 (0.59‰)	*donc je crois*
		0	*donc je ne crois pas*
		2 (0.17‰)	*d'abord je crois*
		0	*d'abord ne je crois pas*

The results of the co-occurrences for *I believe* and *je crois* with more than one occurrence are juxtaposed in Table 3. As in Table 2, the rows are organised according to frequency, and the juxtaposed columns are organised according to semantic-pragmatic equivalence. The figures given denote absolute frequency as well as frequency per 10,000 words.

As with *I think* and *je pense*, the most frequent co-occurrence of *I believe* and *je crois* is the additive discourse connective *and/et*. In (21), the politician accepts the interviewer's claim in an explicit, non-mitigated manner boosted by epistemic necessity. The syntagmatic configuration *and I believe* introduces a proposition which tops the previous claim by qualifying it with (a) the speaker's explicit belief, and (b) the epistemic prediction *will do better*. In (22) the reduplicated negative discourse connective *non* introduces a negative context. This is followed by the contrastive discourse connective *mais*, constituting a necessary move in the argumentation.

Finally, *et je crois* is followed by a non-mitigated epistemic expression (*avoir raison*):

(21)   Yes I accept we have to do better. *And* I believe we *will do better*.

[1990c OTR]

(22)   *Non non mais* pour ce qui concerne le congrès on a mis ça de côté *et* je crois qu'on *a eu raison*…   [2002a QO]

I believe and *je crois* co-occur with the discourse connective *yes/oui*. In (23), the syntagmatic configuration *yes I believe* occurs in the local context of a prediction (*it will*) and evidence in its support. As with the discourse connective *and*, the parenthetical occurs in the linguistic context of epistemic prediction, thus boosting the pragmatic force of the utterance. Moreover, in that particular instance, the pragmatic force of the whole contribution is boosted further by the politician providing further evidence ("interview with good managers") in support of his claim. In (24), *je crois qu'* co-occurs with a discourse connective expressing acceptance (*oui*) followed by a complement that contains an impersonal construction (*il est*) and an evaluation (*anormal*) triggering a subjunctive mood containing a modal verb of possibility (*puissent*). Because of its function as a backing, the parenthetical boosts the force.

In (25), the syntagmatic configuration *but I believe* occurs in the linguistic context of a *personal view*, expressing subjectivity, supplemented by collective self-reference and epistemic necessity (*we should*), boosting the pragmatic force. The excerpt (26) begins with a negative context containing a reduplicated negative discourse connective (*non non*) and a cognitive verb (*sais*). The discourse connective is reduplicated (*mais*) and *je crois que* co-occurs with an expression of epistemic necessity (*obligation*) thus boosting the pragmatic force:

(23)   *Yes* I believe it *will*. You interviewed managers, good managers actually that knew most of them on the screen who understandably wanted to get across to you that things remained pretty well as they are…   [1990e OTR]

(24)   *Oui* je crois qu'*il est* anormal dans notre pays que en toute occasion les consommateurs *puissent* être pris en otages…   [2002a FR2E]

(25)   *My personal view* is that if people have seen to have seriously misbehaved then the House of Commons should take a severe view of it. *But* I believe *we should* have the report, *we should* have the report, *we should* have the examination, *we should* have the representations, *we should* have the considerations, *we should* have the debate about that consideration and then *we should* make up our mind.   [1997d PEI]

(26) *Non non mais je sais bien. Mais* **je crois que** aujourd'hui Rocard a une
      obligation, c'est d'essayer de reconstruire son parti…   [1993 HDV]

In (27), the syntagmatic configuration *now I believe* occurs in the linguistic context of necessity (*can't, have got to*) and possibility (*can*), boosting the force of the
politician's intention of making "a real start on education":

(27) We *can't* just go on taxing spending more. We've *got to* look at how we spend
      that money and we've *got* to look at where the tax burden falls. *Now* **I believe**
      we can make *a real start on education* in this country and let me tell you …
                                                                      [1997f PEI]

(28) I don't anticipate lots of them having wisdom teeth operations but I'm glad
      you acknowledge they're all going to be here after the election. *Because* **I
      believe** *they are too*…   [1997c PEI]

(29) *Toutes les* branches de la sécurité sociale et *tous les* comptes sociaux *sont* en
      déficit. Ne chipotons pas sur les chiffres *parce que* **je crois que** les Français
      attendent un débat d'un autre niveau.   [2007 QO]

In (28), the syntagmatic configuration *because I believe* occurs in a linguistic context containing a non-mitigated verb (*they are too*), which is realised after discussing a particular state of affairs, with which the politician agrees implicitly. This
implicit agreement is made explicit by the politician's providing the reason for the
implicit agreement, viz. "that they are too". The making explicit of the politician's
belief in that particular context boosts the pragmatic force of the utterance. In (29),
there is a premise with two indefinite determiners and definite articles (*toutes/tous
les*) used with a copula (*sont*). The conclusive statement contains two parts: a negative imperative (*ne chipotons pas*) and a discursive connective expressing cause
(*parce que*). Here, *je crois que* boosts the pragmatic force of the wish expressed.

  In (30) and (31) the negated parenthetical *I don't believe* occurs in a negative
context containing the negative discourse connectives *no* and *well*. In (30), it is
repeated, thus boosting the pragmatic force. In (31) it co-occurs with the negative discourse connective *well* signifying some degree of reluctance on the side
of the speaker. In (32), *je crois que* occurs twice, first with the contrastive discourse connective *bon* and a prediction expressing necessity (*va falloir*), fulfilling
a boosting function. The following argumentative move begins with an imperative
(*commençons*) and ends with a stressed first person pronoun (*moi*), *je crois que*
and an intensifier (*bien*), thus boosting the pragmatic force. In (33), *je crois que*
begins the argumentative sequence, preceded by the negative discourse connective
non. This is followed by another token of *je crois que* and the reformulation device
en l'occurrence giving a definition of the politician's previous functions. Both instances have a boosting function:

(30) *No* I do not believe, *I do not believe* for the purposes…   [2001d PEI]

(31) *Well* I don't believe anybody is looking for industrial action in the health
      service.   [1990e OTR]

(32) Quand il s'attaque au vrai problème, *bon je crois* qu'il y a un moment *il
      va falloir* parler des résultats. *Commençons* par la sécurité sociale et le
      financement de la retraite. Moi *je crois qu'*il a *bien* fait de faire les 40 ans *bon*.
                                                                                  [1994 HDV]

(33) *Non,* je crois que vis-à-vis de personne qui vous succède dans les fonctions
      que vous avez exercées *en l'occurence* je crois que j'ai quatre successeurs
      culture communication université éducation…   [1993 7sur7]

In (34) and (35) the linguistic context contains discourse connectives expressing
result and consequence as well as the discourse connectives *alors* and *donc* boosting the pragmatic force. In (34) the syntagmatic configuration *alors je crois* is followed first by an epistemic verb (*savez*) pointing to the co-speaker and then by
expressions denoting epistemic necessity (*véritable*) and possibility (*peut*). In (35)
the discourse connective *donc* announces a consequence on a previous elaboration
about the role of a politician. The syntagmatic configuration *donc je crois que* is
followed by an expression of necessity (*doit*), vagueness marker (*un certain nom-
bre de*) and a second part with a discourse connective *mais* expressing contrast
and containing a verb expressing possibility in negative form (*ne peut pas*). In the
last example (36), the discourse conjunct *d'abord* introduces an utterance where *je
crois que* is followed by an expression of necessity (*il faut*) thus having a boosting
function.

(34) *Alors* je crois *vous le savez* mieux que quiconque qu'il y a eu une **véritable**
      organisation, on *peut* dire soviétique de l'opinion.   [2002g FR2E]

(35) C'est la noblesse du rôle du ministre, c'est la noblesse du rôle de responsable
      politique. *Donc* je crois qu'on on *doit* distinguer *un certain nombre de*
      situations, distinguer *un certain nombre de de* choses, *mais* qu'on *ne* **peut**
      pas euh rejeter le le la dimension de la responsibilité et politique euh et
      médicale.

(36) *D'abord* je crois qu'*il faut* parler du fond de sa politique.

The qualitative analysis of the parentheticals *I believe* and *je crois* has supported
their status as expressions of epistemic modality, boosting the pragmatic force of
an utterance. However, the expression of epistemic modality does not primarily
have the function of expressing the speaker's attitude towards the proposition and
qualifying them accordingly. Rather, the patterned co-occurrences of *I believe* and

je crois with the argumentative discourse connectives *and/et, yes/oui, but/mais, because/parce que, no/non, well/ben* and *now, d'abord, alors* and *donc* show that the two cognitive-verb-based parentheticals have an intersubjective function, instructing the addressee how the speaker intends her/his contribution to be taken up.

4.3 Contrastive analysis revisited

The quantitative and qualitative contrastive analysis of the parentheticals *I think, I believe, je crois* and *je pense* in argumentative political discourse has provided interesting results for language-preferential co-occurrence patterns with respect to distribution, co-occurrence and function. Both languages make use of the parentheticals and both languages display similar co-occurrences, but there seem to be language-specific preferences for the selection of parentheticals and for the selection of co-occurring discourse connectives and other cognitive-verb-based parentheticals. *I think* is undoubtedly the preferred parenthetical for English and *je crois* is the preferred for French, but the two do not share the same preferences for their co-occurring discourse connectives. Here, *I think* and *je pense* have similar preferences, as is reflected in the almost even distribution for the connectives *and/et, but/mais, because/parce que, no/non* and *so/alors, donc* and *yeah/oui*. The negative discourse connective *well* co-occurs frequently with *I think*, but not with *I believe*, and its French counterpart *ben/bon* is significantly less frequent with *je pense*, while it is more frequent with *je crois*. Thus, there seems to be less language-specificity for the selection of co-occurring argumentation-anchored discourse connectives, but more language-specificity for the selection of cognitive-verb-based parentheticals in argumentative discourse.

While *I believe* has only a boosting function in the data at hand, *I think* may both attenuate and boost the pragmatic force, depending on its local linguistic context. In French *je pense que* is used in contexts where the force of the contribution can be boosted or attenuated, and its functions depend strongly on their local linguistic contexts. The parenthetical *je crois* has a boosting function only with the discourse connectives analysed, like its English semantic equivalent. Generally speaking, *I think, I believe, je pense* and *je crois* reinforce the initial orientation of the conversational contribution they qualify.

A discourse-anchored contrastive corpus analysis needs to accommodate both quantitative and qualitative methodologies to capture the multifaceted, complex connectedness between distribution, co-occurrence and function. Against that background, the cognitive-verb-anchored parentheticals under investigation underlie language-preferential constraints with respect to distribution and function, while the argumentation-anchored discourse connectives seem to display more independence.

5. Conclusion

This integrated, discourse-based contrastive analysis has shown that cognitive-verb-anchored parentheticals are frequent in argumentative discourse. They fulfil an important function in the negotiation of validity of arguments by signifying intersubjective positioning and allowing for intersubjective manoeuvring. This is particularly true of *I think* and *I believe*. While the former is a versatile device boosting and attenuating pragmatic force, the latter is a booster only. In French, *je pense* has both the function of boosting and attenuating the pragmatic force, while *je crois* boosts the pragmatic force in contexts where it co-occurs with discourse connectives.

Think- and *believe-*, and *penser-* and *croire-*based parentheticals display patterned co-occurrences with discourse connectives and other cognitive-verb-anchored parentheticals. Both English and French show a clear preference for the discourse connective *and/et*. Negative and contrastive connectives come second and third in line in the English data, while causality-markers come second in line for the French data. These rather explicit argumentative devices are less frequent in English.

The intersubjective function of cognitive-verb-anchored self-references is inherent in argumentative discourse. Their patterned co-occurrences with discourse connectives, other cognitive-verb-based parentheticals and other-oriented contextualization devices show the fine-tuned interplay in the orchestrating of signifying and negotiating intersubjective meaning.

Notes

* We are deeply grateful to the editors and referees for their important input, and to the Academy of Finland and the German Academic Exchange Service for their financial support.

1. The four cognitive verbs are the most frequent ones in our data with 29 instances per 10,000 words for *I think*, 4.95 instances per 10,000 words for *I believe*, 16.41 instances per 10,000 words for *je crois* and 8.58 instances per 10,000 words for *je pense*. Self-references with the cognitive verbs *assume, feel, guess, suppose* and *suspect* are 0.1 for *I assume* and *I guess*, 0.6 for *I suspect*, 0.3 for *I suppose* and *I feel* per 10,000 words. In French, there were 1.26 occurrences of *je trouve* and 2.52 of *je vois* per 10,000 words. There were 0.08 occurrences for *je suppose*, while other verbs like *présumer, (se) douter* were not found at all.

2. In this contribution, the term 'discourse connective' is used as an umbrella term, referring to pragmatic markers, discourse markers, discourse particles and pragmatic expressions, to name but the most prominent ones (e.g. Aijmer & Simon-Vandenbergen 2006, Celle & Huart 2007 and Fischer 2006).

3. I would like to thank Peter Bull (University of York) for sharing the pre-election interviews with me (A. F.).

4. The French indefinite pronoun *on* also refers very often to the speaker. However, it requires a specific contextual analysis in order to find out who is included or excluded from the scope of its reference (Helasvuo & Johansson 2008).

5. To facilitate readability, the transcription adheres to orthographic standards and employs the corresponding punctuation devices. The parentheticals under investigation are printed in **bold**. Other relevant linguistic devices, such as discourse connectives and cognitive verbs are formatted in ***bold italics***.

6. The excerpts (1)–(3) are analysed from a very detailed micro-perspective. Because of external constraints that degree of explicitness cannot be upheld for the analysis of the other excerpts. There, we concentrate on the most important features only.

References

Aijmer, K. 1997. "I think — an English modal particle". In T. Swan & O. Jansen (Eds.), *Modality in Germanic Languages*. Berlin: de Gruyter, 1–47.

Aijmer, K. (Ed.) 2009. *Contrastive Pragmatics*. Special Issue of *Languages in Contrast*, 9 (1).

Aijmer, K. & Simon-Vandenbergen, A.-M. 2006. "Introduction". In K. Aijmer & A.-M. Simon-Vandenbergen (Eds.), *Pragmatic Markers in Contrast*. Amsterdam: Elsevier, 1–10.

Andersen, H. L. 1996. "Verbes parenthétiques comme marqueurs discursifs". In C. Muller (Ed.), *Dépendance et Intégration Syntaxique: Subordination, Coordination, Connexion*. Tübingen: Max Niemeyer Verlag, 307–315.

Anscombe, J.-Cl. & Ducrot, O. 1983. *L'Argumentation dans la Langue*. Mardaga: Bruxelles.

Apothéloz, D. 2003. "La rection dite 'faible': Grammaticalisation ou différentiel de grammaticité?" *Verbum*, XXV (3), 241–262.

Benveniste, E. 1966. *Problèmes de Linguistique Générale*. Tome I. Paris: Gallimard.

Berlin, L. 2008. "*I think, therefore…*: Commitment in political testimony". *Journal of Language and Social Psychology*, 27 (4), 372–383.

Biber, D. 1988. *Variation across Speech and Writing*. Cambridge: Cambridge University Press.

Blanche-Benveniste, C. & Willems, D. 2007. "Un nouveau regard sur les verbes 'faibles'". *Bulletin de la Société de Linguistique de Paris*, Tome CII, Fascicule 1, 217–254.

Brinton, L. J. 2001. "From matrix clause to pragmatic marker". *Journal of Historical Pragmatics*, 2 (2), 177–199.

Bußmann, H. 1996. *Routledge Dictionary of Language and Linguistics*. London: Routledge.

Celle, A. & Huart, R. (Eds.) 2007. *Connectives as Discourse Landmarks*. Amsterdam/Philadelphia: John Benjamins.

Chesterman, A. 1998. *Contrastive Functional Analysis*. Amsterdam/Philadelphia: John Benjamins.

Dostie, G. 2004. *Pragmaticalisation et Marqueurs Discursifs. Analyse Sémantique et Traitement Lexicographique*. Bruxelles: De Boeck, Duculot.

Ducrot, O. 1980 [1975]. "*Je trouve que*". In O. Ducrot et al. (Eds.), *Les Mots du Discours*. Paris: Editions du Minuit, 57–92.

Ducrot, O. 1984. *Le Dire et le Dit*. Minuit: Paris.

Fetzer, A. 2000. "Negotiating validity claims in political interviews". *Text*, 20 (4), 1–46.

Fetzer, A. 2008. "'And I think that is a very straight forward way of dealing with it.': The communicative function of cognitive verbs in political discourse". *Journal of Language and Social Psychology*, 27 (4), 384–396.

Fischer, K. (Ed.) 2006. *Approaches to Discourse Particles*. Oxford: Elsevier.

Givón, T. 1993. *English Grammar: A Function-based Introduction*. Amsterdam/Philadelphia: John Benjamins.

Halliday, M. A. K. 1994. *Introduction to English Functional Grammar*. London: Arnold.

Helasvuo, M.-L. & Johansson, M. 2008. "Construing reference in context: Non-specific reference forms in Finnish and French discussion groups". In M. L. A. Gómez-Gonzáles, J. L. Mackenzie & E. M. González Álvarez (Eds.), *Current Trends in Contrastive Linguistics: Functional and Cognitive Perspectives*. Amsterdam/Philadelphia: John Benjamins, 27–50.

Horn, L. 1989. *A Natural History of Negation*. Chicago: Chicago University Press.

Hunston, S. 2007. "Using a corpus to investigate stance quantitatively and qualitatively". In R. Englebretson (Ed.), *Stancetaking in Discourse*. Amsterdam/Philadelphia: John Benjamins, 27–48.

Ifantidou, E. 2001. *Evidentials and Relevance*. Amsterdam/Philadelphia: John Benjamins.

Jucker, A. 1986. *News Interviews*. Amsterdam/Philadelphia: John Benjamins.

Kärkkäinen, E. 2003. *Epistemic Stance in English Conversation*. Amsterdam/Philadelphia: John Benjamins.

Kerbrat-Orecchioni, C. 1997 [1980]. *Enonciation*. Paris: Arman Colin.

Krzeszowski, T. 1989. "Towards a typology of contrastive studies". In W. Oleksy (Ed.) *Contrastive Pragmatics*. Amsterdam/Philadelphia: John Benjamins, 55–72.

Leech, G. 1983. *Principles of Pragmatics*. London: Longman.

Nuyts, J. 2001. "Subjectivity as an evidential dimension in epistemic modal expressions". *Journal of Pragmatics*, 33 (3), 383–400.

Quirk, R., Greenbaum, S., Leech, G. & Svartvik, J. 1985. *A Grammar of Contemporary English*. London: Longman.

Schiffrin, D. 1987. *Discourse Markers*. Cambridge: Cambridge University Press.

Schneider, S. 2007. *Reduced Parenthetical Clauses as Mitigators: A Corpus Study of Spoken French, Italian and Spanish*. Amsterdam/Philadelphia: John Benjamins.

Simon-Vandenbergen, A. M. 2000. "The functions of *I think* in political discourse". *International Journal of Applied Linguistics*, 10 (1), 41–63.

Simon-Vandenbergen, A. M., White, P. & Aijmer, K. 2007. "Presupposition and 'taking-for-granted' in mass communication". In A. Fetzer & G. Lauerbach (Eds.), *Political Discourse in the Media*. Amsterdam/Philadelphia: John Benjamins, 31–74.

Stein, D. & Wright, S. (Eds.) 1995. *Subjectivity and Subjectivisation*. Amsterdam/Philadelphia: John Benjamins.

Thompson, S. & Mulac, A. 1991. "A quantitative perspective on the grammaticization of epistemic parentheticals in English". In E. Traugott & B. Heine (Eds.), *Approaches to Grammaticalization*. Amsterdam/Philadelphia: John Benjamins, 313–327.

Traugott, E. 1995. "Subjectification in grammaticalization" . In D. Stein & S. Wright (Eds.), *Subjectivity and Subjectivisation*. Amsterdam/Philadelphia: John Benjamins, 31–54.

Urmson, J. O. 1952. "Parenthetical verbs". *Mind*, 61, 480–496.

Van Bogaert, J. 2006. "*I guess, I suppose* and *I believe* as pragmatic markers: Grammaticalization and functions". *Belgian Essays on Language and Literature*, 129–149.

Verhagen, A. 2005. *Constructions of Intersubjectivity*. Oxford: Oxford University Press.

Verschueren, J. 1996. "Functioning in a multi-cultural world. Contrastive ideology research: Aspects of a pragmatic methodology". *Language Sciences*, 18 (3–4), 589–603.

Vet, C. 1994. "Croire et savoir". *Langue Française*, 102, 56–68.

Appendix: Data sources

Table 4. The British political interviews

Date	Words	Interviewee
2001a PEI	12,818	T. Blair (Labour)
2001b PEI	10,825	T. Blair (Labour)
2001c PEI	12,427	W. Hague (Conservative)
2001d PEI	11,029	W. Hague (Conservative)
2001e PEI	11,570	Ch. Kennedy (Liberal Democrats)
2001f PEI	10,207	Ch. Kennedy (Liberal Democrats)
1997a PEI	1,714	J. Major (Conservative)
1997b PEI	6,211	J. Major (Conservative)
1997c PEI	5,411	J. Major (Conservative)
1997d PEI	7,343	J. Major (Conservative)
1997e PEI	7,277	J. Major (Conservative)
1997f PEI	7,300	T. Blair (Labour)
1997g PEI	5,964	T. Blair (Labour)
1997h PEI	7,141	T. Blair (Labour)
1997i PEI	5,745	T. Blair (Labour)
1997k PEI	1,628	T. Blair (Labour)
1997l PEI	8,030	P. Ashdown (Liberal Democrats)
1997m PEI	6,962	P. Ashdown (Liberal Democrats)
1997n PEI	5,439	P. Ashdown (Liberal Democrats)
1997o PEI	4,462	P. Ashdown (Liberal Democrats)
1990a OTR	5,157	M. Heseltine (Conservative)
1990b OTR	4,159	J. Prescott (Labour)

Table 4. *(continued)*

Date	Words	Interviewee
1990c OTR	1,434	J. Cunningham (Labour)
1990d OTR	2,485	J. Gummer (Conservative)
1990e OTR	4,047	K. Clarke (Conservative)
1990f OTR	2,364	D. Trippier (Conservative)
1990g OTR	4,695	T. Blair (Labour)
1990h OTR	2,411	C. Moynihan (Conservative)
1990i OTR	2,457	N. Lamont (Conservative)
	178,712	

Table 5. The French political interviews

Date	Words	Interviewee
2007 QO	24,235	N. Sarkozy (Union for a Popular Movement), Ségolène Royal (Socialists)
2003a QO	1,720	L. Fabius (Socialists)
2003b QO	1,878	Fr. Hollande (Socialists)
2003c QO	1,693	A. Madelin (Union for a Popular Movement)
2003d QO	1,992	Fr. Mer (businessman, Economy Minister/Conservative)
2003e QO	1,790	D. Perben (Union for a Popular Movement), (José Bové)
2003f QO	2,006	N. Sarkozy (Union for a Popular Movement)
2003g QO	1,853	H. Vedrine (Socialists)
2002a QO	2,233	L. Fabius (Socialists)
2002b QO	1,933	Fr. Fillon (Union for a Popular Movement)
2002c QO	2,103	Fr. Hollande (Socialists)
2002d QO	1,566	A. Juppé (Union for a Popular Movement)
2002e QO	1,601	J.-M. Le Pen (Front National)
2002f QO	1,449	J. Lang (Socialists)
2002g QO	3,145	J.-M. Messier (businessman, Economy Minister/Conservative)
2002a FR2E	4,742	J. Chirac (Rally for the Republic)
2002b FR2E	7,100	J. Chirac (Rally for the Republic)
2002c FR2E	3,161	Ph. Douste-Blazy (Christian Democrate)
2002d FR2E	2,993	V. Giscard d'Estaing (former President, Independent Republicans)
2002e FR2E	3,183	B. Gollnisch (Front National)
2002f FR2E	5,161	J.-M. Le Pen (Front National)

Table 5. *(continued)*

Date	Words	Interviewee
2002g FR2E	3,265	J.-M. Le Pen (Front National)
1994 HDV	11,268	M. Aubry (Socialists)
1993 HDV	11,109	B. Tapie (Radical party of the Left)
1994 7sur7	8,197	M. Barzach (Rally for the Republic)
1993 7sur7	7,449	J. Lang (Socialists)
	118,825	

Mood and modality in finite noun complement clauses

A French-English contrastive study*

Issa Kanté
University Paris 13

The present paper presents a corpus-based contrastive analysis of modality in English and French finite noun complement clauses. On the one hand, we claim on the basis of cross-linguistic and semantic evidence that modality is a common intrinsic feature of nouns that license *that/que* complement clauses, and, as a consequence, that head nouns are modal stance markers. On the other hand, this paper shows that indicative-subjunctive alternation in *that/que* noun complement clauses is determined by the modality type of the governing noun. Contrastive analysis of French and English provides evidence to substantiate these claims.

1. Introduction

This paper is a corpus-based study investigating the lexico-semantic relation between *that/que* noun complement clauses and modality. The link between *that*-clauses and modality has been widely described in the literature, but the source of modality has not been fully identified. The types of clauses focused on in this study are illustrated in the examples (1)–(4) below:

(1) *The certainty that the abnormality of this relationship with Johnny could do her harm* was, for a fraction of a second, clear and undisputed in her mind.
(BYU-BNC)

(2) These findings support *the hypothesis that autonomic neuropathy affects motility throughout the gastrointestinal tract.* (BYU-BNC)

(3) *J'étais bien décidé à ne pas souffler mot de mon histoire; mais <u>la certitude que ma mère allait me demander des éclaircissements</u> ne laissait pas de m'exaspérer.* (Frantext)

"I was determined not to whisper a word of my story; but the certainty that my mother would ask for clarifications irritated me."   (My translation)

(4)   *Nous pouvons faire l'importante remarque que la double démonstration que nous venons de donner s'appuie uniquement sur l'hypothèse que les particules ont une trajectoire et que l'équation de continuité est valable.*   (Frantext)
"We can point out that the double demonstration we have done is based solely on the hypothesis that the particles have a trajectory and that the continuity equation is valid."   (My translation)

Our starting point was the observation that a noun like *linguistics* cannot govern a complement *that*-clause (example 5), whereas one like *hypothesis* can (example 2):

(5)   **These findings support (the) linguistics that autonomic neuropathy affects motility throughout the gastrointestinal tract.*

Therefore, the first part of this paper (Section 3) investigates whether the non-modal value [–modality] of the term *linguistics* and the modal (epistemic) value [+modality] of *hypothesis/evidence* can explain why the former cannot govern *that*-clauses whereas the latter can. Previous linguistic studies have shown that such *that/que*-clauses, through the head noun, do involve modality (cf. Perkins 1983; Palmer 1986; Biber et al. 1999; Mélis 2002; Ballier 2007 & [forthcoming] for English, Chevalier & Léard 1996 for French).

The second part of our study (Section 4) explores how mood selection in a subordinate clause is influenced by the head noun, and how the choice of a particular mood affects the overall modal meaning of the construction (cf. Lyons 1977: 848, 1995: 255; Huddleston & Pullum 2002: 172; Riegel et al. 1994: 287). Particularly in French, mood alternation (indicative or subjunctive) is used as a 'modality orientation' marker in complement clauses.[1] As Riegel et al. (1994: 287) note, mood is defined as the category which expresses the speaker's attitude towards his/her utterance. It can be hypothesized that the indicative/subjunctive alternation in *that/que* complement clauses is correlated to the modal class of the governing head noun.

All of the hypotheses in this paper are tested using French and English monolingual corpora (cf. Section 2). These provide authentic utterances from each language to substantiate our claims about the modality of head nouns in Section 3, and will enable us to statistically investigate whether the distribution of mood after head nouns is dependent on the nouns' modality class.

2.   Corpora

Authentic occurrences were selected from two monolingual corpora of French and English, viz. Frantext and Brigham Young University British National Corpus (BYU-BNC). Frantext is a 210-million word corpus (4,000 texts), including literary (80%) as well as scientific and technical texts (20%).[2] The corpus spans five centuries (16th to 21st), but the search was limited to the 20th century. The BYU-BNC (1980's to 1993), an interface designed by Mark Davies at Brigham Young University, consists of 100 million words and is composed of texts from fiction, popular magazines, academic discourse and newspapers; the spoken part was ignored in this study.

Instead of extracting all *that/que*-clauses from these two corpora, we decided to focus only on *that/que*-clauses which are governed by one of the following head nouns, which are assumed to be prototypical representatives of the three modality types **epistemic**, **deontic** and **alethic**: *assertion, certainty, fact* and *hypothesis* for English, *affirmation, certitude, fait* and *hypothèse* for French (epistemic nouns); *constraint, demand, request* and *requirement* for English, *contrainte, demande, exigence* and *obligation* for French (deontic nouns); *likelihood, necessity, possibility* and *probability* for English, *vraisemblance, nécessité, possibilité* and *probabilité* for French (alethic nouns; this term and others are defined in Section 3.3).[3] The selection and modal classification of these nouns were mainly based on the studies of Perkins (1983: 86–87), Chevalier & Léard (1996: 55), Biber et al. (1999: 647–648) and Ballier (2007: 69–70). These authors describe head nouns as involving modality and argue that they could be classified into modal classes (see Sections 3.1 and 3.2 for arguments).[4]

From the BYU-BNC and Frantext corpora, we extracted all *that/que*-clauses that are adjacent to one of the selected head nouns: [(*V/Prep*) *the N that-clause*] and [(*V/Prep*) *le, la, l' N que-clause*]. For both English and French, pre-predicate *that*-clauses (examples 6 and 7) and non-complement *that*-clauses, such as relative clauses [*the N that Rel.*] (example 8), were excluded:

(6)   *That Saints managed to cause an upset with nothing more than direct running and honest endeavour* bodes well for Great Britain   (cf. Biber et al. 1999: 676)

(7)   *Que le vieil Horace est le personnage principal de la tragédie*, c'est la vérité
                                                                    (Soutet 2000: 50)
      "That old Horace is the main character of the tragedy, is the truth."
                                                                    (My translation)

(8)   *The hypothesis that can explain bat navigation* is a good candidate for explaining anything in the world.

Additionally, when a head noun was followed by two *that/que*-clauses, only the first was included in the data. In example (9), for instance, only *que je choisisse à l'avance mes textes* was included in the results.

(9)   *Les points de repère pourraient d'ailleurs être déterminés par <u>le fait que</u>*
      <u>je choisisse à l'avance mes textes et que je les relie par mes commentaires</u>.
      (Frantext)

      "In fact, the bench marks could be determined by the fact that I choose in
      advance my texts and that I connect them by comments."   (My translation)

The corpus query in BYU-BNC yielded 779 *that*-clause occurrences: 319 epistemic, 302 alethic and 158 deontic noun *that*-clauses. For French, the data include 327 nominal *que*-clauses governed by epistemic nouns, 39 governed by alethic nouns and 4 governed by deontic nouns — a total of 370 occurrences. Note that in Frantext, the searches for deontic *exigence* and *obligation* yielded a very limited set of occurrences: three occurrences for the former and one for the latter. As for *contrainte, demande* and alethic *vraisemblance* there were no occurrences at all of *que*-clauses.

As we had only four complement clauses governed by deontic nouns, we extracted data from another corpus, in order to complement the data set. WebCorp Linguist's Search Engine was used to retrieve *que*-clauses governed by these nouns. WebCorp LSE is a "tailored linguistic search engine for accessing the web as corpus" created by the Research and Development Unit for English Studies (RDUES) at Birmingham City University.[5] The test corpus consists of 70 million words from web-extracted texts. WebCorp LSE yielded 10 occurrences of *que*-clauses governed by *vraisemblance* and 30 governed by the deontic nouns *exigence, obligation, contrainte* and *demande*. When added to the occurrences from Frantext, the additional data brought the total to 410 *que*-clauses.

From a contrastive and methodological standpoint, it must be acknowledged that there are stylistic and genre differences between the French and English data. The best contrastive method would have been to compare two corpora that were built on the same sampling techniques and had an equal size. On the one hand, the BNC and Frantext have not the same size and on the other hand, they neither cover the same time period nor contain equally the same genre of texts. However, these differences are unlikely to have any significant negative impact on our analyses, since the main purpose of the statistics is not to demonstrate that the uses of the subjunctive or the indicative in French and in English are proportionally comparable, but to show that, in each language, the proportion of their usage is related to the modality type of the head noun.

3.   Head nouns as modality markers

3.1 Theoretical background

One of the main constraints in *that* noun complement clauses is head noun se-lection. The question is obviously why a *that*-clause can be governed by certain nouns but not by others. A consensus seems to exist on the interpretation of the finite noun complement, but not on the issue of head noun selection constraints. Biber et al. (1999:648) and Mélis (2002:141–145), among others, claim that head nouns or/and their complement *that*-clauses are used by speakers to express their stance or attitude towards the propositional content (cf. Perkins 1983 and Ballier 2007 for English, Chevalier & Léard 1996 for French). Biber et al. (1999:648) ob-serve that "the *that* clause reports a proposition, while the head noun reports the author's stance towards that proposition". Ballier (2007:69) describes the function of (epistemic) head nouns as a testimonial cursor which enables the speaker to express his/her stance on the (modal) status and the plausibility of the state of af-fairs expressed in the *that*-clause. Palmer (1986:126–131) argues that complement clauses, governed by a lexical subordinator, are either used to indicate the atti-tudes and opinions of the speaker (*I think he's there*) or to report the attitudes and opinions of the subject of the main clause, i.e. the original speaker (*he requested that they should arrive early*). In his study, Palmer (1986) focuses on verbs and adjectives as subordinators that express epistemic and deontic modality. Perkins (1983:86) clearly ascribes a modal value to noun complement clauses in structures like *there is a N to/that* in particular.

All these studies acknowledge that head nouns and their complement clauses involve the speaker or another speaker's stance/attitude. Nevertheless, although they help us to understand one of the discursive values of *that*-clauses, they tell us little about the underlying mechanisms of the phenomenon, viz. the issue of head noun selection.

Huddleston & Pullum (2002:965) provide a sample of 58 head nouns and ob-serve that head nouns are either derived from verbs and adjectives or are "mor-phologically derivative". These authors thus seem to link the ability of nouns to govern *that*-clauses to their derivative status. In other words, head nouns govern *that*-clauses because they derive from syntactic categories which are themselves *that* taking items. In their description of noun complement clauses, so-called 'ap-positive clauses', Quirk et al. (1985:1260–61) claim that to govern such a clause, "the noun phrase must be a general abstract noun". It should be pointed out that these accounts might not be entirely convincing since not all head nouns are ab-stract (*picture, sign, slogan*, etc.), nor are all of them derived from verbs or adjec-tives (*fact, idea, story*, etc.) (cf. Ballier 2004).[6]

In contrast, other approaches, such as Nomura (1993), Schmid (2000) and Bowen (2005) carry out a functional analysis to explain how nouns govern *that*-clauses. In these approaches (Nomura 1993 and Schmid 2000 in particular), nouns are classified into different lexical categories such as UTTERANCE nouns, COGNI-TIVE nouns, MODAL nouns, etc. The underlying assumption of such an analysis is that head nouns have to be understood in terms of their use but not necessarily in terms of their inherent semantic properties. This position is essentially the one adopted by Schmid (2000: 13) in the following passage:[7]

> Why are *A-nouns*, *carrier nouns* and *shell nouns* so hard to define? The reason is that they are not defined by inherent properties but constitute a functional lin-guistic class. This means that whether a given noun is a shell noun or not does not depend on inalienable characteristics inherent in the noun, but on its use. A noun is turned into a shell noun when a speaker decides to use it in a shell-content complex in the service of certain aims.

Against this position, however, it can be argued that head nouns can be defined and characterized by their inherent semantic properties. In fact, contrary to the ap-proaches discussed so far, other analyses assume that modality appears to be a prop-erty which plays a significant role in the selection of head nouns in *that*-clauses. For instance, Boone (1996: 48–49) and Chevalier & Léard (1996: 54–55) claim that head verbs and nouns, respectively, are modality markers in *que*-clauses. This claim led them to classify *que*-clause governing verbs (Boone 1996) and nouns (Chevalier & Léard 1996) in three classes of modality, i.e. *epistemic*, *alethic* and *deontic* modality.

The assumption underlying this paper is that modality might be one of the features that provide the finite clause licensing property to head nouns. In other words, it is claimed that head nouns can be semantically and/or pragmatically in-terpreted as involving a modality feature; therefore they can be classified as nomi-nal modal categories.

3.2 Semantic and pragmatic arguments

The claim that head nouns involve inherent modality properties can be supported by the following observation about the polysemic difference between words like *philosophy* and *linguistics*. *The Concise Oxford Dictionary* defines these two words as follows:

> Linguistics: pl. n. [treated as sing.] the scientific study of language and its struc-ture.
> Philosophy: n. (pl. -ies) 1 the study of the fundamental nature of knowledge, re-ality, and existence. 2 the study of the theoretical basis of a branch of study or experience. 3 a theory or attitude that guides one's behaviour.

While both words refer to fields of study, *philosophy* can also refer to "*a theory or attitude that guides one's behaviour*". This meaning is the one expressed in the sentence below:

(10) a. Franklin subscribes to the Apple *philosophy that if you can encourage children to use your products, they will continue to use them when they are adults.*   (BYU-BNC)

In this sentence, the speaker evaluates the propositional content (*that if you can encourage…*) as a *philosophy*, as a theory that guides Apple's policy. When we manipulate the sentence and replace *philosophy* with *linguistics*, the result is not acceptable at all:

(10) b. Franklin subscribes to the Apple **linguistics that if you can encourage children to use your products, they will continue to use them when they are adults.*

In contrast, if we insert a noun such as *idea, assertion, doctrine* etc., the sentence is always correct, although the degree of epistemic commitment will be different with each noun. Our postulate is that *linguistics* is unacceptable precisely because it has no evaluative property similar to the one *philosophy* has as a *that* taking noun. Thus, the word *philosophy* governs a *that*-clause thanks to its polysemic status, *study of* vs. *opinion* or *attitude*. In contrast, apparent co-hyponyms such as *linguistics, geography, chemistry* cannot take *that*-clauses because these words lack the semantic feature *opinion* or *attitude*.

The idea underlying this observation is that head nouns intrinsically involve modal features that allow the speaker to express his/her opinions or attitudes. For instance, it is obvious that nouns like *certainty, requirement* and *(dis)advantage* have semantic properties of, respectively, epistemic, deontic and attitudinal-evaluative modality. This can be perceived in the following sentences:

(11) Such evidence must be balanced with *the certainty that stone of the appropriate type does occur in the Drift of eastern England (Penny 1974, p. 248) (Figure 2.20).*   (BYU-BNC)

(12) *The requirement that all motor vehicles (except invalid carriages, police and local authority vehicles) used on a road must be covered by third party insurance* is fundamental to the lawful operation of any haulage business.   (BYU-BNC)

(13) This logic has *the advantage that it protects the more efficient contractor and exposes the less efficient and is thus conducive to efficiency in the long run.*   (BYU-BNC)

In (11), the *that*-clause is epistemically qualified; the speaker expresses his/her commitment to its plausibility in terms of certainty. In (12), instead of expressing epistemic commitment through the *that*-clause, the speaker reports on the state of affairs in terms of desirability or obligation. In (13), the speaker adopts an attitudinal standpoint towards the state of affairs expressed in the clause. In this case, the evaluation is positive, but the attitudinal evaluation can be negative as well, as in:

(14)   Washed sand or gravel should settle immediately, but these have *the disadvantage that they do not provide mineral nutrients for the plants.* (BYU-BNC)

In addition, nouns that govern *that*-clauses do not only denote the speaker's own commitment or assessment, as in (11)–(14), but also another person's commitment (attitudes and opinions):

(15)   However, Culpitt's *assertion that the post-war collectivist welfare state and its value premises* are now obsolete is clearly open to question. (BYU-BNC).

Notice that the comment *is clearly open to question* is expressed by the speaker him/herself. In such utterances, the speaker reports another person's assertion or modal commitment and then comments on it.

These observations are in line with many analyses of modality. Palmer (1986: 96, 121), for instance, suggests that epistemic (including alethic) and deontic modality have in common "the involvement of the speaker". And Nuyts (2005: 17) goes a step further in claiming that epistemic (with alethic), deontic, and boulomaic modality (notions to be defined below) all indicate the extent to which the speaker or another person is committed to the state of affairs expressed in the *that*-clause. According to Nuyts (2005), they indicate the degree of existential, moral and affective commitment, respectively. In fact, modality appears to play a major role in *that* complement clauses; the following section therefore defines what we mean by "modality".

3.3 Definitions of modality

Modality has been given a considerable number of definitions, ranging from a broad concept in which any sort of assertion may contain modality to a narrow concept in which only modal verbs and some adverbs can convey modality (see also Salkie 2008: 78). Le Querler (1996: 49–61), summarising different views on modality, claims that between these two conceptions there is another which considers modality as the expression of the speaker's attitude towards the propositional content. This view is in line with Palmer's (1986: 16) definition when he says that modality is "the grammaticalization of speakers' (subjective) attitudes and opinions". According to Le Querler (1996: 63–64), the definition of modality, in relation to the speaker, requires its classification in three kinds of modality: *subjective, intersubjective* and *objective*. She defines these types, respectively, as *the relation between the speaker and the propositional content, the relation between the speaker and another speaker*, and *the relation between the propositional content and another proposition*. If we take this view, subjective modality orientation seems to be the type expressed in most finite noun complement constructions. This would particularly be the case if we view finite subordination in general and *that*-clause noun complementation in particular as the expression of the speaker's position towards the plausibility or the desirability of the propositional content (Heyvaert 2003: 82–83; Chevalier & Léard 1996: 53; Martin 1983: 97–98). However, it should be noted that objective modality can also be expressed in nominal *that*-clause constructions such as:

(16)   a.   There is always *the possibility that the input pronunciation will differ from the pronunciation in the lexicon.*   (BYU-BNC)

     b.   *Un tel état de masse négative n'a évidemment aucun sens physique, mais il peut être réinterprété dans le cadre d'une théorie de champ quantique pour l'électron, c'est-à-dire une théorie qui envisage la possibilité que des électrons soient aussi créés ou détruits.*   (Frantext)
        "Such a state of negative mass does not have obviously any physical sense, but it can be reinterpreted within the framework of a quantum theory of field for the electron, i.e. a theory which considers the possibility that electrons are also created or destroyed." (My translation)

As we pointed out in Section 3.1, Chevalier & Léard (1996) distinguish between three types of modality in head nouns: epistemic, alethic and deontic. In addition to these types, we can distinguish another type involved in noun complementation: evaluative/attitudinal modality. Nouns such as *problem, (dis)advantage, worry* convey an attitudinal or evaluative commitment of the speaker or another speaker towards the propositional content. According to Nuyts (2005: 12), "[t]his category [boulomaic] indicates the degree of the speaker's (or someone else's) liking or disliking of the state of affairs".

Another category, dynamic modality, is distinguished in many modality studies (Palmer 1986, 2001; Perkins 1983; Nuyts 2005). With regard to the actual status of this category, Salkie (2008, 2009) and others argue that ability *can*, which is considered as conveying dynamic modality, should in fact be relegated to the periphery of modality categories. According to Salkie (2008: 85–88; 2009: 81–89), dynamic modality is a peripheral/low degree modality category since it does not meet most of the criteria he establishes, including possibility/necessity, epistemic/deontic and subjectivity. He argues that dynamic modality, unlike epistemic or deontic modality, neither involves any possibility/necessity in terms of "possible worlds", nor any subjectivity in terms of a high degree of commitment. Interestingly, nouns to which dynamic properties can be ascribed, such as *ability* or *capacity*, hardly take *that*-clauses. For instance, these two nouns would not be acceptable in (16a/b), whereas others, such as *necessity*, *probability* or *evidence*, can appear in such utterances. In this study, we limit our investigation to epistemic, alethic and deontic modality while excluding boulomaic/attitude modals (for reasons of space) as well as dynamic modal expressions (as they are only marginally relevant).

First of all, epistemic modality refers to the types of semantic judgments or assessments that concern the speaker's knowledge or belief of the proposition. Through nominal epistemic items, speakers express their degree of certainty or belief with regard to a state of affairs as in (11) in English or as in (17) in French.

(17)   *J'ai acquis la certitude que dans le cul-de-sac temporel où je me suis fourvoyé il n'y a pas âme qui vive.*   (Frantext)
         "I got the certainty that in the temporal cul-de-sac where I was misled there is not a living soul."   (My translation)

Secondly, alethic modality concerns the speaker's estimation of the (degree of) logical necessity or possibility of the proposition, as illustrated in (16a/b) and (18):

(18)   *La persistance des espèces parasites est dominée par la nécessité que l'animal jeune ou la larve rencontre, à une phase définie de son existence, l'espèce le plus souvent strictement déterminée où il doit pénétrer et évoluer.*   (Frantext)
         "The persistence of the parasitic species is dominated by the need that the young animal or the larva, in a specific phase of its existence, meet the most strictly determined species where it must penetrate and evolve."
                                                                                (My translation)

Finally, deontic modality involves permission, obligation or moral desirability of the proposition. Thus, any head noun that conveys any of these semantic features is considered deontic in this study (for more on these definitions see Lyons 1977, 1995; Palmer 1986; Huddleston & Pullum 2002; Nuyts 2005, among others). In (12) and in (19), the speaker qualifies the *that*-clause as, respectively, a requirement and an obligation.

(19)   *Ainsi la voie fut ouverte pour convoquer une conférence constitutionnelle sur requête de la majorité, tandis qu'était maintenue l'obligation que tout amendement fût ratifié par les membres permanents du conseil de sécurité...*
                                                                                (Frantext)
         "Thus the way was open to convene a constitutional conference on request of the majority, while the obligation was maintained that any amendment be ratified by the permanent members of the Security Council." (My translation)

As far as the first two modality classes (epistemic and alethic) are concerned, some scholars, Palmer (1986) for instance, make no distinction between them. The decision to distinguish between them in this study is motivated by two reasons: first, nouns that involve alethic and epistemic modality do not behave similarly when selecting mood; prototypically they do not select the same mood in the same proportion. For instance, Martin (1983: 118–124) claims that in French, epistemic expressions generally select the indicative, while alethic modality, like deontic modality, mostly selects the subjunctive. The second reason for distinguishing between epistemic and alethic modality is that this distinction mirrors the distinction between the concepts of objectivity and subjectivity. Nuyts (2005: 9, 13–14), in discussing Lyons' (1977) account, observes that "the distinction between alethic and epistemic modality shows some similarity to that between objective and subjective epistemic modality."

4.   Head nouns and mood selection

4.1 Outline

The aim of this second part is to show that the use of the indicative or the subjunctive in complement *that*-clauses is correlated to the lexical item governing the subordinate clause. More particularly, it is hypothesized that the correlation between the lexical head and mood alternation depends on the head's modality type. This hypothesis is tested through a corpus-based comparative analysis of mood alternation in French and in English.

4.1.1   *English subjunctive*

There are basically three distinctive uses of the subjunctive in English: mandative, formulaic and volitional use (also called 'were-subjunctive', cf. Quirk et al. 1985), as illustrated in examples (20), (21) and (22):

(20)   I suggest that he <u>leave</u>.   (Berk 1999: 149)

(21)   God <u>save</u> the Queen. / God <u>be</u> with you.   (Berk 1999: 150)

(22)   I wish I <u>were</u> a bird.   (Berk 1999: 150)

As these examples show, the main formal characteristic of mandative and formulaic subjunctives (both are also called present subjunctives) is the lack of the third person singular concord of the indicative mood on the main verb. As a consequence, the present subjunctive and the present indicative forms are indistinguishable in all the other persons except in the third person singular. According to

Quirk et al. (1985: 156), the mandative is considered "the most common use of the subjunctive, [and] occurs in subordinate *that* clauses".

Next to the subjunctive forms, language users can also opt for the so-called "putative (mandative) *should*" (cf. Quirk et al. 1985: 157, 784) in complement *that*-clauses, as illustrated in example 23.

> (23)   The suggestion that the new rule <u>should</u> be adopted came from the
>   chairman.   (Quirk et al. 1985: 1262)

As Quirk et al. (1972: 784) state, putative *should* "is used quite extensively in *that*-clauses to express not a subordinate statement of fact, but a 'putative' idea". Furthermore, the same authors (1972: 784) point out that *should* appears "in contexts where, historically speaking, a present subjunctive might be expected", which is to say that putative *should* can be considered as a substitute for the present subjunctive. Therefore, the two forms (putative *should* and the present subjunctive) were combined in some of the data processing.

4.1.2   *French subjunctive*

Formally, French has four subjunctive tenses: present, past, imperfect and pluperfect subjunctive. But in practice only two forms (present and past) are commonly used, with the other two playing only a marginal role in literary or very formal language (cf. Riegel et al. 1994; Soutet 2000).

The French subjunctive can either appear in independent/main clauses (examples 24 and 25) or in subordinate clauses (examples 26–28):

> (24)   *Que le ciel vous <u>protège</u>! / <u>Vive</u> le roi!*   (Riegel et al. 1994: 322)
>   "May heaven protect you! Long live the king!"   (My translation)

> (25)   *Moi, que je <u>fasse</u> une chose pareille!*   (ibid.: 323)
>   "Me, that I should do such a thing!"   (My translation)

> (26)   *Je veux/ordonne/souhaite/ qu'il <u>vienne</u>.*   (ibid.: 324)
>   "I want/order/wish that he come."   (My translation)

> (27)   *La chatte est sortie   sans   que je ne   m'   en <u>aperçoive</u>.* (ibid.: 326)
>   the cat   AUX go.out.PTCP without that I   NEG REFL it   realize.SUBJ
>   "I did not notice that the cat left."   (My translation)

> (28)   *Je cherche pour les vacances un livre qui me <u>plaise</u>.*   (ibid.: 326)
>   "For the vacation, I am looking for a book that I like."   (My translation)

In contrast to examples 24 and 25, where the use of the subjunctive is not required by any explicit formal item, its use in (26) and (27) is governed by a lexical item (*vouloir/ordonner/souhaiter* and *sans que* respectively). Even for an example like

(28), Soutet (2000: 117) argues that the use of the subjunctive is to some extent required by the verb *chercher* (which involves an idea of investigation), although he acknowledges that the modal force is weaker in this case than in (26). According to Soutet (2000), *chercher* and other verbs like *vouloir* (volition) in (29) or *avoir besoin de* (necessity) in (30) are the items that require the subjunctive in utterances such as:

(29)   *Pierre veut une secrétaire qui sait/sache le chinois.*
       "Pierre wants a secretary who speaks/speak Chinese."   (My translation)

(30)   *Pierre a besoin d'une secrétaire qui sait/sache le chinois.*
       "Pierre needs a secretary who speaks/speak Chinese."   (My translation)

These observations about the English and French subjunctive suggest that in both languages, the use of the indicative and the subjunctive in subordinate clauses appears to be related to the governing item, viz. the head noun in the present study. The correlation between these moods and the governing nouns is analysed in the following subsections to determine whether the modal category of the governing noun is significant in the use of one mood or the other.

4.2 Hypotheses

The analyses in this section are based on the following hypothesis: the choice of mood (indicative/subjunctive) is related to the modality type of the governing head. As Martin (1983: 117) suggests, we deal with mood alternation in terms of tendency:

> L'emploi du subjonctif obéit à des tendances beaucoup plus qu'à des règles, et, ainsi, les conceptions rigides se vouent elles-mêmes à l'échec. [...] Les travaux des dix dernières années apportent même des exemples d'indicatif où on ne l'attendait guère; et inversement de subjonctif.

> "The use of the subjunctive obeys tendencies much more than rules, and, thus, rigid concepts are bound to fail. [...] Studies carried out during the last decade even point out examples with the indicative in contexts where it would not have been expected; the same goes for the subjunctive."

He illustrates his claim by examples (31) and (32) among others:

(31)   *Il semble qu'il a/ait fait telle chose.*   (Martin 1983: 117)
       "It seems that he did / do (subjunctive) such a thing."   (My translation)

(32)   *Il est possible qu'on parviendra un jour à greffer un cœur neuf ou du moins en bon état.*   (Martin 1983: 117)
       "It is possible that one day one will manage to transplant a new heart or at least one in good condition."   (My translation)

Kupferman (1996:142) also supports this position when he asserts that the contrast between the subjunctive and the indicative is basically a matter of tendency. According to Martin (1983:118), the use of the indicative and the subjunctive can be explained on a probability scale, as illustrated in Figure 1:

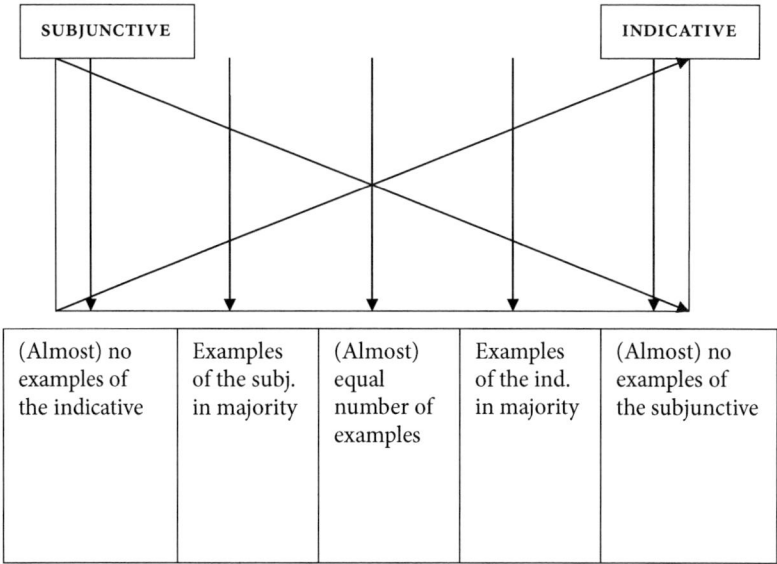

Figure 1. Use of the subjunctive and the indicative in French (after Martin 1983:118)

The common ground between Martin's (1983) and Kupferman's (1996) positions is that mood alternation should not be viewed as a question of which predicate requires which mood, but rather which predicate tends to license which mood. Therefore, Martin (1983) suggests that the use of the indicative and the subjunctive should not be regarded as a clear-cut dichotomy but as a gradience like in Figure 1 above. Note that the types of utterances discussed by Martin (1983:116–139) include *que*-clauses governed by a verb (*il semble qu'il a/ait fait telle chose*), noun clauses (*attirons l'attention sur le fait qu'il a/ait pris une telle décision sans nous informer*) or adjective clauses (*Pierre n'est pas certain que Sophie viendra/vienne*), and relative clauses (*je suis à la cherche d'un emploi qui me permette/permettra de...*).

In addition to this probability tendency, Martin (1983:119–124) argues that mood alternation should be understood in terms of "possible worlds" and "universes of belief". According to him, alethic and deontic modalities exist in the space of "possible worlds", where the proposition they govern is not considered as what it is, but as what it *could be* or *should be*. Thus, alethic and deontic expressions mostly select the subjunctive to indicate that the proposition belongs to those worlds. As for epistemic predicates, Martin (1983:133–139) postulates that they govern either the indicative or the subjunctive depending on their polarity. If we assume that these observations are correct, we can put forward the following hypotheses:

a. *That/que*-clauses governed by epistemic nouns will primarily select the indicative but also accept the subjunctive according to their pragmatic interpretation; hence, a high frequency of the indicative is to be expected after these expressions.
b. *That/que*-clauses governed by alethic and deontic nouns primarily select the subjunctive or related structures, although the indicative is not completely excluded; hence, a high frequency of the subjunctive is to be expected after these heads.

These hypotheses are tested using corpus analysis and statistics. Specifically, we aim to examine, first, whether mood alternation is a matter of tendency correlated with modality classes, and, second, the extent to which a particular mood is used with each of the three types of modality (i.e. alethic, deontic or epistemic). While it might seem problematic to apply an analysis of French mood to English, this will in fact allow us to determine whether the findings apply cross-linguistically. Although the subjunctive does not necessarily appear under the same qualitative and quantitative conditions in the two languages, the relevance of modality properties in mood selection should be observable cross-linguistically.

4.3 Data analysis

Data collected from the English and French corpora are presented in Tables 1 and 2, respectively.

First of all, let us bear in mind that the corpora investigated are very different in size and composition; differences in text type might influence the choice for a particular mood. However, it should also be kept in mind that the purpose of these statistics is not to compare the English and French figures directly, but to show that in each of the two languages the use of the indicative and the subjunctive can be related to the modality type of the head noun. In this respect, as we have already said, tendencies can be identified and the relative frequencies of the categories can be compared. Nevertheless, we should point out that the subjunctive seems much more alive in French than in English. In comparing its use in our data set, we note considerable differences — Table 3 summarises them.

One can observe that out of 779 occurrences in the English material, only 94 contain subjunctive forms or *should*, while in the French data 72 occurrences of the subjunctive out of a total of 410 occurrences of *que*-clauses (12.1% against 17.6%).

The data in Tables 1 and 2 reveal two important observations: first, the English data set does not contain instances of an epistemic noun licensing the subjunctive,

Table 1. English data

Modality classes	Nouns	Occ.	Indicative	Subjunctive	should	Modal aux.	Ambiguous cases[8]
Epistemic nouns (319)	assertion	79	69 (87%)	0	2 (3%)	8 (10%)	
	certainty	40	32 (80%)	0	0	8 (2%)	
	fact	100	92 (92%)	0	1 (1%)	7 (7%)	
	hypothesis	100	86 (86%)	0	0	14 (14%)	
Total		319	279 (87.5%)	0	3 (0.9%)	37 (11.6%)	
Alethic nouns (302)	likelihood	100	67 (67%)	0	1 (1%)	32 (32%)	
	necessity	2	0	0	2 (100%)		
	possibility	100	42 (42%)	1 (1%)	0	57 (57%)	
	probability	100	86 (86%)	0	0	14 (14%)	
Total		302	195 (64.6%)	1 (0.3%)	3 (1%)	103 (34.1%)	
Deontic nouns (158)	constraint	12	3 (25%)	0	4 (33.3%)	4 (33.3%)	1 (8.4%)
	demand	30	4 (13.3%)	13 (43.3%)	9 (30%)	2 (6.7%)	2 (6.7%)
	request	16	1 (6.2%)	6 (37.5%)	6 (37.5%)	0	3 (18.8%)
	require-ment	100	10 (10%)	23 (23%)	26 (26%)	27 (27%)	14 (14%)
Total (779)		158	18 (11.4%)	42 (26.6%)	45 (28.5%)	33 (20.9%)	20 (12.6%)

and even the use of putative *should* is extremely low (0.9%). In both English and French, the indicative is by far the most frequently used mood with epistemic nouns in *that*-clauses, i.e. 87.5% in English against 75.8% in French. The main difference between the two languages is that the subjunctive is used in around 6.10% of occurrences in the French data set in contrast to the English data set. This first observation lends cross-linguistic support to our first hypothesis (i.e. epistemic nouns mostly select the indicative); in English, purely epistemic nouns do not even seem to accept the subjunctive at all.

The second general observation relates to findings across categories: the English data show a fall in the use of the indicative, ranging from 87.5% in the epistemic category over 64.6% in the alethic category to 11.4% in the deontic category. In the French data, the indicative is also most frequently used with epistemic nouns (75.8%) compared to deontic nouns (17.6%) and alethic nouns (10.2%). Conversely, the use of the subjunctive and *should* is significantly higher after deontic nouns (55.1% subjunctives + *should* in English and 55.9% subjunctives in

Table 2. French data

Modality classes	Nouns	Occ.	Indicative	Subjunctive	Conditional	Ambiguous cases
Epistemic nouns (327)	*affirmation*	42	38 (90.5%)	0	4 (9.5%)	
	certitude	94	82 (87.2%)	0	12 (12.8%)	
	fait	100	65 (65%)	12 (12%)	1 (1%)	22 (22%)
	hypothèse	91	63 (69.2%)	8 (8.8%)	8 (8.8%)	12 (13.2%)
Total		327	248 (75.8%)	20 (6.1%)	25 (7.7%)	34 (10.4%)
Alethic nouns (49)	*vraisemblance*	10	1 (10%)	7 (70%)	0	2 (20%)
	nécessité	7	1 (14.3%)	4 (57.1%)	0	2 (28.6)
	possibilité	23	2 (8.7%)	18 (78.3%)	0	3 (13%)
	probabilité	9	1 (11%)	4 (44.5%)	0	4 (44.5%)
Total		49	5 (10.2%)	33 (67.3%)	0	11 (22.5%)
Deontic nouns (34)	*contrainte*	10	5 (50%)	2 (20%)	0	3 (30%)
	exigence	11	0	9 (81.8%)	0	2 (18.2%)
	demande	5	0	4 (80%)	0	1 (20%)
	obligation	8	1 (12.5%)	4 (50%)	2 (25%)	1 (12.5%)
Total (410)		34	6 (17.6%)	19 (55.9%)	2 (5.9%)	7 (20.6%)

Table 3. Frequencies of the subjunctive in the English and French corpora

Corpora	Occ.	Indicative	Subjunctive (+ *should*)	Modal verbs	Ambiguous cases[9]
English	779	492 (63.15%)	94 (12.1%)	173 (22.2%)	20 (2.55%)
French	410	259 (63.20%)	72 (17.6%)	27 (6.5%)	52 (12.7%)

French) than after epistemic nouns (0.9% in English and 6.1% in French). Alethic nouns have a much lower subjunctive selection rate in English (1.3% subjunctive + *should*) than in French (67.3%).

The question to be addressed next is how to interpret these observations. Beyond generalisations, it is likely that a close look at the lexical classes should reveal the mechanisms underlying these mood selection tendencies among lexical nominal classes and the properties that favor one mood or the other.

4.3.1   *Epistemic nouns favor the indicative*

As noted above, the 319 English *that*-clauses governed by epistemic nouns do not include a single one that licenses the formal subjunctive. As Heyvaert (2003: 82) claims, there is a tight link between indicative and epistemic modals since they both express "the speaker's position with respect to the plausibility of the propositional content of the clause". Thus, one can assume that they can be considered as part of the same semantic conceptual continuum. This suggests that the high/exclusive use of the indicative with epistemic nouns is a phenomenon to be expected. This tendency is observable in both our English and French data, even if French epistemic nouns tend to accept around 6% of subjunctive. Martin (1983) and others (Riegel et al. 1994; Soutet 2000) have attempted to explain this phenomenon. Martin (1983) justifies the use of the subjunctive after expressions like *le fait que* by arguing that they mark the proposition as an existing reality, while also indicating that this reality could have been different. In other words, in an utterance like *le fait que Pierre soit venu est tout de même bon signe* (Martin 1983: 131), ("the fact that Pierre be here is nevertheless a good sign" — my translation) the speaker asserts reality (*Pierre-come back*), but places it in a counterfactual world, where (*Pierre might not have come*). Thus, when the proposition is asserted as a reality existing in a factual world, the head noun governs the indicative. However, when the proposition denotes an existing reality that is perceived as potentially counterfactual, the head noun selects the subjunctive. For instance, in a sentence such as (33), the speaker uses the subjunctive to indicate that the state of affairs described by the propositional content is not necessarily what was or could be expected.

> (33)   *Les points de repère pourraient d'ailleurs être déterminés par le fait que*
> *je choisisse à l'avance mes textes et que je les relie par mes commentaires.*
> (Frantext)
> "In fact, the bench marks could be determined by the fact that I choose my texts in advance and that I connect them by comments."   (My translation)

Thus, the subjunctive indicates that the state of affairs could have been different, i.e. *ne pas choisir mes textes* ("not to choose my texts"), which explains its use in (33).

4.3.2   *Deontic and alethic nouns favor the subjunctive*
Analysis reveals that French and English deontic nouns choose the subjunctive/ *should* more frequently than the indicative. Chi-square results for deontic nouns requiring the subjunctive/*should* are highly significant in both English (χ^2 = 45.343 (df = 1), p < 001) and French (χ^2 = 6.76 (df = 1), p < .01); this suggests that part of our second hypothesis — deontic nouns would mainly license the subjunctive — is verified for both languages. As for the other part of the second hypothesis — *alethic nouns would also select the subjunctive more frequently* — this is supported for French (10.2% indicative vs. 67.3% subjunctive) but not for English (64.6% indicative vs. 1.3% subjunctive/*should*). The chi-square result confirms Martin's (1983) observation that the French alethic category more frequently selects the subjunctive. In sum, French deontic and alethic nouns more frequently select the

subjunctive. In English, the deontic class selects the subjunctive more frequently, whereas the alethic class, like the epistemic class, mostly requires the indicative.

The notion of modality "class" is important here, since, within these classes, individual nouns vary with respect to the mood selection proportion. For instance, in French, nouns from the deontic class, such as *contrainte* or *obligation*, are frequently used with the indicative, even though the class as a whole, or the other nouns in it, selects the subjunctive. Notice that French *contrainte* is used with 50% indicative vs. 20% subjunctive in our data, and that English *constraint* is the deontic noun which has the highest use of the indicative (25%).

4.3.3 *Gradience in modality classes*

Is the contrast observed in the previous section, i.e. that the epistemic class more frequently selects the indicative and the deontic or alethic class more frequently selects the subjunctive, related to any gradience in modal class or to a lexical-semantic interpretation of the nouns? Indeed, different nouns may belong to the same class, but not share the same degree of being an element of that class. For instance, in the alethic class, *necessity* in both its occurrences selects mandative *should* in English against 14.3% indicative, 57.1% subjunctive and 28.6% of ambiguous cases in French. As for *probability/probabilité*, it favors the indicative (86% indicative vs. 0% subjunctive and *should* in English; 11% indicative vs. 44.5% subjunctive in French; the other 44.5% are non-distinctive forms).

Such discrepancies within the same class can be explained by Heyvaert's (2003:82–85) approach (cf. Section 4.3.1 above). It could even be argued that modality as a semantic property allowing mood selection can be considered as a system set in an integrated continuum. If we assume that epistemic, alethic and deontic classes are the fundamental constituents of modality, then the integrated continuum is a tripartite circular system; the three modality types in relation to mood selection form a system, as Figure 2 illustrates.

One can see that this system, in relation to mood selection, would have the epistemic class as the starting point of the circular continuum, followed by the alethic class and then by the deontic class. This hypothesis would explain the discrepancies in Tables 1 and 2. In fact, nouns may belong to a particular modality class without sharing the same degree of class membership. In other words, an alethic noun like *probability* is closer to the epistemic class than *necessity*, which is semantically closer to the deontic class. An utterance such as (34) clearly shows that the former is closer to epistemic *fact/evidence*, while the latter, in (35), has greater affinity with deontic *requirement/obligation*.

(34)   If he suspected Pascoe, Rain had to concede <u>the probability</u> that he <u>was</u>
       right.   (BYU-BNC)

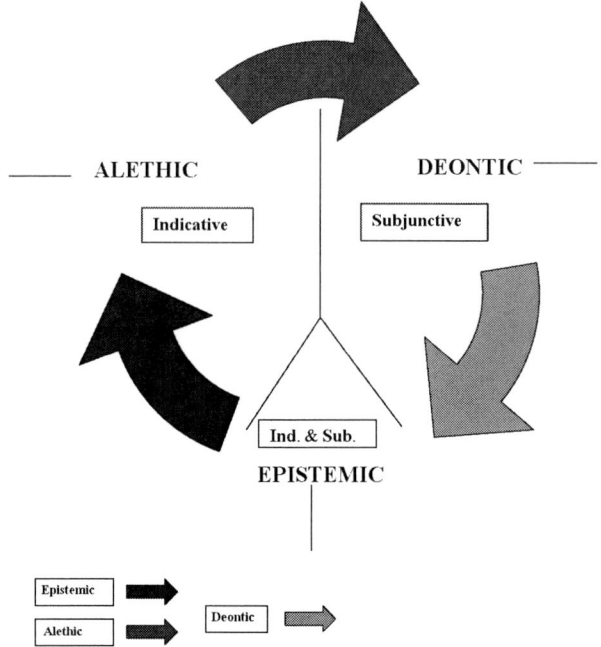

Figure 2. Lexical Modality classes continuum

(35)   In trying to find answers, managers — whether they were heads or
governors — were caught between the need to make progress and to prepare
for broad changes which had been widely publicized by central government
and to prepare for <u>the necessity</u> that they <u>should</u> lead changes.   (BYU-BNC)

Therefore, as the analysis above reveals that the epistemic class is the one that
mostly accepts the indicative, it becomes possible to understand why *probability* has a high indicative percentage (86% against 14% used with modal verbs in
English). Similarly, it is not surprising that *necessity* should license the mandative subjunctive/*should* more frequently than the indicative (its two occurrences
are used with *should*), because it is close to the deontic class (nouns that involve
obligation, permission, etc.) — a class which tends to choose the subjunctive. In
French *nécessité* ("necessity") is used in similar proportions: 14.3% indicative and
57.1% subjunctive, with the remaining 28.6% non-distinctive forms.

5.   Conclusion

This paper has argued that the presence of a modality feature is a common intrinsic property of *that* taking nouns. The lexical classification of nouns into modality

classes has proved to be an efficient method to underpin our claims. First, the analysis has revealed that the presence of a modality feature is a necessary condition for a noun to govern a *that*-clause. However, further investigations need to be carried out as to whether it is a sufficient condition.

Second, corpus analysis and statistics have provided support for the hypotheses and have revealed explicit mechanisms guiding the choice of mood in English and French noun complement clauses. Again, the classification of head nouns into lexical modality groups appears to be an efficient procedure in determining which modality class favors which mood. Thus, epistemic nouns (in both English and French) mostly or exclusively select the indicative. Alethic and deontic nouns favor one mood or the other depending on their degree of modality class membership. Both classes seem to favor the subjunctive in French, whereas in English the former chooses the indicative while the latter selects the subjunctive. The closer a noun is to the epistemic class, the more likely it is to license the indicative. Conversely, the further removed a noun is from the epistemic class, the more likely it is to license the subjunctive. Accordingly, the results support the concept of a scalar continuum in mood alternation, as put forward by Martin (1983) — see Figure 1. Further studies should elaborate this concept in greater detail.

Finally, with regard to the interpretation of modality in overall *that* noun complementation, three fundamental modality levels can be observed. The head noun conveys the first type of modality, which indicates the speaker's attitude/commitment as *epistemic*, *alethic* or *deontic*. The second modality ascription is performed at the subordination level, which marks modality orientation. The type of modality conveyed by the head noun is generally subjective, since it is the speaker who expresses/describes his/her personal or another speaker's stance towards the propositional content. Yet, modality orientation can also be objective, viz. when the speaker uses alethic expressions or logical constructions. And the third level of modality encoding concerns mood in relation to the head noun. It marks the proposition as being asserted/factual through the use of the indicative or as non-asserted/unreal when the subjunctive is used.

Notes

* Special thanks to Nicolas Ballier, Raphael Salkie, Catherine Léger and Eleanor Hendricks for their advice and perceptive comments on earlier versions of this paper. Any remaining errors are mine. Many thanks to Emmanuel Ferragne for his advice and comments on the Chi-square test.

1. For the concept of "modality orientation", see Halliday (1994).

2. Source: http://www.atilf.fr/atilf/produits/frantext.htm (accessed September 2009).

3. *Probability* may also be considered as epistemic in the literature. Notice that in most linguistic studies on modality, there is no distinction between epistemic and alethic modal expressions (Palmer 1986 for instance).

4. Biber et al. (1999) and Ballier (2007) describe head nouns as expressing the speaker's modal stance, but do not put them explicitly in modality classes.

5. Source http://www.webcorp.org.uk/webcorp_linguistic_search_engine.html (accessed September 2009). For further information see:, http://www.webcorp.org.uk/guide/, http://wse1.webcorp.org.uk/preview/ (accessed September 2009).

6. Examples of *picture, sign, slogan* used as head nouns:

With a 10% increase in sales over the last study period, we have *a clear picture that the Chinese book market is being more gradually influenced by the translated books.* (Webcorp)

Madeleine picked up her fork and began to eat. This was *the sign that the children could start eating too.* (BYU-BNC)

This positive part of conventionalism most plainly corresponds to *the popular slogan that judges should follow the law and not make new laws in its place.* (BYU-BNC)

7. Schmid (2000) uses the terms 'A-nouns', 'carrier nouns' and 'shell nouns' to refer to what is also called head nouns.

8. Example: *I wrote up these notes immediately after each occasion and as soon as they were typed, sent copies to those involved with the request that they verify that the substance and the spirit of each occasion were accurately and adequately recorded.* (BYU-BNC).

9. By "ambiguous cases", we mean the non-distinctive forms of the verb between the indicative and the subjunctive.

References

Ballier, N. 2004. "Deverbal nouns as heads of noun complement clauses in English". In J. J. Lecercle (Ed.), *Dossier en Vue de l'Habilitation à Diriger des Recherches.* Unpublished Habilitation thesis, Vol.1. Université de Paris X, 4–35.

Ballier, N. 2007. "La complétive du nom dans le discours des linguistes". In D. Banks (Ed.), *La Coordination et la Subordination dans le Texte de Spécialité.* Paris: l'Harmattan, 55–76.

Ballier, N. Forthcoming. "La complétive du nom, un dictum pris en charge par personne?". In N. Ballier, A. Blanc & J. V. Lozano (Eds.), *Les Représentations Linguistiques de la Personne.* Rouen: Presses Universitaires de Rouen et du Havre.

Berk, L. M. 1999. *English Syntax: From Word to Discourse.* New York: Oxford University Press.

Biber, D., Johansson, S., Leech, G., Conrad, S. & Finegan, F. 1999. *Longman Grammar of Spoken and Written English.* Essex: Longman.

Boone, A. 1996. "Les complétives et la modalisation". In Cl. Muller (Ed.), *Dépendance et Intégration Syntaxique: Subordination, Coordination, Connexion.* Tübingen : Niemeyer, 45–51.

Bowen, R. 2005. *Noun Complementation in English. A Corpus-based Study of Structural Types and Patterns*. Göteborg: Göteborg University.

Chevalier, G. & Léard, J. M. 1996. "La subordination nominale: Classes, sous-classes et types sémantiques". In Cl. Muller (Ed.), *Dépendance et Intégration Syntaxique: Subordination, Coordination, Connexion*. Tübingen : Niemeyer, 53–65.

Halliday, M. A. K. 1994. *An Introduction to Functional Grammar*. London: Edward Arnold.

Heyvaert, L. 2003. *A Cognitive-Functional Approach to Nominalization in English*. Berlin: Mouton de Gruyter.

Huddleston, R. & Pullum, G. 2002. *The Cambridge Grammar of the English Language*. Cambridge: Cambridge University Press.

Kupferman, L. 1996. "Observations sur le subjonctif dans les complétives". In Cl. Muller (Ed.), *Dépendance et Intégration Syntaxique: Subordination, Coordination, Connexion*. Tübingen: Niemeyer, 141–151.

Le Querler, N. 1996. *Typologie des Modalités*. Caen: Presses universitaires de Caen.

Lyons, J. 1977. *Semantics*. Cambridge/New-York: Cambridge University Press.

Lyons, J. 1995. *Linguistic Semantics*. Cambridge/New York: Cambridge University Press.

Martin, R. 1983. *Pour une Logique du Sens*. Paris: Presses Universitaires de France.

Mélis, G. 2002. "Nominalisateurs et prise en charge". In C. Delmas & L. Roux (Eds.), *Construire et Reconstruire en Linguistique Anglaise. Syntaxe et Sémantique*. C.I.E.R.E.C Travaux 107, Publications de l'Université de Saint-Etienne, 139–150.

Nomura, M. 1993. "The semantics of the content clause construction in English". *English Linguistics*, 10, 184–210.

Nuyts J. 2005. "Modality: Overview and linguistic issues." In F. William (Ed.), *The Expression of Modality*. Berlin: Mouton de Gruyter, 1–26.

Palmer, F. R. 1986. *Mood and Modality*. Cambridge: Cambridge University Press.

Palmer, F. R. 2001. *Mood and Modality*. 2nd ed. Cambridge: Cambridge University Press.

Perkins, M. R. 1983. *Modal Expressions in English*. London: Frances Pinter.

Quirk R., Greenbaum, S., Leech G. & Svartvik, J. 1972. *A Grammar of Contemporary English*. London: Longman.

Quirk, R., Greenbaum, S., Leech G. & Svartvik, J. 1985. *A Comprehensive Grammar of the English Language*. London/New York: Longman.

Riegel, M., Pellat, J.-C. & Rioul, R. 1994. *Grammaire Méthodique du Français*. Paris: PUF.

Salkie, R. 2008. "Modals and typology: English and German in contrast". In M. L. A. Gómez-González, J. L. Mackenzie & E. M. González Álvarez (Eds.), *Current Trends in Contrastive Linguistics: Functional and Cognitive Perspectives*. Amsterdam/Philadelphia: John Benjamins, 77–98.

Salkie, R. 2009. "Degrees of modality". In P. Busuttil, R. Salkie & J. van der Auwera (Eds.), *Modality in English: Papers from ModE2*. Berlin: Mouton de Gruyter, 79–104.

Schmid, H.-J. 2000. *English Abstract Nouns as Conceptual Shells: From Corpus to Cognition*. Berlin: Mouton de Gruyter.

Soutet, O. 2000. *Le Subjonctif en Français*. Paris: Ophrys.

The Concise Oxford English Dictionary. 2001. Pearsall J. & P. Hanks (Eds.). Oxford/New York: Oxford University Press.

Corpora

Davies, M. 2004: online. *BYU-BNC: The British National Corpus.* Available at: http://corpus.byu.
edu/bnc (accessed September 2009).
Frantext Corpus: online. Available at: http://www.frantext.fr (accessed September 2009).
Webcorp Linguist's Search Engine (Webcorp LSE): online. Available at: http://www.webcorp.
org.uk/webcorp_linguistic_search_engine.html (accessed September 2009).

Choice of strategies in realizations of epistemic possibility in English and Lithuanian

A corpus-based study*

Aurelia Usoniene and Audrone Šoliene
Vilnius University

The paper deals with the qualitative and quantitative parameters of equivalence between the realizations of epistemic possibility in English and Lithuanian. The focus of the contrast is on the auxiliary and adverb strategies (van der Auwera et al. 2005) in English (*can, could, may, might* vs. *maybe, perhaps, possibly*) as opposed to the corresponding modal verb and adverb/particle strategies in Lithuanian (*galėti* "can/could/may/might" vs. *gal, galgi, galbūt, rasi, lyg ir* "maybe/perhaps/possibly"). The purpose of the corpus-based study is to find out which means of expression are preferable in the two languages and what the scope of their meanings is. The paper will also look at the frequency of epistemic and non-epistemic use of the modal expressions in the original and in translation.

1. Introduction

Since the category of modality is not isomorphic and fine-grained cross-linguistic differences are difficult to discover by introspection or analysis of contrived examples, the corpus-based approach adopted in this study helps to reveal patterns which would be difficult to find otherwise. The possibility of combining comparable and parallel corpora allowed us to map the correspondences between the formal and functional features in the source language (SL) and target language (TL) texts and define parallels between them.

The present study will look at the qualitative and quantitative dimensions of correspondence between the two basic types of realizations of epistemic possibility in English and Lithuanian. The axis of contrast runs across the auxiliary and adverb strategies in English — *can, could, may, might* vs. *maybe, perhaps, possibly* — (see van der Auwera et al. 2005) and across the corresponding modal verb and adverb/particle strategies in Lithuanian (*galėti* "can/could/may/might" vs. *gal, gal-gi, galbūt, rasi, lyg (ir)* "maybe/perhaps/ possibly"). The research carried out by van der Auwera et al. (2005) demonstrates that, despite the existing similarity in terms of the auxiliary and adverb strategies available for the realization of epistemic meanings, speakers of English and Slavonic languages do not use these strategies with equal frequency. The results of the investigation of the Slavonic translational equivalents for the English auxiliaries and adverbs of epistemic possibility show that the degree of polyfunctionality of the English auxiliaries seems to explain some of the reasons why Slavonic modal adverbs are more common as equivalents for the English auxiliary *might* than for *could*. As van der Auwera et al. (2005) note, this feature appears to be more typical of the South and West Slavonic languages.

Contrastive analyses based on parallel corpus data (Aijmer 1997, 1999; Løken 1997; Johansson 2001, 2007; Simon-Vandenbergen & Aijmer 2007) show that in a cross-linguistic perspective the percentage of 'congruent' (lexical) correspondence in expressions of epistemic modality is not very high. An assumption is made that the proportion of lexical correspondence can be very low when dealing with realizations of grammatical categories cross-linguistically. The purpose of this parallel corpus-based study is to find out what means of expression are preferable in the given languages and what the scope of their meanings is. The paper will also look at the frequency of epistemic and non-epistemic use of the modal expressions under analysis.

2.   Data and method

The research is based on the analysis of data obtained from a self-compiled bi-directional parallel corpus — *ParaCorp$_{E\text{-}LT\text{-}E}$*. The corpus is designed following the ENPC model (Johansson & Hofland 1994, Johansson 2007). The *ParaCorp$_{E\text{-}LT\text{-}E}$* was compiled from original English fiction texts and their translations into Lithuanian and original Lithuanian fiction texts and their translations into English. The present size of the corpus is 1,572,498 words (see Table 1).

The advantage of such a corpus model is that it allows different sorts of comparison and can be used both as a parallel corpus and a comparable corpus (Johansson 2007: 11).

Table 1. Size of the two sub–corpora *ParaCorp$_{E \to LT}$* and *ParaCorp$_{LT \to E}$*

	Original	Translation	Total
ParaCorp$_{E \to LT}$	486,871	386,640	873,511
ParaCorp$_{LT \to E}$	296,759	402,228	698,987

It must be admitted, however, that there is an imbalance between the two sub-corpora. Our aim was to build a balanced bidirectional corpus; however, the matching of original texts in terms of size was difficult as the number and range of texts that have been translated from English into Lithuanian is far greater than those of translations from Lithuanian into English. A similar situation has been observed in other languages as well (cf. Johansson 2007: 13). Mainly due to this reason, the included literary texts vary in their length and number: the $ParaCorp_{E \rightarrow LT}$ includes full texts (6 novels and 2 short stories), whereas the $ParaCorp_{LT \rightarrow E}$ is comprised of both full texts and extracts (3 full text novels, 39 short stories and 14 extracts). Moreover, the English texts have been translated by 8 translators (5 women and 3 men); the Lithuanian texts have been translated by 19 translators (13 women and 6 men). Most of the texts included in the corpus were written, translated, and published in the period of 1980–2006. However, there are some texts that were published before 1980: the $ParaCorp_{LT \rightarrow E}$ includes the novel *Hestera* (*Esther*) by V. Kavaliūnas and some short stories, and the $ParaCorp_{E \rightarrow LT}$ includes G. Orwell's novel *1984*. A list of all the texts can be found in the Appendix.

The texts and their translations were aligned using the aligning tool LYGIA (developed at the Centre of Computational Linguistics of Vytautas Magnus University). The alignment was performed first at the paragraph level, then at the sentence level. Then, in order to generate concordance lines, we used the multilingual browser ParaConc (Barlow 1995). Though the search was automatic, the analysis of concordances was carried out manually, since the $ParaCorp_{E\text{-}LT\text{-}E}$ is not annotated.

Since the corpora differ in size, the raw frequency numbers have been normalized per 1,000 words to make the comparison statistically valid. Moreover, in order to check whether the similarities and differences are statistically significant, we have also performed the log-likelihood (LL) test, which is commonly judged to be a more statistically reliable test than the chi-square test (cf. Dunning 1993). The cut-off value for statistical significance at the 1% level used in this research is 6.63 ($p < 0.01$). In this study, the widely accepted terms 'overuse' and 'underuse' are used in a pure quantitative sense — to refer to higher and lower frequencies of modal possibility markers in the two languages under contrast. By no means do we imply that the terms 'overuse' or 'underuse' have the connotation of "deviant from the norm". However, frequencies of particular patterns and uses are of crucial importance to us, since we maintain that frequency is an important factor in specification of meaning (Leech 2003, Simon-Vandenbergen & Aijmer 2007).

Though the use of parallel corpora in contrastive studies was criticised by some scholars as giving only a mirror image of their source language (Teubert 1996: 247), our views are very much in line with the opinion expressed in Mauranen (2002), Noël (2003) and Simon-Vandenbergen & Aijmer (2007) that translations are part of natural language in use and the output of translators "varies on a number of parameters, as does that of any language user, whether bilingual or monolingual" (Mauranen 2002: 164). Thus, the analysis of various translational paradigms can contribute to providing a fine-grained picture of the various senses of the words in the source language too. Naturally, the fact that the language data under study have been collected from fiction limits the scope of our conclusions to a certain extent, but one has to agree that a literary text encompasses a variety of registers and a broad variation of linguistic style. The choice of corpus-based contrastive methodology used in the given investigation (Aijmer & Simon-Vandenbergen 2004, Altenberg & Granger 2004) seems to be a most efficient and reliable tool capable of diagnosing language-specific variation in the conceptualisation of the notion of modal possibility, revealing its varied linguistic realizations.

2.1 Data selection criteria

When the overall distribution of the modal possibility markers in the two languages was considered, the first step was to isolate all occurrences of the English *can*, *could*, *may*, *might*, *maybe*, *perhaps* and *possibly* and the corresponding Lithuanian modal verb *galėti* "can/could/may/might" and epistemic stance adverbials *gal*, *galgi*, *galbūt* "maybe/perhaps", *galimas daiktas/dalykas* "conceivably", *rasi* "perhaps", *bene* "possibly", *vargu/bemaž/kažin* "possibly" and *lyg/tartum/tarytum/tarsi* "as if/like" in the parallel corpus. For the sake of convenience, the Lithuanian *galėti* will be glossed as "can/may" throughout the paper. The translationally related sentence pairs (LT → E or E → LT) given as examples in the paper come from the *ParaCorp*$_{E-LT-E}$ and they have not been glossed, whereas the Lithuanian sentences given as single instances have been glossed. The examples from the *ParaCorp*$_{E-LT-E}$ carry a reference code which accompanies an original sentence.

It must be noted that there have been two stages of selected data analysis carried out and the sets of selected language data were not identical for each stage. In the first stage of the quantitative analysis, we aimed to investigate which linguistic markers of modal possibility (without any specification into epistemic and non-epistemic possibility) are prevalent in both languages. So, the first stage of the analysis was concerned with the overall occurrences of all modal possibility verbs (both positive and negative forms) and adverbials in the two languages with no selection criteria taken into account. The Lithuanian prefixed forms of the verb *galėti* "can/may" were also counted, e.g.:

(1) *...jis **te-gal-i**   jum perduo-ti mano nutarimus.*   (SB)
     he PREFcan.3PRS you pass.INF my   decisions
     "he can pass on my decisions."

As no unanimous agreement has been reached thus far regarding the distinction between the word classes of modal particles and adverbs in Lithuanian linguistics, we will be referring to Lithuanian modal expressions like *galimas daiktas/dalykas* "possible thing=conceivably", *galbūt* "maybe", *rasi* "maybe" and particles like *gal* "perhaps", *lyg/tarsi* "as if" as epistemic stance adverbials (Biber et al. 1999:854). Thus, the key issue analysed in this study will undergo a slight terminological variation in the Lithuanian data analysis, i.e. we shall call it the 'verb-adverbial' strategies.

The second stage of the analysis was a combination of both quantitative and qualitative analysis. At this stage, the emphasis has been laid on the distinction between the epistemic and non-epistemic use of the modal realizations under study. The initial language data-set has been filtered further and analysed taking into account the criteria given in Sections 2.1.1–2.1.5.

2.1.1 *Full vs. elliptical sentences*

Since our analysis was restricted to the sentential level, we eliminated elliptical sentences where the proposition was not fully fledged, as in the examples under (2) and (3):

(2) **I may.** (OG)
   "O man gal."

(3) **Perhaps** the children — (OG)
   "Gal vaikai..."

2.1.2 *Negative and positive environments of use*

The interaction of modality and negation and as a result thereof the ambiguity of scope interpretation have been widely discussed in the literature (de Haan 1997; van der Auwera 2001; Palmer 1995, 2003). When making a distinction between epistemic and non-epistemic meanings, we considered only the positive occurrences of the verbs, as sometimes it is difficult to determine whether the negative has scope over the main verb or modality, which can result in different modal meanings. Consider the following Lithuanian example:

(4) *Jis negali   būti   namie.*
   he NEGcan.3PRS be.INF at home
   "He cannot be at home."

This sentence can receive an epistemic reading ("It is not possible that he is at home"); it can be interpreted deontically ("It is not possible for him to be at home") or dynamically ("The circumstances or inherent qualities of the subject are such that he cannot be at home").

Since our study primarily focuses on the interpretation of modal possibility in terms of the epistemic and non-epistemic distinction, and the interaction of negation and modality is more relevant for studies of modal necessity (e.g. the misplacement of the negative in *You mustn't come* and *You needn't come* (Palmer 1995: 468)), we will limit our research to the positive occurrences of the modal verbs under study.

2.1.3   *Subject specification*

The correlation of the grammatical subject with epistemic interpretation was taken into account. As already noted by Coates (1983: 97), impersonal *you* is very common as the subject in sentences yielding a non-epistemic reading as in the following examples under (5).

> (5)   *Gali dabar **prašyti** ir **melstis**, gali **verkti** kruvinom ašarom.*   (MI1)
>   "You **can pray** and **plead** now; you **can weep** tears of blood."

We also set out to analyse how strong the correlation of epistemic modality with 1st, 2nd and 3rd-person subjects was (Heine 1995: 25). Therefore, special attention was given to the Lithuanian 3rd and 2nd person forms *gali* ("can/may".3PRS) and *gali* ("can/may".2PRS.SG) since they are homographs. To capture this distinction the data had to be sorted manually. The two forms differ in their accentuation in speech, whereas in the written language, it is the context of use that has to be taken into account. Some sentences with the predicate *gali* contain an overt NP in the subject position as in (6) or a pronoun as in (7), which eases the ascription of *gali* to a third or second person form group.

> (6)   *Žmogus   gali   daug padaryti.*   (MI)
>   man.NOM can.3PRS much do.INF
>   "A person can do a lot."

> (7)   *Tu gali   man įsakinėti ar ne, kaip nori.*   (KST)
>   you can.2PRS.SG me   order.INF or not as   want.2PRS.SG
>   "You can order me or not, just as you please."

However, when the sentences contained a zero subject their interpretation needed a slightly wider context than a one-sentence frame to establish co-referential links, e.g.:

> (8)   *Žmogaus akis — puikus instrumentas.*
>   *Gali   pridaryti, gali   atidaryti...*   (MI)
>   can.2PRS.SG close.INF can.2PRS.SG open.INF
>   "A man's eye is a wonderful instrument. It can squint; it can open wide..."

Also, the animacy of the subject seems to be an important but not decisive factor in distinguishing between epistemic and non-epistemic meaning. For example, sentences (6) and (7) with animate subjects clearly receive a non-epistemic interpretation, but this is not always the case. There is no doubt that the factors determining the epistemic or non-epistemic interpretation converge. For instance, sentence (9) has an animate subject, but still is epistemic, as it contains a stative verb; the correlation of stativity and epistemic modality is discussed below.

(9)   My father **might be** at home.

A number of scholars associate use of an inanimate subject, impersonal *it/this* and existential *there* with an epistemic reading (Coates 1983, Heine 1995, Wärnsby 2004). Bybee et al. (1994), for example, observe that the presence of impersonal *it* in a subject position precludes a non-epistemic reading in cases like (10):

(10)   It **may be** some days before I can get hold of one. (OG)

In the same vein, Wärnsby (2004) claims that sentences containing existential subject *there* are unquestionably epistemic, e.g.:

(11)   **There** could be no doubt that Fluffy was still alive. (RJK)

Thus, in the process of data analysis the singled out sentences have been considered from the point of view of how much the subject specification can determine an epistemic reading of a sentence.

2.1.4   *Stativity vs. non-stativity of complements*
The meaning of the modal verbs can be directly dependent upon the semantics of the main verb figuring in the sentence. Prototypical instances of epistemic modality are characterized by stative verbs (Coates 1983, Fachinetti 2003, Heine 1995, Wärnsby 2004). In the present study, epistemic and non-epistemic readings of modal verbs have been tested in terms of the presence of stative verbs and the *be*-phrase (henceforth *be*-P) construction too. For example, in sentence (12), the Lithuanian stative construction *gali būti-P* can yield an epistemic reading:

(12)   *Šis skaitymas* **gali būti** *paskutinis, paskutinis...*   (LA)
       "This reading **might be** his last..."

However, not all *be*-P complements are stative and not all sentences of this complementation type receive an epistemic reading. In Lithuanian, as in English, *būti-P* ("be"-P) units and especially the ones with adjective phrases (henceforth APs) **can** denote dynamic situations like *būti mandagiam* "be polite" as opposed to a stative proper *būti užmigusiam* "be asleep" (Usoniene 1988).

As has been mentioned above, we can speak of synergy of several constraints determining an epistemic or non-epistemic sentence interpretation. For example, in the literature on modality the epistemic status of the English modal auxiliary *can* has been frequently put in question. A general tendency is to acknowledge the epistemic status of *can* in non-assertive contexts, mostly in rhetorical questions (Coates 1995, Hoye 1997), as in sentence (13):

(13)   **Can** that be true?
       "Is it possibly the case that that is true?"

In such cases, there is a clear relationship with the use of epistemic *can't*. Such sentences can be glossed as "it can't be true (it must be false)" (Coates 1995:63). However, there is wide disagreement as to whether *can* should be used epistemically in affirmative contexts. Some authors express a rather categorical view arguing against the epistemicity of *can* (Coates 1983, Gresset 2003), while other scholars are in favour of the epistemic interpretation of *can*. For example, Perkins (1983:35) claims that there are cases where *can* might be regarded as expressing an epistemic sense as in sentence (14):

(14)   Cigarettes **can** seriously **damage** your health.

Despite the fact that we would regard sentences as in (14) as expressing dynamic possibility, we subscribe to the view that in some contexts *can* could acquire an epistemic interpretation and there might be an indication that *can* is starting to appear in epistemic contexts where several factors determining an epistemic reading of a sentence converge, such as the use of existential, impersonal and dummy subjects, and of stative complements. For example, Coates (1995:63) gives the following example of possibly epistemic *can*:

(15)   We hope this coding system **can be** useful [to other linguists working in the field].

2.1.5   *Adverb/adverbial scope specification*

For the English adverbs, we only included uses with sentence scope, as in example (16), since it is only in these contexts that there is a choice between the adverbial and the auxiliary strategies. We excluded such sentences as (17). Here and in the following scope will be indicated by square brackets:

(16)   **Perhaps** [they had heard it all before].   (MI)

(17)   He's a very unhappy man, **maybe** [even suicidal], and I didn't have a clue.
                                                                                                    (HN)

As far as the Lithuanian epistemic stance adverbials are concerned, their position is free and they can also have variable scope — from entire clauses to (parts of) NPs. We will only deal with parenthetical uses of the epistemic stance adverbials, i.e. when they are not integrated into clausal syntax and have a clausal scope as in (18) and (19):

(18) *[Gintė teisinsis]* **gal**...   (KR)
      "Gintė **might** make excuses."

(19) ***Gal** [visąlaik gudriai apsimetinėjo, slapčia Jiems kenkdamas].*   (GR2)
      "Or **maybe** he was clever and was fooling Them the entire time, all the while secretly hurting Them."

It should be noted that the Lithuanian *gal* "perhaps" can function both as an inter-rogative particle and as an epistemic stance adverbial. So in certain contexts it can be rather difficult to make a distinction between a question proper and a modal-ized utterance to convey the speaker's attitude towards what is being said. The information conveyed can range from probability to an imperative command, e.g.:

(20) ***Gal** jau eisiu.* ("Perhaps I'll go.")
      ***Gal** eisi?* ("Will you go?")
      ***Gal** užsičiauptum!* ("Shut up, will you!")

In the opposition illustrated under (21) where the use and meaning of the Lithuanian question particle *ar* "whether" is contrasted to *gal* "perhaps" used in the position of a question marker, *gal* "perhaps" will be regarded as a marked member of the opposition, unambiguously indicating the speaker's doubt and ten-tativeness. Therefore the given instances of use with *gal* occurring initially in ques-tions were counted as epistemic and included into the analysis.

(21) ***Ar** tu ateisi šiandien?*   vs. ***Gal** tu ateisi šiandien?*
      "Are you coming over tonight?" vs."**Perhaps** you are coming over tonight?"

The basic difference between *ar* and *gal* can be seen in terms of fixed and free posi-tion in the sentence. *Gal*, like the majority of epistemic adverbials in Lithuanian, can move freely around the sentence, while the position of the question particle *ar* "whether" is fixed. Compare the following modifications to the examples in (21):

(22) * *Tu **ar** ateisi šiandien?*   vs. *Tu **gal** ateisi šiandien?*
      * *Tu ateisi **ar** šiandien?*   vs. *Tu ateisi **gal** šiandien?*

Instances where the Lithuanian epistemic lexical markers modify NPs did not fall under the scope of the present study. *Gal* "perhaps" is extremely frequent in the context of listing (cf. Simon-Vandenbergen & Aijmer 2007:283) where several NPs are enumerated as in (23):

(23) *Turėję pastogę, namus, tėvus, seseris, brolius, **gal** [žmoną], **gal** [vaikus]...* (SB)
      "They had a shelter, a home, parents, sisters, brothers, — **maybe** a wife,
      maybe children."

The basic domain of use of the Lithuanian *tarsi/tartum/tarytum/lyg* "as if/like" is
the constructions of comparison (Wiemer 2007). The sentences in which these
words are used as comparative particles (24) or conjunctions (25) have been eliminated from the analysis:

(24) *Martynas irzlus ir isteriškas **tarsi** [terjeras].*   (GR)
      "Martynas is short-tempered and hysterical **like** a terrier."

(25) *Vaitkus pajuto, [**tartum** du žydri plonyčiai siūlai įsitempė ore]...*   (GrR)
      "Vaitkus felt **as if** two light blue threads [...] had been drawn tightly in the
      air."

Only epistemic uses have been selected for further analysis, like the one in the following example:

(26) *Žmonės **lyg ir** suvokia, jog pasaulis yra kaip tik toks[...]*   (GR)
      "Humans **seem to understand** that such is the world [...]"

3. The expression of modal possibility in Lithuanian

There are no modal auxiliaries in Lithuanian. The majority of modal verbs are
fully conjugated lexical verbs and there are a few verbs with a defective paradigm
— like *reikia* "need".3PRS, *teko* "get".3PST — that can be regarded as semi-modal
auxiliaries. The latter are mainly so-called 'verbal impersonals', i.e. third person or
'zero-coded forms' of the verb which are uninflected verb stems and unmarked for
number. They are used in impersonal constructions (Siewierska 2008). As in many
pro-drop languages, in Lithuanian these are not only meteorological verbs like *lyti*
"to rain", but also verbs of appearance like *(at)rodyti* "to seem" and modal verbs the
use of which can be illustrated in the following examples:

(27) ***Reikia**   eiti.*
      need.3PRS go.INF
      "It is necessary to go."

(28) ***Teko**   palaukti.*
      get.3PST wait.INF
      "One has got to wait."

Modal verbs in Lithuanian are polyfunctional and they can be used to express both epistemic and non-epistemic types of modality, e.g.:

(29) *Gali/galėsi*   *eiti*   *namo,*   *jei nori.*
      may.2SG.PRS/FUT go.INF home.ADV if want.2SG.PRS
      "You may go home if you want."

(30) *Turi*   *man padėti.*
      have.2SG.PRS I.DAT help.INF
      "You have to help me."

(31) *Jis gali/turi*   *būti*   *jau*   *namie.*
      he may/must.3PRS be.INF already home
      "He might/must be at home already."

Epistemic modality can be also expressed by using a great variety of modal particles and a few adverbs to indicate a low/high degree of speaker's confidence regarding the truth-value of the proposition as in (32) below (as we have already indicated above, we shall use the term 'epistemic stance adverbials' to refer to the Lithuanian modal particles and adverbs):

(32) *Jis gal/galbūt/turbūt/lyg ir*   *namie.*
      he perhaps/maybe/probably/as if home.ADV
      "Perhaps/maybe/probably he is at home."

Morphologically, there are only a few modal adverbs in Lithuanian — *tikriausiai/ greičiausiai/veikiausiai* "most probably" among them (Ambrazas 1997: 393) — and they are used to express high probability, i.e. epistemic necessity.

There has not been any research carried out on the issues of grammaticalization and lexicalization of the Lithuanian particle *gal* "perhaps" and the two modal words *turbūt* "probably" and *galbūt* "maybe"; however, it is absolutely clear that *gal* is related to the verb *gal-ėti* ("can/may".INF), while the words *turbūt* and *galbūt* are derived from *turi būti* ("have".3PRS "be".INF) and *gali būti* ("can/may".3PRS "be". INF) accordingly. As in Scandinavian languages (Norde 2006) the latter phrase can function as a predicate in the matrix clause, e.g.:

(33) *Gali*   *būti,*   *kad jis teisus.*
      may.3PRS be.INF that he right.M.SG.NOM
      "It may be that he is right."

The source of origin of some of the epistemic possibility adverbials is rather transparent, for instance, *kažin* is derived from *kas žino* "who knows", *rasi* is a form of the verb *rasti* "find", *tarsi/tarytum/tartum* are related to the verb *tarti* "utter", *lyg* comes from the adverb *lygiai* or the adjective *lygus* "equal". However, the origin of such particles as *bene* is more difficult to trace back to any of the words in Modern Lithuanian. Zinkevičius (1981:196) links *bene* to *be-g(u)-ne* meaning "whether not" / "perhaps". A variety of other modal realizations as the use of the neuter adjectives *galima* "possible", *įmanoma/įmanu* "possible", the nouns *galimybė* "possibility", the verbs of propositional attitude and the verbs of probability (or verbs of appearance) taking clausal complements will not be dealt with in the present paper because the point of departure of contrast is English auxiliaries and their correspondences in Lithuanian.

The key verb to express modal possibility is *galėti* "can/may", which is one of the most frequent verbs in the language. In the frequency list produced for the Lithuanian language (Grumadienė & Žilinskienė 1997), the verb *galėti* takes a top position: it is the 13th word and the second most frequent verb in a lemmatized frequency list of the 1,2-million-word corpus of written Lithuanian. The verb *turėti* "have", which functions both as a verb of possession and a modal verb of necessity is the 18th word and the third most frequent verb in the list. Other modal verbs like non-epistemic *(su)gebėti* "manage/be able to" and *privalėti* "must" appear very low in the list. The particle *gal* "perhaps/maybe/whether" is at 99th place. In the frequency list produced by the compilers of the whole 60-million-word Corpus of Contemporary Lithuanian Language (CCLL), *galbūt* "maybe", an epistemic stance adverbial, takes a higher position (388) than *turbūt* "probably" which comes much lower in the list (758). Thus, the Lithuanian realizations of modal possibility seem to dominate over the realizations of modal necessity in written Lithuanian. A more detailed account of the quantitative results will be given in the section below.

4. Findings

The first observation to be made is very general and concerns the overall distribution of the modal auxiliaries/verbs and adverbs/adverbials under analysis in the source language (SL) texts, i.e. the texts written in the original: Lithuanian-original (LT-orig) and English-original (E-orig). The first quantitative opposition was based on the overall number of occurrences of four basic English modal auxiliaries of possibility (*can, could, may, might*) against the number of occurrences of key possibility adverbs (*perhaps, maybe, possibly, conceivably*). The contrast of normalised frequencies showing a predominant use of modal auxiliaries in English is given in Table 2.

In Lithuanian, the normalized frequency of overall occurrences of all the conjugated forms of the modal possibility verb *galėti* "can/may" is 4.56 and if we add the frequency of the other two non-epistemic possibility verbs *(su)gebėti* "manage/be able to", and *mokėti* "know how", the final value is 5.23.[1] It is also higher than

Table 2. Normalised frequency of possibility-auxiliaries (E-AUX) vs. possibility-adverbs (E-ADV) in E-orig

E-AUX (poss)	f/1,000	E-ADV	f/1,000
can	2.1	*perhaps*	0.42
could	3.0	*maybe*	0.37
may	0.2	*possibly*	0.16
might	0.8	*conceivably*	0.01
Total	**6.1**	**Total**	**0.95**

the normalised frequency of modal possibility adverbials (2.09). As can be seen in Table 3, the most frequent adverbial is *gal* "perhaps" which accounts for half of all the adverbial frequency.

The ratio of the normalised frequency values between the English auxiliaries and adverbs is significantly high, 6:1 (AUX-6.1 : ADV-0.95). In Lithuanian, it is 2:1 (V-5.23 : ADV-2.09), which means that the frequency ratio between the use of epistemic adverbials in English vs. Lithuanian is approximately 1:2. A summary of these values is presented in Table 4.

Moreover, the log likelihood score (+27.05) indicates a statistically significant difference in the frequency of epistemic modal auxiliaries in original English as compared to modal verbs in original Lithuanian. However, the most marked

Table 3. Normalised frequency of possibility-adverbs (LT-ADV) vs. possibility-verb (LT-V) *galėti* in LT-orig

LT-ADV	f/1,000	LT-V	f/1,000
gal(gi)	1.40	*gal-iu/ime* (1PRS.SG/PL)	0.85
galbūt	0.14	*gal-i/ite* (2PRS.SG/PL)	0.47
bene	0.10	*gal-i* (3PRS)	0.98
galimas daiktas/dalykas	0.04	*gal-ėjau/ėjome/ėdavau/ėdavome* (1PST/FRQ.SG/PL)	0.39
kažin	0.04	*gal-ėjai/ėjote/ėdavai/ėdavote* (2PST/FRQ.SG/PL)	0.08
vargu	0.03	*gal-ėjo/ėdavo* (3PST/FRQ)	1.08
rasi	0.02	*gal-ėsiu/ėsime/ėčiau/ėtumėme* (1FUT/SUBJ.SG/PL)	0.26
bemaž	0.01	*gal-ėsi/ėsite/ėtum/ėtumėte* (2FUT/SUBJ.SG/PL)	0.13
lyg(ir/tai), tarsi/tartum/tarytum	0.31	*gal-ės/ėtų* (3FUT/SUBJ)	0.33
Total	**2.09**	**Total**	**4.56**

Table 4. Normalised frequency and LL of modal possibility realizations in the E-orig and LT-orig sub-corpora

	AUX	ADV
E-orig	6.1	0.95
LT-orig	5.23	2.09
LL	+ 27.05	−167.01

difference is in the choice of adverb/adverbial strategies in the two languages. The log likelihood score (−167.01) of the frequencies observed in the two sub-corpora signals that Lithuanian clearly favours epistemic stance adverbials when compared with English. There are many possible explanations for the significantly lower frequency of modal possibility verbs in Lithuanian. One of the reasons might be a well-known language-specific feature of English, namely a predominant use of modal *can/could* in descriptions of various acts of sense perception to denote actualization of the possibility and actual performance of seeing, hearing, feeling, etc. Thus, all the translational correspondences of *can/could see, can/could hear* in the LT-trans sub-corpus are plain forms of verbs of perception. Compare the following examples, (34)–(35), from the parallel corpus (*ParaCorp$_{E-LT-E}$*):

(34)   I **can hear** the diesel engines rumbling towards us even as we speak.   (HN)
       *"Jau dabar, mums kalbantis, **girdžiu** artėjančių ratų bildesį."*

(35)   Her back was to the door, but Sophie **could see** she was crying.   (BD)
       *"Ji stovėjo nugara į duris, bet Sofi **matė**, kad ji verkia."*

On the contrary, in Lithuanian, modal possibility verbs, if used at all with verbs of sense perception, mainly denote a potential performance or non-fact past, as in the following examples:

(36)   *Jis atsigulė, kaip jaunystėje, kad prieš užmigdamas ir pabusdamas **galėtų***
       ***matyti** kalnų viršūnes.*   (VB)
       "He lay down the way he had as a child, so that he **could see** the mountain through the window before he fell asleep."

(37)   *Jie **galėjo** mus **pamatyti**.*   (KST)
       "They **could have seen** us."

A normalised frequency of this type of use in the LT-orig sub-corpus is extremely low (0.02), while in the E-orig sub-corpus, the normalised frequency of *can/could see, can/could hear* and *can/could feel* collocations reaches 0.5. Thus, the prevailing use of *can/could* with verbs of sense perception in English might be regarded as one of the reasons of a higher count of possibility auxiliaries in the E-orig sub-corpus. A predominance of stance adverbials in Lithuanian might be an areal feature of circum-Baltic languages (cf. Aijmer 1996, Johansson 2001, Mortelmans 2009). It can also be explained by a much lesser degree of grammaticalization of modal verbs in Lithuanian.

The second task in the study was to calculate the frequency of the epistemic and non-epistemic readings in the use of the basic possibility modal verbs in the two languages and to check their frequency against that of epistemic stance adverbials. Following the selection criteria stated above, the results obtained are in line with the claims made by Coates (1995), Heine (1995), Biber et al. (1999), Facchinetti (2002), Wärnsby (2004). The epistemic use of *can* is rare in our data. It constitutes only 4%. Epistemic *can* is basically found in interrogative constructions, in existential sentences with introductory subject *there*, and with *be*-P complements, as in (38) and (39):

(38)   What **can** it possibly **mean?**   (HN)

(39)   I do not think there **can be** much pride left in you.   (OG)

The most frequent modal possibility auxiliaries in English are *could, may* and *might* and the ratio of epistemic vs. non-epistemic use is shown in Figure 1.

The two most frequent epistemic auxiliaries *may* and *might* usually take 3rd-person subjects (53%), existential *there* or impersonal *it/this* (26%) and the remaining 21% co-occur with 1st and 2nd-person subjects taken together.

The Lithuanian possibility verbs *(su)gebėti* "manage/be able to" and *mokėti* "know how" are never epistemic and it is only the key verb *galėti* "can/may" that is used to express epistemic possibility. The aim of the study was to find out just how epistemic it is and what forms are most commonly used with the given reading. Following Heine's (1995:25) observation that "epistemic modality correlates most

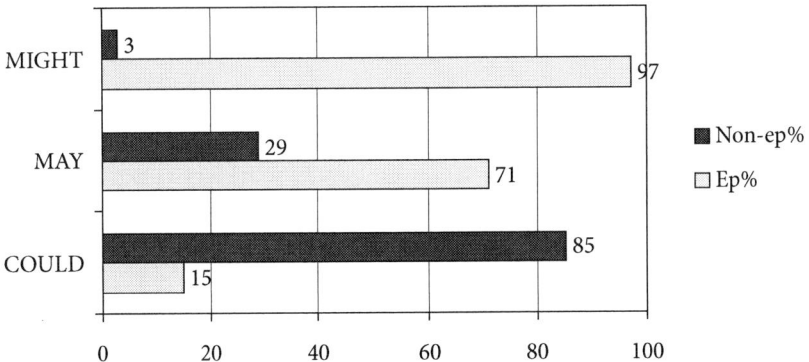

Figure 1. Epistemic vs. non-epistemic readings of possibility auxiliaries in E-orig

strongly with third-person and least strongly with first-person subjects" our next task was to find out what the distribution of the so-called personal forms of the Lithuanian modal possibility verb *galėti* "can/may" is. As can be seen in Table 5, the overall frequency of 3rd-person forms of *galėti* "can/may" is higher than the frequency of 1st/2nd-person forms, which also allows us to assume that 3rd-person forms might have more epistemic use than 1st/2nd-person forms.

Table 5. Overall distribution of *galėti* finite forms in LT-orig

gal-*ėti* "can/may"	f/1,000	%
1st/2nd-person forms	2.17	47
3rd-person forms	2.39	53
Total	4.56	100

The assumption was not corroborated by further qualitative and quantitative analysis. Frequency counts of epistemic readings of modal possibility with 3rd-person forms have been found to be rather low, which will be shown in Table 6 and explained below. No occurrences have been found where 1st/2nd-person verb forms have an epistemic reading, which is in accordance with Heine's observation on German modals (Heine 1995: 26). A further distinction was made between the 3rd-person *galėti* "can/may" forms (present/past/past frequentative/future tense forms and subjunctive) taking main verb infinitives and *būti*-P ("be"-P) as complements, e.g.:

(40)   *Jis galėtų būti lenkas.*   (MI)
     "He **can be** a Pole."

(41)   *...užsiminė, kad kai kam iš tikrųjų tas užrašas gali labai nepatikti, bet pats*
     garsiausiai kvatojo, vaišino visus ...   (KJ)
     "Uncle Hans hinted discreetly that somebody **might dislike** the inscription indeed, but laughed too..."

All the cases of use where the verb *galėti* "can/may" followed by *būti*-P ("be"-P) has a non-epistemic reading take an AP complement and an animate subject, e.g.:

(42)   *Visiškai nesvarbu, kas ką myli, ar mylimasis vertas, leidžiasi, moka, gali būti*
     mylimas.   (IJ)
     "It doesn't matter who loves whom and whether the loved one is willing, worthwhile or **capable of accepting love**, it's important how you love."

(43)   *Kol yra vagių, policija gali būti rami, — ji turės duonos, — turės ką gaudyti,*
     ką saugoti. (SB)
     "But so long as there are thieves, the police **can rest** assured that they'll have a job and bread on the table, something to chase, something to guard."

As can be seen in Table 6 below, in both types of patterns taken together the Lithuanian possibility verb *galėti* "can/may" predominantly functions as a non-epistemic modal verb. It is only approximately one third of its use that has been found to be epistemic.

Table 6. Distributions of epistemic vs. non-epistemic readings of 3rd-person forms of *galėti* "can/may" in LT-orig

Patterns with 3rd-person forms	Epistemic		Non-epistemic	
	f/1,000	%	f/1,000	%
gal* + INF	0.26	18	1.16	82
gal* + *būti*-P	0.11	77	0.03	23
Total	0.37	24	1.19	76

As was expected, Lithuanian statives of the type *būti*-P ("be"-P), where P stands for NP, AP or PP, give a higher degree of epistemic readings and the ratio between epistemic and non-epistemic frequency is 0.11 : 0.03. However, in total, epistemic use with the possibility verb *galėti* "can/may" is rather low, namely 0.37 (f/1,000). When compared to the overall normalised frequency of adverbials in Table 3, the ratio becomes very significant, because it shows that adverbial usage is about 5 times higher than that of epistemic possibility use of the verb *galėti* "can/may" in Lithuanian, as shown in Table 7.

Table 7. Normalised frequency of epistemic possibility realizations in LT-orig: Adverbials vs. possibility verb *galėti* "can/may"

LT-orig	ADV	V
(f/1,000)	2.09	0.37

If we look only at the frequency of the Lithuanian epistemic possibility adverbials *gal/galgi/galbūt* "perhaps/maybe" as opposed to the epistemic use of the verb *galėti* "can/may", it is nearly four times higher than that of the given verb forms, e.g.:

(44)   LT-orig → *gal/galgi/galbūt*-1.54 vs. V-0.37

To sum up the basic findings obtained in the analysis of qualitative and quantitative parameters of modal realizations of possibility in the English and Lithuanian sub-corpora of the texts in the original, the statistical data analysed support our hypothesis that the Lithuanian language shows a significantly higher frequency of epistemic adverbials as contrasted with the use of the auxiliary and adverb strategies in English.

The following stage of our contrastive study was to find more evidence to support or discard our hypothesis about an overwhelming priority given by the speakers of Lithuanian to the adverbial use to express their epistemic stance regarding the possibility of the situation described by looking at the translational correspondences in the two languages.

The two most widely used English epistemic possibility auxiliaries *may/might* have been found to correspond to adverbials in translation into Lithuanian more often than to the Lithuanian modal verb *galėti* "can/may". The most frequent correspondence of the English *may/might* has been found to be the Lithuanian adverbial *gal(būt)* "perhaps/maybe", which makes up 26.5% of all the translational correspondences of *may/might* in the LT-trans sub-corpus. The other Lithuanian epistemic possibility adverbials under analysis in the given study constitute only 5% of the correspondences used. On the contrary, the translational correspondences of *could* contain Lithuanian adverbials rather rarely (only 4%). The translators' preference has been given to the Lithuanian verb *galėti* "can/may", which makes up 69%. Mention should be made of the fact that a considerably high percentage of zero-correspondences has been observed. However, we will not comment on the reasons for this phenomenon in this paper. Other translational correspondences include adjectives and various forms of the subjunctive mood in Lithuanian. The frequency of the translational correspondences illustrating the choice of the adverbial and verb forms strategies in translation from English into Lithuanian is given in Table 8.

Table 8. Frequency of translational correspondences of *may/might/could* in LT-trans: Choice of strategies

E-orig	LT-trans (ADV)	LT-trans (V + INF/*būti*-P)
Ep-*may/might*	31.5%	22%
Ep-*could*	4%	69%

An illustration of the translational correspondences discussed can be seen in Table 9.

Frequency counts of the English correspondences — both in translation and in the original — for the most frequent Lithuanian epistemic adverbials *galbūt* "maybe" and *gal* "perhaps" have shown that there is an overuse of the English adverbs *perhaps* and *maybe* in English as a target language, while the frequency of verb use decreases respectively, as illustrated in Table 10.

The frequency of zero correspondences is not exactly the same in the translated texts and the original ones. There might be various explanations for this mismatch and some of the preliminary observations allow us to assume that one of the reasons is language-specific conceptualization of probability (cf. Nuyts 2001). The absence of any means of expression on the level of the aligned sentences might

Table 9. Illustration of *may/might* translational correspondences in LT-trans

SL → E-orig	TL → LT-trans
\<s>You **may be** right.\</s> (BD)	\<s> — ***Galbūt** jūs ir teisus.*\</s>
\<s>We believe these numbers **may be** the key to who killed him.\</s> (BD)	\<s>*Mes manome, kad šie skaičiai **galėtų būti** informacijos, kas jį nužudė, raktas.*\</s>
\<s>We **might have** a better idea if we could get some information from you first.\</s> (BD)	\<s>***Gal** geriau susivoktume, jeigu pirmiausia gautume šiek tiek informacijos iš jūsų.*\</s>
\<s>We've had a tip-off that he **might be** there.\</s> (AM)	\<s>*Turime žinių, kad jis **gali būti** pas jus.*\</s>

Table 10. Frequency of correspondences of the Lithuanian epistemic adverbials *galbūt* "maybe" + *gal* "perhaps" in E-orig vs. E-trans

Correspondence	%		f/1,000	
	E-trans	E-orig	E-trans	E-orig
perhaps/maybe	69	47	0.86	0.48
other adverbs	2	4	0.02	0.05
verbs	15	31	0.18	0.31
miscellaneous	3	0	0.03	0.00
Ø	12	18	0.16	0.18
Total	100	100	1.26	1.02

have three explanations: the element of likelihood might be utterly lost, it might be sometimes partially/fully conveyed by some other linguistic means (lexical or syntactic) in the context or the situation described is differently conceptualized in Lithuanian. In this respect, a bi-directional search of correspondences in a parallel corpus gives plenty of evidence in the form of zero correspondence. A distinction can be made between zero correspondence in a TL and zero correspondence in a SL. The latter can be called insertion. Consider the following examples:

(45) OK, so ØE I got the number wrong.   (HN)
  *"Na gerai, **gal** aš supainiojau skaičių."*
  (Lit. "OK, **perhaps/maybe** I got the number wrong.")

(46) ØE 'Ave to teach you the A, B, C next.   (OG)
  *"**Gal** dar ir abėcėlės turėsiu tave mokyti?"*

Thus insertion of modal particles and adverbs in Lithuanian seems to correspond to cases of zero correspondence of English modal auxiliaries in Lithuanian. For example, in the *ParaCorp*$_{E \to LT}$ the zero correspondences of epistemic *might* make up 20% and those of *may* 21%. On the other hand, cases of "inserted" *gal* "maybe/ perhaps" in translated Lithuanian constitute 20%. The given phenomenon of insertion is directly related to 'overuse', which is used to refer to a mismatch of an element's frequency in the target texts as compared to the source texts (Simon-Vandenbergen & Aijmer 2002/2003: 16). These quantitative results would suggest that it is appropriate for a translation to follow target language conventions. The insertion of modal expressions in the target language can be interpreted as a sign of normalization, i.e. bringing the translation closer to the norms of the target language (Schmied & Schäffler 1996: 50; Teich 2003: 145).

5.   Concluding remarks

Users of English and Lithuanian seem to have a very similar potential of choice at their disposal for the encoding of their epistemic attitude of possibility towards the situations described. The purpose of the study was to find out what choices are made by the speakers of the two languages under analysis. Despite the existence of the same adverb and verb strategies, their implementation is very different. On the basis of the analysis carried out on the distinction made between qualitative and quantitative parameters of modal realizations of epistemic and non-epistemic possibility in English and Lithuanian, it can be observed that in the Lithuanian language, epistemic adverbials dominate as realizations of epistemic possibility. The main function of the key Lithuanian modal verb *galėti* "can/may" can be considered to be a key marker of non-epistemic possibility and its epistemic meaning is mainly dependent upon its use with Lithuanian *būti*-P ("be"-P) statives (cf. Wärnsby 2004). The results of the English data analysis are in line with the observations made by van der Auwera et al. (2005) that the use of modal auxiliaries is more frequent than that of adverbs and that this higher frequency seems to correlate with their degree of grammaticalization. Similar conclusions are drawn in Mortelmans (2009). Her research on the realizations of epistemic and evidential (inferential) necessity in English, German and Dutch has shown that German makes less use of epistemic *müssen* — which is considerably less grammaticalized than its English counterpart *must* — and seems to turn to modal adverbs and modal particles instead.

Meanwhile it is difficult to give a clear answer on the conditions and reasons that have predetermined the present architecture in the domain of modal realizations in Lithuanian. It is difficult to delineate our argumentation by relating it to areality issues or to the differences due to the processes of grammaticalization or lexicalizations, because there has been no relevant research carried out in

Lithuanian linguistics and there is scarce or no data that could shed light on the diachronic development of the phenomena.

Methodologically, the study can be seen as one offering more evidence on the importance and plausibility of corpus-based contrastive methodology in linguistic research. As has been shown in the paper, findings obtained in the analysis of translational correspondences fully support and corroborate the results of the interlinguistic contrast based on similarities and differences detected in original English and original Lithuanian. It is worthwhile noting that it is not only information on authentic language use that corpus-based studies provide but also frequency information by laying "emphasis on typical forms of expression rather than on the range of possible forms of expression" (Barlow 2008: 103). Moreover, though not directly, the subject dealt with in the paper is related to the issue of translation equivalence, or to be more precise, touches upon the problem of congruent and non-congruent correspondences in the domain of grammatical categories.

First, it is obvious that the translational paradigm indicates language-specific differences in the process of grammaticalization. The study's quantitative findings on the frequency of the use of the auxiliary-adverb strategies in English and Lithuanian are in line with a suggestion made by van der Auwera et al. (2005: 202) that English auxiliaries are much more strongly grammaticalized than those of Slavonic languages.

Second, and in parallel, the preliminary results obtained by contrasting Lithuanian-English epistemic modal correspondences support the viewpoint that the meaning of modal adverbials is very much context dependent and that they have to be analysed both in terms of modality and of discourse, as is claimed by Aijmer (2001).

Third, a relatively significant proportion of zero correspondence has been observed by many linguists; for instance the percentage of zero correspondences of *seem* in Norwegian texts is about 16% (Johansson 2001: 238), that of Swedish *visst* "seems/of course" is about 16.9% (Aijmer 1996: 411), and that of Swedish *väl* "probably/perhaps" is 38% (Aijmer 1996: 415). The abundance of inserted modal adverbials (particles and adverbs) in Lithuanian might be a compensatory way to bridge the language-specific differences in modal meaning realization. Alongside the processes of grammaticalization and pragmaticalization, the weakening of meaning might also signal differences in use of pragmatic convention.

Notes

* We are sincerely grateful to Ms Ann Kelly for reading our manuscript and offering her kind advice. Our thanks are due to all the anonymous reviewers for their helpful comments and

critical remarks on the original draft, which have substantially improved the final version of the paper.

1. The figures for *(su)gebėti* "manage/be able to" and *mokėti* "know how" have not been provided in Table 3 because their frequency is rather low: the normalised frequency of the overall occurrences of singular and plural person forms of these two verbs with different time reference marking is only 0.67. Moreover, their use is purely non-epistemic (dynamic).

References

Aijmer, K. 1996. "Swedish modal particles in a contrastive perspective". In K. Jaszczolt & K. Turner (Eds.), *Semantics and Pragmatics: Meanings and Representations*, Vol. 1. Oxford/ N.Y./Tokyo: Pergamon, 393–427.

Aijmer, K. 1997. "I think — an English Modal Particle". In T. Swan & O. J. Westvik (Eds.), *Modality in Germanic Languages: Historical and Comparative Perspectives*. Berlin/N.Y.: Mouton de Gruyter, 1–47.

Aijmer, K. 1999. "Epistemic possibility in an English-Swedish perspective". In H. Hasselgård & S. Oksefjell (Eds.), *Out of Corpora. Studies in Honour of Stig Johansson*. Amsterdam: Rodopi, 301–326.

Aijmer, K. 2001. "Epistemic modal adverbs of certainty in an English-Swedish perspective". *SPRIK Reports, No 5*. Available at http://www.hf.uio.no/forskningsprosjekter/sprik/docs/ pdf/aijmer.pdf (accessed November 2006).

Aijmer, K. & Simon-Vandenbergen, A.-M. 2004. "A model and a methodology for the study of pragmatic markers: The semantic field of expectation". *Journal of Pragmatics*, 36 (10), 1781–1805.

Altenberg, B. & Granger, S. 2004. "Recent trends in cross-linguistic lexical studies". In B. Altenberg & S. Granger (Eds.), *Lexis in Contrast: Corpus-based Approaches*. Amsterdam/ Philadelphia: John Benjamins, 3–48.

Ambrazas, V. (Ed.) 1997. *Lithuanian Grammar*. Vilnius: Baltos lankos.

van der Auwera, J. 2001. "On typology of negative modals". In J. Hoeksema, H. Rullmann, V. Sanchez-Valencia & T. van der Woulden (Eds.), *Perspectives on Negation and Polarity Items*. Amsterdam/Philadelphia: John Benjamins, 21–48

van der Auwera, J., Schalley, E. & Nuyts, J. 2005. "Epistemic possibility in a Slavonic parallel corpus — a pilot study". In B. Hansen & P. Karlik (Eds.), *Modality in Slavonic Languages: New Perspectives*. München: Sagner, 201–217.

Barlow, M. 1995. *A Guide to ParaConc*. Athelstan: Houston.

Barlow, M. 2008. "Parallel texts and corpus-based contrastive analysis". In M. L. A. Gómez-González, J. L. Mackenzie & E. M. González Álvarez (Eds.), *Current Trends in Contrastive Linguistics: Functional and Cognitive Perspectives*. Amsterdam/Philadelphia: John Benjamins, 101–121.

Biber, D., Johansson, S., Leech, G., Conrad, S. & Finegan, E. (Eds.) 1999. *Longman Grammar of Spoken and Written English*. London: Longman.

Bybee, J., Perkins, R. D. & Pagliuca, W. 1994. *The Evolution of Grammar. Tense, Aspect and Modality in the Languages of the World*. Chicago: University of Chicago Press.

Coates, J. 1983. *The Semantics of Modal Auxiliaries*. London: Croom Helm.

Coates, J. 1995. "The Expression of root and epistemic possibility in English". In J. Bybee & S. Fleischman (Eds.), *Modality in Grammar and Discourse*. Amsterdam/Philadelphia: John Benjamins, 55–66.

Dunning, T. 1993. "Accurate methods for the statistics of surprise and coincidence". *Computational Linguistics*, 19 (1), 61–74.

Facchinetti, R. 2002. "*Can* and *could* in contemporary British English: A study of the ICE-GB corpus". In P. Peters, P. Collins & A. Smith (Eds.), *New Frontiers of Corpus Research. Papers from the 21st International Conference on English Language Research on Computerized Corpora Sydney 2000*. Amsterdam/New York: Rodopi, 229–246.

Facchinetti, R. 2003. "Pragmatic and sociological constraints on the functions of *may* in contemporary British English". In R. Facchinetti, M. Krug & F. Palmer (Eds.), *Modality in Contemporary English*. Berlin/New York: Mouton de Gruyter, 301–327.

Gresset, S. 2003. "Towards a contextual micro-analysis of the non-equivalence of might and could". In R. Facchinetti, M. Krug & F. Palmer (Eds.), *Modality in Contemporary English*. Berlin/New York: Mouton de Gruyter, 81–99.

Grumadienė, L. & Žilinskienė, V. 1997. *Dažninis dabartinės lietuvių kalbos žodynas. Frequency Dictionary of Modern Written Lithuanian*. Vilnius: Mokslo aidai.

de Haan, F. 1997. *The Interaction of Modality and Negation: A Typological Study*. New York: Garland.

Heine, B. 1995. "Agent-oriented vs. epistemic modality: Some observations on German modals". In J. Bybee & S. Fleischman (Eds.), *Modality in Grammar and Discourse*. Amsterdam/Philadelphia: John Benjamins, 17–53.

Hoye, L. 1997. *Adverbs and Modality in English*. London/New York: Longman.

Johansson, S. 2001. "The English verb *seem* and its correspondences in Norwegian: What seems to be the problem". In K. Aijmer (Ed.), *A Wealth of English. Studies in Honour of Göran Kjellmer*. Göteborg: Acta Universitatis Gothoburgensis, 221–245.

Johansson, S. 2007. *Seeing Through Multilingual Corpora: On the Use of Corpora in Contrastive Studies*. Amsterdam/Philadelphia: John Benjamins.

Johansson, S. & Hofland K. 1994. "Towards an English-Norwegian parallel corpus". In: U. Fries, G. Tottie & P. Schneider (Eds.), *Creating and Using English Language Corpora*. Amsterdam/Atlanta, GA: Rodopi, 25–37.

Leech, G. 2003. "Modality on the move: The English modal auxiliaries 1961–1992". In R. Facchinetti, M. Krug & F. Palmer (Eds.), *Modality in Contemporary English*. Berlin/New York: Mouton de Gruyter, 191–240.

Løken, B. 1997. "Expressing possibility in English and Norwegian". *ICAME Journal*, 21, 43–59.

Mauranen, A. 2002. "Will 'translationese' ruin a contrastive study?". *Languages in Contrast*, 2 (2), 161–86.

Mortelmans, T. 2009. "Modal verbs, modal adverbs and modal particles in English, German and Dutch. What markers of epistemic necessity and inferential evidentiality might express". *Book of Abstracts: 42nd Annual Meeting of the Societas Linguistica Europaea*. Universidade de Lisboa, 67.

Noël, D. 2003. "Translations as evidence for semantics: An illustration". *Linguistics*, 41 (4), 757–785.

Norde, M. 2006: online. "The grammaticalization of adverbs: Two case studies". Abstracts of *Colloque "Perspectives Contrastives et Grammaticalisation", Département de Français, Université de Fribourg, 2 et 3 octobre 2006*. Available at: http://www.unifr.ch/fns_form-hybride/publications/Abstracts_Perspectives_contrastives.htm#mn (accessed December 2007).

Nuyts, J. 2001. *Epistemic Modality, Language, and Conceptualization: A Cognitive-Pragmatic Perspective*. Amsterdam/Philadelphia: John Benjamins.

Palmer, F. 1995. "Negation and the modals of possibility and necessity". In J. Bybee & S. Fleischman (Eds.), *Modality in Grammar and Discourse*. Amsterdam/Philadelphia: John Benjamins, 453–473.

Palmer, F. 2003. "Modality in English: Theoretical, descriptive and typological issues". In R. Facchinetti, M. Krug & F. Palmer (Eds.), *Modality in Contemporary English*. Berlin/New York: Mouton de Gruyter, 1–17.

Perkins, M. R. 1983. *Modal Expressions in English*. London: Frances Pinter.

Schmied, J. & Schäffler, H. 1996. "Approaching translationese through parallel and translation corpora". *Synchronic Corpus Linguistics. Papers from the 16th International Conference on English Language Research on Computerized Corpora, Toronto 1995*. Amsterdam: Rodopi, 41–56.

Siewierska, A. 2008. "Ways of impersonalizing". In M. L. A. Gómez-González, J. L. Mackenzie, E. M. González Álvarez (Eds.), *Current Trends in Contrastive Linguistics: Functional and Cognitive Perspectives*. Amsterdam/Philadelphia: John Benjamins, 3–26.

Simon-Vandenbergen, A.-M. & Aijmer, K. 2002/2003. "The expectation marker *of course* in a cross-linguistic perspective". *Languages in Contrast*, 4 (1), 13–43.

Simon-Vandenbergen, A.-M. & Aijmer, K. 2007. *The Semantic Field of Modal Certainty: A Corpus-based Study of English Adverbs*. Berlin/New York: Mouton de Gruyter.

Usoniene, A. 1988. "Lietuviškų statyvų problemos". *Kalbotyra*, 39 (1), 110–117.

Teich, E. 2003. *Cross-linguistic Variation in System and Text*. Berlin/New York: Walter de Gruyter.

Teubert, W. 1996. "Comparable or parallel corpora?". *International Journal of Lexicography*, 9 (3), 238–264.

Wärnsby, A. 2004. "Constraints on the interpretation of epistemic modality in English and Swedish". In R. Facchinetti & F. Palmer (Eds.), *English Modality in Perspective. Genre Analysis and Contrastive Studies*. Frankfurt am Main: Peter Lang, 163–190.

Wiemer, B. 2007. "Lexical markers of evidentiality in Lithuanian". *Rivista di Linguistica*, 19 (1), 173–208.

Zinkevičius, Z. 1981. *Lietuvių kalbos istorinė gramatika*. D. 2. Vilnius: Mokslas.

Appendix: Data sources

The reference codes used in quoting the examples consist of the initials of the authors' names. In order to economize on space and for the sake of convenience, the short stories written by the same author have not been listed separately. Only the titles of short story collections and the number of the translated short stories or extracts included into the corpus have been indicated.

The English-Lithuanian Parallel Corpus (ParaCorp$_{E \to LT}$)

AM — Albom, M. 1997. *Tuesdays with Morrie*. New York: Doubleday. (*Antradieniai su Moriu* tr. by S. Dagys)

BD — Barthelme, D. 1981. *The School*. New York: G P Putnam's Sons. (*Mokykla* tr. by S. Repečka)

BrD — Brown, D. 2003. *The Da Vinci Code*. New York: Doubleday. (*Da Vinčio kodas* tr. by I. Žakevičienė)

HN — Hornby, N. 2002. *How to Be Good*. London: Penguin Books. (*Kaip būti geru žmogumi* tr. by R. Drazdauskienė)

MM — Marchetta, M. 1999. *Looking for Alibrandi*. New York: Orchard Books. (*Kas tu, Alibrandi?* tr. by R. Vidugirienė)

MI — McEwan, I. 1998. *Amsterdam*. London: Jonathan Cape. (*Amsterdamas* tr. by R. Rudaitytė)

OG — Orwel, G. 1949. *1984*. London: Secker & Warburg. (*1984-ieji* tr. by A. Sabonis)

RJK — Rowling, J. K. 1997. *Harry Potter and the Sorcerer's Stone*. London: Bloomsbury. (*Haris Poteris ir išminties akmuo* tr. by Z. Marienė)

The Lithuanian-English Parallel Corpus (ParaCorp$_{LT \to E}$)

AP– Andriušis, P. 1997. *Anoj pusėj ežero*. Vilnius: Baltos lankos. (A short story tr. by A.T. Klimas)

AJ — Aputis, J. 2005. *Vieškelyje džipai*. Vilnius: Lietuvos rašytojų sąjungos leidykla. (3 short stories tr. by V. Kelertas, R. Dapkus, Gr. M. Grazevich and L. Sruoginis)

BB — Baltrušaitytė, B. 1981. *Po pietvakarių dangum*. Vilnius: Vaga. (5 short stories tr. by J. Avižienis)

GR — Gavelis, R. 2006. *Tylos angelas*. Vilnius: Tyto alba. (4 short stories tr. by V. Kelertas, A. Samalavičius and J. Avižienis)

GR1 — Gavelis, R. 2002. *SUN-TZU gyvenimas šventame VILNIAUS MIESTE*. Vilnius: Tyto alba. (An extract tr. by L. Sruoginis)

GR2 — Gavelis, R. 1989. *Vilniaus pokeris*. Vilnius: Vaga. (An extract tr. by L. Sruoginis)

GrR — Granauskas, R. 2006. *Novelės*. Vilnius: Žaltvykslė. (5 short stories tr. by V. Kelertas, R. Dapkus, Gr. M. Grazevich, M. Girniuvienė, D.V. Kupčinskaitė and I. Geniušienė)

GL — Gutauskas, L. 2003. *Plunksnos. Kazbek*. Vilnius: Tyto alba. (An extract tr. by D.J. Ross)

IE — Ignatavičius, E. 1988. *Chrizantemų autobuse*. Vilnius: Vaga. (A short story tr. by V. Kelertas, R. Dapkus and Gr. M. Grazevich)

IJ — Ivanauskaitė, J. 1985. *Pakalnučių metai: Novelės*. Vilnius: Vaga. (2 short stories tr. by L. Sruoginis and K. Sakalavičiūtė)

IJ1 — Ivanauskaitė, J. 2003. *Placebas*. Vilnius: Tyto alba. (An extract tr. by D.J. Ross)

IM — Ivaškevičius, M. 2002. *Žali*. Vilnius: Tyto alba. (An extract tr. by D.J. Ross)

JA — Jakučiūnas, A. 2005. *Servijaus Galo užrašai*. Vilnius: Lietuvos rašytojų sąjungos leidykla. (An extract tr. by L. Sruoginis)

JJ — Jankus, J. 1973. *Užkandis*. New York: Ateitis. (A short story tr. by A.T. Klimas)

JV — Juknaitė, V. 2001. *Šermenys*. Vilnius: Alma Littera. (A short story tr. by L. Sruoginis)

JV1 — Juknaitė, V. 2002. *Išsiduosi. Balsu*. Vilnius: Lietuvos rašytojų sąjungos leidykla. (An extract tr. by L. Sruoginis)

KV — Kavaliūnas, V. 1974. *Hestera*. Chicago: Lietuviškos knygos klubas. (*Esther* tr. by J. Kavaliūnas; R. Hamner (Ed.))

KR — Klimas, R. 1981. *Gintė ir jos žmogus*. Vilnius: Vaga. (2 short stories tr. by Gr. M. Grazevich and R. Dapkus)

KST — Kondrotas, S.T. 2004. *Meilė pagal Juozapą*. Vilnius: Lietuvos rašytojų sąjungos leidykla. (2 short stories tr. by L. Simutis and A.T. Klimas)

KJ — Kunčinas, J. 1993. *Tūla*. Vilnius: Lietuvos rašytojų sąjungos leidykla. (An extract tr. by L. Sruoginis)

KH — Kunčius, H. 2001. *Ekskursija: Casa Matta*. Vilnius: Lietuvos rašytojų sąjungos leidykla. (An extract tr. by L. Sruoginis)

LA — Landsbergis, A. 1979. *Muzika įžengiant į neregėtus miestus*. Michigan: Ateitis. (A short story tr. by L. Sruoginis)

LR — Lankauskas, R. 1970. *Šiaurės vitražai*. Vilnius: Vaga. (A short story tr. by G. M. Slavėnas)

MI — Meras, I. 1988. *Lygiosios trunka akimirką*. Vilnius: Vaga. (*Stalemate* tr. by J. Zdanys)

MI1 — Meras, I. 1995. *Apverstas pasaulis*. Chicago: Algimanto Mackaus Knygų Leidimo Fondas AM & M Publications. (3 short stories tr. by L. Sruoginis, M.M. De Voe and S. Sužiedėlis)

PS — Parulskis, S. 2004. *Trys sekundės dangaus*. Vilnius: Baltos lankos. (An extract tr. by L. Sruoginis)

SB — Sruoga, B. 1989. *Dievų miškas*. Kaunas: Šviesa. (*Forest of the Gods* tr. by A. Byla)

ŠS — Šaltenis, S. 1986. *Apysakos*.Vilnius: Vaga. (3 extracts tr. by L. Sruoginis and V. Kelertas)

ŠR — Šerelytė, R. 1995. *Žuvies darinėjimas*. Vilnius: Lietuvos rašytojų sąjungos leidykla. (2 short stories tr. by M.M. De Voe)

ŠA — Šlepikas, A. 2005. *Lietaus dievas*. Vilnius: Lietuvos rašytojų sąjungos leidykla. (A short story tr. by D.J. Ross)

VB — Vilimaite B. 1996. *Užpustytas traukinys*. Vilnius: Lietuvos rašytojų sąjungos leidykla. (4 short stories tr. by L. Sruoginis)

ZM — Zingeris, M. 2002. *Grojimas dviese*. Vilnius: Baltos lankos. (An extract tr. by D.J. Ross)

Index